14-28

PROBLEMS AND PERSPECTIVES IN HISTORY
EDITOR: H. F. KEARNEY MA PHD

Origins of the English Parliament

A list of titles in the
PROBLEMS AND PERSPECTIVES IN HISTORY series
will be found on the back cover of this book

Origins of the English Parliament

Peter Spufford

LECTURER IN MEDIEVAL HISTORY
UNIVERSITY OF KEELE

BARNES & NOBLE, Inc.
NEW YORK
PUBLISHERS & BOOKSELLERS SINCE 1873

Published in the United States in 1967
by Barnes & Noble, Inc.
105 Fifth Avenue, New York

Printed in Great Britain by Richard Clay (The Chaucer Press), Ltd.,
Bungay, Suffolk

Editor's Foreword

'Study problems in preference to periods' was the excellent advice given by Lord Acton in his inaugural lecture at Cambridge. To accept it is one thing, to put it into practice is another. In fact, in both schools and universities the teaching of history, in depth, is often hindered by certain difficulties of a technical nature, chiefly to do with the availability of sources. In this respect, history tends to be badly off in comparison with literature or the sciences. The historical equivalent of set texts, readings or experiments, in which the student is encouraged to use his own mind, are the so-called 'special periods'. If these are to be fruitful, the student must be encouraged to deal in his own way with the problems raised by historical documents and the historiography of the issues in question and he must be made aware of the wider perspectives of history. Thus, if the enclosure movement of the sixteenth century is studied, the student might examine the historiographical explanations stretching from More's *Utopia* and Cobbett to Beresford's *Lost Villages of England*. At the same time he might also be dealing with selected documents raising important problems. Finally he might be encouraged to realize the problems of peasantries at other periods of time, including Russia and China in the nineteenth and twentieth centuries. In this particular instance, thanks to Tawney and Power, *Tudor Economic Documents*, the history teacher is comparatively well off. For other special periods the situation is much more difficult. If, however, the study of history is to encourage the development of the critical faculties as well as the memory, this approach offers the best hope. The object of this series is to go some way towards meeting these difficulties.

The general plan of each volume in the series will be similar, with a threefold approach from aspects of historiography, documents and editorial consideration of wider issues, though the structure and balance between the three aspects may vary.

A broad view is being taken of the limits of history. Political history will not be excluded, but a good deal of emphasis will be placed on economic, intellectual and social history. The idea has in fact grown out of the experience of a group of historians at the University of Sussex, where the student is encouraged to investigate the frontier areas between his own and related disciplines.

H. KEARNEY

Contents

CONTENTS

CONTENTS

CONTENTS

Acknowledgements

We are grateful to the following for permission to reproduce copyright material:

Basil Blackwell & Mott Ltd for material from Aquinas: *Selected Political Writings*, trans. J. G. Dawson, ed. A. P. d'Entreves; Wm. Blackwood & Sons Ltd for material from *A History of Medieval Political Theory in the West*, Vol. V by R. W. and A. J. Carlyle; Cambridge University Press for material from *The Medieval Coroner* by R. F. Hunnisett and *An Essay on the Origins of the House of Commons* by D. Pasquet; The Catholic Historical Review for material from 'The Parliaments of the Middle Ages and the Early Modern Period' by R. H. Lord, published in the *Catholic Historical Review*, VXI; The Clarendon Press for material from *The Parliamentary Representation of the English Boroughs during the Middle Ages* by M. McKisack, *The Wool Trade in English Medieval History* by E. Power, *The Dominican Order and Convocation* by E. Barker, *Select Charters* and *The Constitutional History of England* by W. Stubbs, *The Northeners* by J. C. Holt, *The Song of Lewes*, ed. C. L. Kingsford, and *King Henry III and the Lord Edward* and *The Thirteenth Century* by F. M. Powicke; Librairie Armand Colin for material from ' "Ordres" ou "Puissances" l'example des Etets de Flandre' by J. Dhont from *Annales Economies Sociétés Civilisations*; Columbia University Press for material from Marsilius of Padua: *The Defender of the Peace*, trans. A. Gewirth; the author for 'Justice in Early English Parliaments', published in the *Bulletin of the Institute of Historical Research*, xxvii (1954) and for material from *Historian and the Medieval English Parliament* by Sir J. Goronwy Edwards; Harvard University Press for material from *Studies in Early French Taxation* by J. L. Strayer and Taylor; The Johns Hopkins Press for material from *Studies in the History of the English Feudal Barony* by S. Painter; Houghton Mifflin Company for material from 'Taxation and Representation in the Middle Ages' by C. Stephenson from *Anniversary Essays in Medieval History by Students of Charles Homer Haskins*; the author for 'La Société d'Ancien Régime' by Professor Emile Lousse; Manchester University Press for material from *Chapters in the Administrative History of Medieval England* by T. F. Tout; the author for material from *Il Parlamento in Italia* by Professor Antonio Marongiu (published in the English language by Eyre & Spottiswoode

Ltd – trans. S. Woolf); The Merlin Press Ltd for material from 'The Legislators of Medieval England' by H. M. Cam from *Law Finders and Law Makers in Medieval England*; Methuen & Co. Ltd for material from *Principals of Government and Politics in the Middle Ages* by W. Ullmann; the author and the Past and Present Society for material from 'The English Economy in the Thirteenth Century' by Professor E. Miller, published in *Past and Present*, No. 28 (July 1964): World Copyright the Past and Present Society; Sir Charles Morris, K.C.M.G. for material from *Medieval Representation and Consent* by M. V. Clarke; Public Record Office for material from the unpublished *Coram Rege Roll* (Crown Copyright); the author for material from 'The Problem of the Attendance of the Lords in Medieval Parliaments' by Professor J. S. Roskell, published in the *Bulletin of the Institute of Historical Research*, xxix (1956); Routledge & Kegan Paul Ltd and The University of Chicago Press for material from *Feudal Society* by M. Bloch; Routledge & Kegan Paul Ltd and Alfred A. Knopf, Inc. for material from *Medieval Political Ideas* by Ewart Lewis; the Selden Society for material from *The Mirror of Justices* edited by W. J. Whittaker and F. W. Maitland (Selden Society, Volume 7 for 1893); Stevens & Sons Ltd for material from *Parliaments and Great Councils in Medieval England* by H. G. Richardson and G. O. Sayles; the author for material from 'The Nature of Parliament in the reign of Henry III', published in *English Historical Review*, lxxiv, 1959, and 'The Knights the period of Reform and Rebellion 1258–67: A Critical Phase in the rise of a New Class' published in the *Bulletin of the Institute of Historical Research*, xxi (1946), both by Professor R. H. Treharne; the Editor of the *Wisconsin Law Review* for material from 'A Roman legal theory of consent, *quod omnes tangit*, in medieval representation' by G. Post; Dr. H. Wright for 'Bastard Feudalism' by K. B. McFarlane published in the *Bulletin of the Institute of Historical Research*, xx (1945), and Yale University Press for material from *Taxation in Medieval England* by S. K. Mitchell.

We have been unable to trace the copyright owners in 'Buzones' by the late G. T. Lapsley, published in *English Historical Review*, xlvii (1932) and would welcome any information that would enable us to do so.

Preface

In the compilation of this small volume I have incurred a number of debts of gratitude. I should like to thank John Illsley for his aid in selecting suitable passages, Professor Edward Miller for critically reading my introduction and saving me from a number of pitfalls, Eric Hill for rigorously criticizing my translations from Latin and saving me from further pitfalls, Carolyn West for so much typing, and my wife, Margaret Spufford, for radically improving the volume by her perceptive historical comments.

PETER SPUFFORD

Cambridge
August 1966

Introduction

In 1965 the nominal seven hundredth anniversary of parliament was celebrated with much enthusiasm, the issue of commemorative postage stamps, and other manifestations of the publicist's art. It is well therefore to look at the thorny question of the true origins of parliament. The notion that the English parliament began in 1265 must, of course, be dismissed at once as a publicist's fiction. It is as false as the idea which found currency for many years in textbooks that parliament began with the so-called 'Model Parliament' of 1295. Dating the origins of parliament is no simple matter, and no single occasion can be pinpointed as the first parliament. Scholars even differ on the century, let alone the year, in which the beginning of parliament as an institution can be found. Mr Richardson has argued that the use of the word 'parliament' as a technical term provides evidence that parliament was already an institution in the strict sense of the word by the middle of the thirteenth century (see no. 2). For him

The step to be explained is the transition from the occasional plenary sessions of the king's court held at no regular intervals to the regular and ordered meetings described by Humbert de Romans (see no. 4), to which the name of parliament is applied and which we find in existence from the middle years of the thirteenth century.

Whereas Mr Richardson and Professor Sayles have declared that parliament was already an institution before 1258, Professor Plucknett and Miss McKisack, on the other hand, have hesitated to suggest that parliament had even become an institution, in the full sense, by the early years of Edward III's reign (1327–77). Professor Powicke has sidestepped the issue by suggesting that dating of origins is a false trail, and that it is impossible to date the appearance of any institution at all exactly (see no. 67).

All that can be said with any certainty is that, from the early thirteenth century, occasional political assemblies summoned by the kings of England gradually acquired the name of parliaments, and that, at least by the middle of the fourteenth century, the characteristics of these assemblies became sufficiently recognizable for parliaments to be thought of as established institutions. By the end of Edward III's reign parliaments had a known, and more or less regular, composition, function and routine.

As fallacious as the idea that the origins of a medieval institution can be pinned down and dated to a particular year is the equally publicized notion that the English parliament was unique. How this misconception has arisen is not altogether clear, for historians have always been aware that the English parliament was only one particular national version of a whole range of assemblies which were called into existence throughout western Europe in the thirteenth and fourteenth centuries. In general, wherever a kingdom or a semi-autonomous principality developed its own central administrative system it also developed these assemblies for the whole kingdom or principality (see no. 6). In most parts of Europe, however, important assemblies also appeared on a regional level at the same time, or even earlier. In France such assemblies generally corresponded to areas with a common feudal background, such as the 'estates' of the former duchy of Normandy, but occasionally to newer administrative units such as the 'estates' of the new *senéchaussée* of Beaucaire. In England the only approximations to regional assemblies were the shire courts, in which the communities of the shires gathered (see no. 7), as the community of the realm did in parliament. At the same time as these national and regional gatherings, similar types of assembly were developing within the framework of the church (see nos. 8 and 9), and in the rapidly growing towns. The English parliament perhaps owes its false appearance of uniqueness to the fact that many of these medieval assemblies withered away in the early modern period, and that, except in the Habsburg lands, the remainder were suppressed in the epoch of the French Revolution and its Napoleonic aftermath.

The comparative study of these assemblies on a European scale shows that the earliest examples were not to be found in England, but in the countries which made up the Christian part of the Iberian peninsula (see no. 5). In every country, however, the same problems of definition arise. It is impossible to seize on any one particular moment in the slow development of a feudal council into a national assembly, and point to it as the 'beginning' of a Spanish *cortes*, a French *assemblée d'états*, or a German diet. It is impossible to say when a parliament, a *cortes* or a diet ceases to be only a meeting, an occasion, and became a corporate body, an institution. Ultimately it is only possible to generalize in the vaguest possible terms and to conclude that, elsewhere, as in England, a social occasion became a political institution between the beginning of the thirteenth century and the end of the fourteenth century. Even then, the origins of some of the Spanish *cortes* can perhaps be placed a little earlier, and that of some of the German diets rather later.

Most historians have concerned themselves with the emergence, in this post-feudal period, of a parliamentary type of assembly from the previous feudal councils, which they sometimes designate as 'pre-parliaments'. However, the problem of parliamentary origins is even more complex than this, for if the historian stands back and surveys the problem in rather a longer perspective he finds himself confronted, a few centuries earlier, with a range of pre-feudal assemblies throughout western Europe. In Anglo-Saxon England there had been the Witenagemot and in Visigothic Spain and the Carolingian Empire alike there had been a tradition of holding important councils, just as in tenth- and eleventh-century Iceland there had been the Althing. The suspicion emerges that there may possibly have been some continuity from such pre-feudal assemblies through the feudal period to post-feudal parliaments, *cortes*, estates and diets. Close scrutiny will readily show that there was no strictly institutional continuity, but it is more difficult to deny that there was at least some nebulous continuity of political habit.

The concept of the thirteenth and fourteenth centuries as a post-feudal period may in itself seem shocking to those who have been brought up to believe that feudalism survived until the French or Bolshevik revolutions. In the strict sense, a feudal society is one based on military service, personally performed, in return for the tenure of landed estates or fiefs, *feuda* (see nos. 12 and 13). As early as the twelfth century kings often accepted payments of money and hired mercenaries instead of exacting the actual military service owed by knights and barons for their lands. In the thirteenth century a royal army no longer consisted of the king's tenants and their undertenants, serving by virtue of their feudal obligations. Instead it consisted almost exclusively of paid and professional bannerets, and their contingents of knights bachelor and esquires, all of whom received wages like the supporting infantry. With the professionalization of the army there was a parallel demilitarization of society, and such slight obligations to perform military service as survived through the thirteenth century were usually fulfilled by hiring professional substitutes. A feudal society was a society oriented to fighting. The post-feudal society in which parliaments grew up was no longer primarily military. Its aristocracy included fighting-men, in not inconsiderable numbers, but it was no longer exclusively a military caste.

3

In a feudal, military, society the political decisions to be taken were primarily military decisions, and the advice which the prince took, apart from that within his family and household, was from those who would help him to implement his decisions, his great military tenants. In a post-feudal, demilitarized, society, political decisions came to cover a much wider range and the aid needed to implement decisions was not that of the warrior, but that of the taxpayer, even when the taxes were spent on war. Society was no longer made up of a hierarchy of warriors in a series of lord–vassal relationships, but of king and subjects. In this transformed society the warriors were only a specialized group, who fought, not as and how they agreed and advised, but as they were paid. Political decisions were in the hands of politicians, not of soldiers. Ultimately everything had come to depend on the taxpayers, not on the soldiery.

It was in this changed society that parliaments came into being and replaced feudal councils. The transition is barely perceptible, and the personnel long remained very much the same. In the old feudal councils the natural counsellors were the greater tenants-in-chief, particularly the earls and the bishops, the weight of whose advice depended on the size of their military following. In the new parliaments the natural counsellors were the richer lay and ecclesiastical magnates, whether they were theoretically tenants-in-chief or not. Amongst these the earls still predominated, but their political weight now depended on the extent of their lands and on the taxable wealth and the powers of patronage it gave them.

Successive kings may have been compelled to accept the counsel of the more powerful men of the kingdom, for reasons of custom and expediency, but they also always relied heavily on the advice of their close relatives and on that of the members of their household and administration. At the heart of the old feudal councils were such military officers as the marshal and the constable. At the heart of the new parliaments were the judges, together with the officers of the wardrobe, of chancery and of the exchequer, who were responsible for the central administration and finances of the king and kingdom. Military advisers had been replaced by civil servants and lawyers as the core of the royal counselling body (see nos. 27 to 30).

The course of the twelfth and thirteenth centuries witnessed the progressive extension of the powers of the king as against those of the magnates, itself both cause and effect of the growth and increasing complexity of the royal bureaucracy. In the legal field, not only were

4

new courts called into existence, but royal justice progressively ousted private justice, and written law supplemented and to some extent even replaced customary law. In the field of finance national taxes replaced feudal taxes and demanded new machinery for their assessment and collection. The growing needs and expenses of government could be met less and less adequately by aids, reliefs or scutages based on an increasingly outmoded feudal ordering of society. They were supplemented occasionally in the reign of John, and increasingly frequently from that of Henry III, by taxes on movables, and from 1266 by customs dues also. By the end of the thirteenth century these new forms of taxation had largely replaced the older feudal dues and were responsible for meeting those royal needs which could not be paid for out of the basic revenues derived from the royal lands and the profits of justice. Such enlargements in the sphere of government naturally increased the number of occasions for consultation and the number of opportunities for friction. If at times the early parliaments of the thirteenth century appear very literally as *parleys*, conversations or arguments between two parties, the two sides concerned were the crown, or rather the king and his civil-servants-cum-cabinet-ministers on the one hand, and the community, or at least the politically vocal part of it, particularly the earls and richer magnates, on the other. Like all generalizations, this is an over-simplification, since royal relatives were to be found amongst the earls, and the more important civil servants were frequently rewarded with bishoprics. They, as well as certain other magnates were usually, although not always, to be found on the side of the 'crown' in occasions of dispute with the 'community'.

At the same time as feudal councils became parleys between crown and community and consequently acquired the name of parliaments, a radical change was taking place in the community. Formerly the magnates could equate themselves with the community of the realm, but by the early fourteenth century it had become common to speak of the magnates *and* the community of the realm. The magnates were no longer the only politically vocal elements in England, and with the break-up of the hierarchically ordered feudal society, they could no longer claim to speak for those below them.

Only the king, his ministers and his magnates had been present at the earlier parliaments, but from the middle of the thirteenth century others were occasionally summoned. Surviving documents first record the summons of knights of the shire in 1254 and of representatives of boroughs in 1265. Representatives of the lower clergy are not known to have been called until 1295. Both knights and burgesses may possibly have been present at similar assemblies at dates earlier than these, for example in 1237, for which the evidence is ambiguous.

Although the magnates thus ceased to be the only part of the community to be present in parliament, they were still by far the most important element, and were for long to remain so, in so far as they did not abdicate their natural position by their failure to attend (see no. 31). Within the magnate group itself there were some men of particular importance, notably the score of bishops and the dozen or fewer earls. Even within this inner group there were a very few dominant individuals, a handful of men with outstanding landed endowments. These 'super-earls' were the successive heads of the Clare family, who combined the earldoms of Gloucester and Hertford, the successive heads of the Bohun family, who combined the earldoms of Hereford and Essex, and Edmund and Thomas of Lancaster, who held the earldoms of Lancaster, Leicester and Derby. The last held that of Lincoln also. In and out of parliament alike, these men dominated the political scene in the thirteenth century and the early fourteenth. They did so by virtue of their power as much as by their personalities. Nevertheless it is all too easy for the historian unintentionally to play down the role of the magnates by his interest in the novel elements in thirteenth-century political life. Of these the most striking is the emergence of the members of the knightly class into a position of financial and social independence, in the period between the dissolution of the old feudal network and their entanglement in the fourteenth century in the new meshes of bastard feudal obligation (see nos. 14, 15, 21 and 22).

The knightly or gentry class might still owe the magnates nominal feudal obligations, but these were becoming increasingly tenuous and impersonal as the thirteenth century progressed, and had long been commuted for cash. The gentry were important, not because they were fighting knights, nor because they were dependents of the magnates, but because of their increasing political importance in their own localities. The demilitarization of society had been accompanied by the elaboration of civil government. At the centre successive kings built up a professional civil service and judiciary; but in the country the kings relied upon the gentry class to provide amateur administration. Self-government at the king's command involved the richer gentry in obligations to serve as sheriffs and coroners, as assessors and collectors of taxes, as keepers of the peace, and on juries of recognition and presentment. Government, and hence political power, on a county level was in the hands of those members of the gentry whom Professor Treharne has called a *new* class. To use his words:

> The essential change in the nature of knighthood, the fact which justifies the title 'a new class' is the evolution of the mere Norman soldier into the thirteenth-century landed proprietor, with an essentially civilian mode of life, and a predominantly administrative occupation.

From mere fighting-men the knights had thus developed into a sort of nobility, and in the reign of Edward I there were thought to be some three thousand such landowners who held at least the qualifying minimum of land worth twenty pounds a year. Apart from the earls there were as yet no titles to differentiate the members of this nobility in status, although their wealth ranged from the qualifying twenty pounds a year up to parity with the poorer earls. Differences in landed wealth were, however, significant, for it was from amongst the wealthier members of the class that the king generally chose those to whom individual summons to parliament were sent. There does not originally seem to have been any regular criterion for summoning individuals. The king selected the men he wished to be present at each particular parliament separately. There was as yet no fixed parliamentary peerage. Early baronies by writ were the later invention of misguided antiquarians and the wishful thinking of peerage lawyers and their optimistic clients. Holders of ancient feudal baronies, or fragments of baronies, could not necessarily expect to be summoned individually. The lack of clear dividing lines may be illustrated by the individuals who were on one or more occasions personally summoned to parliament and were present at a later parliament as knights for their shires.

Within each shire there was also differentiation within the gentry class, for only a limited circle of men more or less monopolized the affairs of local government. These were the *buzones*, the weightier gentry in the county, weighty by virtue of their wealth or their personality. In any group of men there will be some who eagerly seek after office and power, and others who will as eagerly avoid it. So it was with the county gentry of the thirteenth and fourteenth centuries. An inner group chose itself from amongst those adequately qualified to perform the functions of local government (see nos. 16–20). It was the same men who were in turn coroners and sheriffs, assessors and collectors of taxes. It was naturally from this inner group of the more powerful and politically experienced gentry that knights of the shire were chosen to represent the shire in parliament. Such men were able to represent their constituents in a much more real and personal sense than their modern counterparts, for their constituencies were not mere geographical expressions devised by the electoral arithmetic of boundary commissioners, but real, organic communities in which they were accustomed to play a significant role. The thirteenth-century shire was a coherent entity, a community which could be seen visibly meeting together in the county court at frequent and regular intervals. As the community of the realm met in parliament, so the community of the shire met in the county court, for general political, legal, financial and social purposes. As central government intensified its activities it naturally took for granted the corporate existence of the community of the shire and gave it increasing corporate responsibilities and obligations. The carrying out of these corporate responsibilities in turn increased the cohesion of the shire as a selfconscious community. The election, or rather choice, of representatives to go to the king in parliament was at this period only one of the many functions of the county court. Although many others might be present at meetings of the county (see no. 7), the effective members of the shire community were the *buzones*, the politically active gentry. Knights of the shire in parliament thus represented real corporate bodies, or rather, the new politically important class who dominated those corporate bodies. Knights of the shire seem to have been included in parliament because the class which they represented had become of political importance. It had become worth while, from the royal point of view, to include them in assemblies so that they might hear policy expounded and act on it. The intermittent appearance of knights of the shire in late thirteenth-century parliaments can perhaps thus be related to the administrative functions and consequent political importance acquired by members of the gentry class over the previous hundred years. This in its turn may be linked with social and economic change over the same period.

The social consequences of the demilitarization of society and the loosening of feudal bonds have already been touched on, but the question has not yet been posed in economic terms. Were the gentry rising in the thirteenth century? It would be pleasant to answer with an unequivocal affirmation that this was so, but it is unfortunately impossible to do so. The answer must be so hedged with caveats that no clear generalization can be made. The basic difficulty is the relative dearth of evidence. We do not often have for the gentry the same means of assessing income as we have for a large number of ecclesiastical landlords and a limited number of lay magnates. The basis of their prosperity was of course their land. We have a limited idea of the extent of this from the enquiries made after their deaths, but very little evidence of how they exploited it. Little as is known of gentry incomes, even less is known of their expenditure, and this, as much as income, influences any growth or decline in prosperity. We do not know for certain whether office-holding was a matter of profit or loss, and whether the country gentleman benefited, or suffered, from a term of office as sheriff.

A general consideration of the whole thirteenth-century economic situation will provide a partial answer (see nos. 14 and 15). The rapid increase in population up to the end of the thirteenth century from at least the end of the eleventh century, and quite probably from the tenth century, was the key to economic change. From this increase in population there followed a rise in prices, particularly of food, a decline in real wages, an increase in the acreage of land under cultivation, and a rise in rents. In addition to rents, whether they were paid in services, goods or money, there was a rising return from manorial perquisites. This was a situation which was obviously disadvantageous to the villein tenant or the rural wage labourer. It was equally advantageous to certain, but not all, landholders.

The economic situation for the manorial lord, who was often a member of the gentry, depended on how much of the manor was in demesne. Only the demesne could be directly farmed at a profit. It could be tilled with cheap wage labour, and its products could be sold at high prices. The portion which was let to villeins might, or might not, be so profitable to the lord. Villein services had largely been commuted by the late thirteenth century, so the profitability of the land depended on how long previously the services had been commuted, and whether the villein payments were frozen in relation to a long past cost of living and had been utterly overtaken by inflation. The proportion of villeins among the tenants dictated the profitability of the manor court and the amount of money received from heriots and merchet and so forth, as well as the income to be obtained from the exploitation of the manorial monopolies of brewing, milling and even baking. Land farmed in demesne and land leased to villeins were therefore both likely to make a manor profitable to its lord. On the other hand the freeholder was the real economic thorn in the side of the manorial lord,

9

for the majority of freeholders held their tenements at what had become, by the thirteenth century, ridiculously low rents, and they were liable for few other payments.

The hundred rolls reveal the incredibly complex state of affairs early in Edward I's reign. Freeholders subdivided and sublet their holdings to other free tenants in acre or half-acre fragments, and the manorial lord had little expectation of the land reverting to demesne unless he made a deliberate effort to regain it. Cartularies of religious houses show that deliberate efforts were made to regain land from free-holders. Many of these houses quite consistently set about buying their freeholders out whenever the opportunity arose, and whenever they could find the resources to do so from other parts of their estates. The feet of fines suggest that some members of the knightly or gentry class, in so far as they had the necessary liquid assets, also set about buying out their freeholders.

The problem of gentry expenditure remains. Was this rising faster than income? Treharne suggests that office-holding was an increasing financial burden, but this is not entirely certain. The efforts of Henry III's government, of the baronial reformers, and of Edward I, alike seem to have been directed towards cutting down the profits of sheriffs. This in itself implies that there were still profits to be made. The gift of shrievalties as favours by Edward I carries the same implication. Nevertheless, men were prepared to pay to be exempt from the office of sheriff and men who died in office often left their dependents in difficulties. Some men could obviously still make a profit from the office of sheriff, but the expenses of others equally obviously exceeded the perquisites. Similarly the financial consequences of holding other local offices and performing other functions in local government depended on variety of opportunity and individual temperament. Of living standards we know nothing, except for a general impression that they were probably rising. We cannot therefore conclude with certainty, although some of the evidence points in that direction, that those who represented the shires, and those who were represented, were an increasingly important element in the country economically as well as politically.

If then, superficially on an administrative and political level, and more fundamentally on a social and economic level, the leading figures among the gentry were becoming of increasing importance, and this new importance lay behind the summoning of knights of the shire to parliament, it prompts the suggestion that similar changes, economic, social, administrative, and political, may have lain behind the summoning of representatives of the boroughs. It would be foolish to pretend that the towns, with the exception of London and perhaps of the Cinque Ports, were individually of much political significance in thirteenth- and fourteenth-century England. This lack of influence is perhaps reflected in the silent role that their representatives played in early parliaments. Nevertheless, intermittently in the thirteenth century, and increasingly regularly in the fourteenth century, burgesses were present in parliament. The crown thought it worth while to summon them. Why? The answer must be sought in terms of wealth and privileged immunity.

The enormous increase in the population of England between the Domesday Book of the late eleventh century and the Hundred Rolls of two centuries later had a variety of economic effects. The consequent combination of rising prices for agricultural produce and declining real wages has already been considered in so far as it favoured those nobility who had control of demesne lands. The next link in the economic chain has yet to be considered. The magnates and gentry were primarily consumers, not producers, and greater wealth in their hands gave them greater opportunities of spending. Those who provided for the needs of this class had therefore an increasing scope for their activities. The growth of towns was in some measure a consequence of the increasing provision of cloth and other manufactured goods for the prospering sector of the gentry and aristocracy, of growing trade in foreign goods, whether wines, silks, furs or other luxuries, for their conspicuous consumption, and of expanding sales of bulk produce from their estates, whether wool or grain (see no. 23). Throughout western Europe towns grew from the tenth century onwards, and were particularly thriving in the twelfth and thirteenth centuries, so much so that many new towns were planted by lords eager to cash in on this patent prosperity.

As the towns prospered they burst out of the decaying shell of feudal society. Townsmen, with their interests focused on trade or manufacture, had no interest in or talent for military duties, and resented outside, unsympathetic, interference in their activities. The financial exigencies of the Angevin kings coincided with the first wave of urban prosperity in England, and in consequence, at the end of the twelfth century, money passed and charters were granted. In this way a limited measure of local autonomy was created in many towns. This might take a variety of forms, including, for example, the right to elect a reeve rather than have one appointed, or the right to answer directly at the exchequer for royal dues rather than have the sheriff extort what he could on the spot. Later, in the 1250s, a number of towns received the right to reply to all royal writs directly to the central government instead of through the sheriff. This particular right brought these towns, from a subordinate position, up to the same level as the shires as local government units to which the central government could give corporate responsibilities and obligations. As in the shires, the carrying out of these corporate responsibilities increased the selfconscious community feeling in the towns, at least among the leading townsmen. However, in some ways the most significant of these grants of autonomy was that by which the town was allowed to compound for all tolls and taxes for a fixed annual payment. Grants of this kind were mostly made in the reign of John, but half a century after the rates of payment were fixed, it became apparent that they were unrealistic. When the original sum was fixed it had usually represented more than the king would otherwise have obtained from the town, and the townsmen were willing to pay the extra as the price for independence. With the twin factors of rising prices and economic growth it became obvious by the middle, and even more so by the end, of the thirteenth century that many towns were being undertaxed. In consequence of their chartered immunities no more taxation could be had without their consent. Consent to additional taxation was sometimes negotiated by the crown with individual town communities, but this was inconvenient, and it was simpler to gather the representatives of all these communities together in time of parliament. Representative burgesses in early parliaments seem to have had little other function than to negotiate the rate of urban taxation (see no. 39).

Taxation as a cause of summons comes out most clearly in the case of urban representatives, but it was also a cogent cause of summoning shire representatives. As Pasquet so clearly pointed out, subsidies on those in the countryside could not be collected without the active participation of at least some members of the gentry class as assessors and collectors, and not at all without the tacit agreement of the whole gentry class to the taxation of themselves and those over whom they had influence (see no. 34). As the magnates implied in 1254, it was no longer possible for them to consent to taxation on behalf of the gentry. The gentry had to give their consent themselves (see no. 64).

As well as representatives of the shires and boroughs Edwardian parliaments sometimes contained representatives of the lower, diocesan, clergy. The background of their summons is again one of taxation.

Henry III and Edward I had sought to tax the temporalities of the clergy on various occasions, and had run into difficulties owing to the theoretical immunity of the clergy from lay taxation. This immunity could be circumvented in two ways. The pope could be asked to make a grant on behalf of the clergy, or alternatively the clergy themselves could be asked directly. For a short time, therefore, in the reigns of Edward I and II it came about that representatives of the diocesan clergy sat in parliament and consented to taxation there. In the long run, however, they slipped out of parliament, and gave their consent to clerical subsidies in convocation.

As well as direct taxes for which the consent of the gentry, the urban oligarchies and the diocesan clergy was necessary, or at least convenient, Edward I sought to meet his increasing financial needs through indirect taxation. His first venture into this field was in his father's lifetime, but the 'new custom' of 1266 raised a great deal of opposition and was replaced by a tax on wool that came to be known later as the 'Great and Ancient Custom'. This was granted to Edward I in his first parliament at the rate of half a mark (6s 8d) per sack on all wool exported. He later tried to obtain grants of further taxation, with varying degrees of success, on wool and other exports, and on imports. He did not, however, ask for these grants in parliaments, but in special assemblies of wool merchants, or of other exporters or importers. The right of these assemblies to grant taxation was strongly contested by the magnates and others in parliament. Throughout the reign of Edward II, and through most of that of Edward III, the struggle over the right to grant indirect taxation continued between a rather amorphous body which became known as the estate of merchants, and the representatives of the shires and boroughs who were coming to form a lower house in parliament (see no. 63).

Continental scholars have coined the doctrine of *puissances* to explain who was present in the political assemblies of the later Middle Ages. By *puissance* they mean those who either individually, or corporately, exercise some measure of political power. The presence of the central administrators in parliament is thus explicable in terms of office. They, above all, ran the state. The presence of the earls and the bishops, and the greater lay magnates and abbots is equally explicable, for they controlled, by virtue of their hereditary or official wealth and lands, states within the state. The presence of the representatives of the gentry who dominated the shire communities is seen in terms of their local power and wealth, those of the representatives of the urban patriciates who

13

dominated the town communities in terms of their wealth and corporate immunities, and those of the clergy similarly in terms of wealth and immunity. Those without power and influence remained without representation, not only in the later Middle Ages, but until recent times. The extension of the suffrage in the nineteenth and twentieth centuries can be correlated with the power and influence, and the ability to bring pressure to bear, of the successive groups admitted to the vote. Disregarding Burkean notions of virtual representation, there was no one in parliament to represent the peasant, the rural labourer, or the urban craftsman in late medieval England. These people had neither individual or corporate means of exerting power and influence, save that of occasional revolt, as in 1381. On a European scale the varying composition of assemblies in different territories and at different times can be related in a similar way to the varying political, and at root, socio-economic, balance in society.

In England the thirteenth century saw the introduction, in a haphazard way, of all the constituents of later parliaments. The fourteenth century saw the regularization of what had already begun. It gradually became customary for particular magnates to be summoned, and not others. By the middle of the century the concept of an hereditary parliamentary peerage had already developed. Richard II acknowledged this development by the creation of hereditary parliamentary barons, although the reaction to the first such creation, in 1387, reveals that the custom was still far from universally accepted. As the ranks of the lay peers became limited to the earls, together with a known traditional parliamentary group from among the barons, so the ranks of the ecclesiastical peers became customarily limited to the bishops, together with a known traditional group from among the abbots. Similarly it became customary to summon knights and burgesses to all parliaments and not merely to some, whilst it ceased to be customary to summon the lower clergy to any parliaments at all. During the century it became customary for certain boroughs to be represented and not others, although it was not until the second half of the fifteenth century that the selection of boroughs represented was so rigidly defined that additional boroughs needed an explicit charter to grant them the privilege, and obligation, of representation. Likewise it was not until the fifteenth century that the electorate was defined for the shires. In the towns it remained variable and governed by local custom right up to the nineteenth century.

The fourteenth century also saw the polarization of the English parliament into two chambers. The gentry began to sit with the bur-gesses in one 'house' and not, surprisingly, with the aristocracy, from whom they were still barely divided. The aristocracy sat, equally sur-prisingly, with the upper clergy in another 'house'. This particular division into two houses, rather than three, or four, was distinctively English. The upper house was, naturally, the more important, and the essential part of parliament, except for matters of taxation. It was there-fore in the upper house that officers of the crown sat, although their numbers decreased as the fourteenth century advanced. It was the pro-ceedings of this house, not those of the lower house, that came to be recorded in the parliament rolls. The lower house at the same time began to grow more formal in its activities, with a chairman, called the speaker, and with certain exclusive privileges, including eventually the sole right to initiate grants of taxation, indirect as well as direct. The two houses met together for certain plenary sessions, such as the open-ing of parliament, or in informal committee for practical purposes, but in general they assembled apart, in their own fixed and separate meeting places, and this perhaps best symbolizes their formal institutionalization.

To ask what a medieval parliament did is to ask an impossible ques-tion. It is improper to say, before the fifteenth century at least, that such and such defined functions were performed *by* parliament. From the thirteenth century the type of functions performed *in time of* parliament can be described, but they were not performed exclusively *in* parlia-ment.

Much argument has been expended over the essential nature of parliament, and over the most important and characteristic function performed in parliament. The source material used very largely dictates the emphasis laid on different functions. If the historian had only the writs of summons to parliaments, he would conclude that early parlia-ments were concerned exclusively with the great business of the realm (see nos. 35 and 36). If he had only the rolls of parliament, he would conclude that, up to 1316, parliaments were concerned almost exclu-sively with judicial business. If he had only the statute roll, he would see parliament as one of the occasions of the promulgation of legislation. If he had to rely solely on the narrative of chroniclers, he would be pre-sented with a combination of politics, legislation and taxation, with politics predominating, and without any mention of justice. The mag-nates who framed great reforming documents such as the Provisions of Oxford in 1258, and the Ordinances in 1311, assumed the primacy of politics in parliament, although they acknowledged that there was a place for the redress of judicial and administrative grievances. On the other hand, the expansion of the membership of parliament, by its very nature, lays the emphasis on taxation. The selection of passages from nineteenth- and twentieth-century historians illustrates the different emphases that have consequently been laid on the nature of early parliaments (see nos. 52 to 68), whilst the narrative of the Hilary Parliament at Lincoln in 1316 (see no. 69) is designed to emphasize the multiplicity of functions performed in parliament.

Finally we must ask not only what was done in parliament, but why it was done there. The importance of relegating certain matters to parliamentary meetings may be explained negatively, in terms of the crown having no real option but to consult with the powerful sections of the community. The same thing may be expressed rather more positively in terms of the community reaching political maturity and claiming a share in the government. The suggestion that the king was in some way forced to consult the community may be made more palatable by saying that the king found consultation convenient and in his own best interests. However this explanation may be expressed, it comes back in some form or other to the fact that the social and economic balance in society changed in such a way that it became convenient, or expedient, or necessary for certain matters, for example taxation, to be dealt with only in consultation with, and with the agreement of, those sectors of the community concerned. A slightly different explanation may be given in theoretical terms, by suggesting that there was a revolution in political thought, and that certain things came to be thought of as morally or even legally right during the course of the thirteenth century (see nos. 41 and 44). In this view the crown was compelled to consult with the community, not because it was convenient to do so, or as a consequence of the political balance of power, but because it was morally right to do so. It is not at all clear how much the expression of moral obligation in the thirteenth century was a consequence of what was happening in practice, and how much it was an influence on practice. Did Aquinas draw his view of the necessity for the whole community to consent to legislation from Aristotle, or did he read it into Aristotle because of what he saw being done in the contemporary world (see no. 42)? The lawyers twisted the doctrine found in Roman private law *Quod omnes tangit* . . . (that which touches all ought to be approved by all), to apply to public, constitutional law. Did they do so on grounds of purely theoretical reasoning, or because of a climate of opinion generated by contemporary practice? When

Edward I quoted this doctrine (see no. 45), it was quite perverted from the original intention enshrined in the *Codex* of Justinian. Edward used it as a justification of his actions, but the doctrine may possibly also have been a contributory cause for his actions. The same problems are raised by the Song of Lewes in which the actions of the barons against the crown in 1265, on behalf of the community, were justified in terms of moral right and wrong (see no. 49). It is not clear whether the song only provided justification after the event, or was a genuine expression of real attitudes of right and wrong, so firmly held that they impelled men to action.

The thirteenth and fourteenth centuries thus not only witnessed the transformation of older councils into parliaments throughout western Europe, but also saw a radical change in the balance of society, and a revolution in the doctrine of authority. How closely these three developments can be correlated still remains a matter of dispute.

Part One

PARLIAMENTS THROUGHOUT MEDIEVAL EUROPE

Common Features of Parliaments
throughout Europe

R. H. Lord read this paper in America in 1929, four years before the project was mooted of forming an International Commission for the History of Representative and Parliamentary Institutions. The work of the commission over the past thirty years has done much to modify in detail what Lord wrote, but it remains, nevertheless, a landmark in the consideration of representative institutions on a comparative basis for the whole of Europe. It is surprisingly enough still the only comparative survey available in English, although more up-to-date surveys exist in other languages. These extracts show how Lord emphasized, and perhaps even over-emphasized, the similarities and the common features between the assemblies, whereas other authors, pre-occupied with one particular country, have often been at pains to emphasize the dissimilarities and the idiosyncracies of their own national institutions.

1 R. H. LORD

It is generally agreed that one of the greatest achievements of the Middle Ages was the development of the representative system and of parliaments. It is largely, though perhaps not sufficiently, recognized that in the general scheme of the evolution of European states, between the age of feudalism and the era of absolute monarchy, there intervenes a period of what may be called parliamentary monarchy, of quasi-constitutionalism, of experiments – practically for the first time in history – with representative institutions. This period extends roughly from the thirteenth to the seventeenth century. The hallmark of it is the fact that the power of the crown was then more or less extensively limited by that of assemblies, in part elective, whose members, though directly and immediately representing only the politically active classes, were also regarded as representing in a general way the whole population of the land. . . . What has not been adequately recognized, in the first place, is the universality of the phenomenon. The fact is that class-parliaments or assemblies of estates arose not merely in the three kingdoms of the British Isles, but in all the realms of the Iberian peninsula, in France and all the French provinces, in the Holy Roman Empire and in nearly all the territorial states of Germany, the Netherlands, and

Italy, in the Scandinavian kingdoms, Hungary, Bohemia, Poland, and Muscovy. Except for the municipal republics of Germany and Italy, where assemblies of estates were obviously out of the question, and the Balkan lands, where the Turkish conquest cut short the natural course of development, parliaments are found in this period in every state in Europe from Scotland to Hungary and from Portugal to Russia.

These hundreds of parliaments, national and provincial, ought to be studied comparatively, if we are ever to have an adequate conception of the constitutional development of Europe as a whole, and not simply a set of generalizations based on the history of three or four of the larger countries. But no such comparative study has ever been made. From the lack of it many misconceptions have arisen: e.g., that the English Parliament was in nearly every respect unique, or that England was the only country in Europe that developed a vigorous and effective parliamentary system, or that England alone preserved its parliament uninterruptedly from the Middle Ages down to the nineteenth century. . . .

The assemblies in question went by various names: 'Parliament', in England, Ireland, Scotland, Sicily, Naples, and the Papal States, and (for certain special assemblies) in Aragon, Catalonia, and Valencia (in Spanish and Italian '*Parlamento*'); '*Cortes*' for the ordinary parliaments of Portugal and the Spanish kingdoms; 'States-General' and 'Provincial Estates' in France and the Netherlands; '*Stati*' in Piedmont, but '*Congregazioni generali*' for the estates representing the whole of the territories of the House of Savoy; '*Reichstag*' in the Holy Roman Empire, and '*Landtag*' in the German territorial states; '*Rigsdag*' in Denmark and Norway; '*Riksdag*' in Sweden; '*Sněm*' and '*Sejm*' ('assemblies') in Bohemia and Poland respectively; '*Országgyülés*' and '*Zemski Sobor*' ('assemblies of the land') in Hungary and Russia – although for all the parliaments of Central and Northern Europe the custom of our language is to say 'Diet'.

These assemblies usually arose in that stage of political evolution when, amid the decay of feudalism, the prince, engaged in building up a more unified and more highly organized national or territorial state, but not yet strong enough to proceed as he liked, autocratically, felt the need of enlisting the support of the politically active classes of the population; when the nobles, no longer able to rule independently in their localities, might still hope by corporate organization and collective action to wield a large power over the common state; and when through the growth of cities a vigorous new social class had come to the front with important interests to defend and often with ambitions to have a voice in public affairs equal to that of the older privileged classes. Between the crown, on the one hand, and the leading social classes on the other, a certain equilibrium had been reached, and collaboration and mutual concessions were necessary. More concretely, it was the ever growing financial needs of the crown – the need of larger revenues than those supplied by the domain lands and the customary feudal aids – that usually conduced most powerfully to the calling of the first parliaments. Other factors that sometimes operated were: disputed successions to the throne (Denmark, Norway); foreign invasion (Scotland, Sweden); the desire of the princes for popular support against the magnates (Hungary, Russia), or against the Papacy (France, Portugal). The crown most commonly took the initiative in the introduction of these assemblies. But cases are not lacking in which the subjects (through 'leagues', 'confederations', 'unions') forced a weak government or a tyrannical ruler to take them into organized consultation (Aragon, Bohemia, various German and Netherlands territories).

The practice of consultation through parliaments seems in most countries to have arisen from a development of the old *curia regis*. Medieval rulers were accustomed, for treating more important public affairs, to expand their ordinary 'court' or 'council' into a large assembly ('*curia solemnis*', '*curia plena*', '*magnum concilium*', '*colloquium*', '*congregatio*', '*Hoftag*', etc.), which might be attended by most or all of the prelates, magnates, and tenants-in-chief, and in some countries by all the nobility. It was natural that, with the urban renaissance, 'men of the good towns' or other spokesmen of the commons should occasionally be called to these gatherings, when matters affecting them were to come up. . . .

The competence of these assemblies can seldom be defined with any accuracy, for it was bounded by no systematic constitutions of the modern sort. The estates almost everywhere did, indeed, at one time or another wring from their rulers written recognition of their rights in this or that respect; and, apart from this, the unwritten law of customs and precedents generally established for them a certain more or less incontestable sphere of activity. But at bottom everything depended on the ever-varying political situation and the ever-shifting balance of power as between the crown and the estates. Whenever the crown felt strong enough, it was prone to forget, to deny, or to ride roughshod over inconvenient parliamentary rights, no matter whether they were based on custom or on sacred charters. And when the prince was weak, or a minor, or badly in debt, or the land in a great crisis, the estates in their turn were likely to take the bit in their teeth, to extend their scope almost without limits, or even virtually to sequestrate the government. When the crown was up, parliament was down, and vice versa – that is the most general rule that can be laid down in the matter.

The most constant and important activity of the estates was the granting of taxes. *Landtage sind Geldtage* – that German adage might have been applied to nearly all these parliaments. Almost everywhere (save in Russia, Denmark, and Norway), the principle came to be recognized that, apart from the old feudal and domain revenues, no taxes could be imposed without the consent of the estates. It was by exploiting the power of the purse that not only the English Parliament but many Continental ones raised themselves to a high degree of power and indispensability. And it may be said that in most countries the sole right of the estates to grant taxes was, on the whole, well maintained down to the seventeenth century. There is, however, the well-known exception of France, where the States-General lost this power from 1440 on, and the Provincial Estates, from about the same period, could do little more than debate how taxes that could not be escaped might best be paid.

The second chief sphere of parliamentary activity was in legislation. All these assemblies had at least some influence in this field, through their right to present petitions and grievances (*cahiers de doléances, greujes, agravís, postulata, gravamina*), which even in countries like France furnished the stimulus and the material for a great deal of royal law-making. The French States-General and the Castilian and Portuguese Cortes in the later period scarcely got beyond this. But nothing could be more erroneous than the assumption often made (by writers whose knowledge of Continental systems hardly extends beyond France or Castile) that the English Parliament was the only assembly of that time that discovered how to gain effective legislative power by making grants of supply depend on redress of grievances, and by drawing up their demands in the form of 'bills' ready to become 'acts' as soon as they received the royal sanction. In fact both these devices came to be practiced in most Continental parliaments: in the eastern Spanish kingdoms, Sicily, the German states, Sweden, Poland, Bohemia, and Hungary. Usually this did not exclude a certain amount of legislation by the crown without the sanction of the estates; but, on the other hand, in Germany at least within certain spheres the estates could legislate without the sanction of the crown. In general, the principle was widespread that all more important laws ought to be made only with the consent and participation of parliament; and there were kingdoms like Poland or Aragon where this principle was very strictly carried out.

Thirdly, there was a vast range of functions which most parliaments sometimes arrogated to themselves, especially in times of crisis and confusion, and some of which were exercised for long periods by some of these assemblies. Foreign relations were a matter in which most estates often claimed a voice. They wished to be consulted about war, peace, alliances, treaties; nay, sometimes they sent and received embassies, raised armies, and concluded peace or alliances quite of their own authority. Similarly, the history of most parliaments shows attempts to dictate the choice of the prince's advisers or to force upon him a council formally elected by the estates (which the Swedish kings had to submit to through much of the eighteenth century). There are many cases of a parliament appointing a regent, fixing the succession to the throne, or even for long periods freely electing its rulers. Even more common was the custom that the estates should prescribe how the taxes they granted should be expended, or should undertake the collection and disbursement through their own agents and treasury. Many parliaments (e.g., the eastern Spanish kingdoms, Languedoc, Brittany, the German states) came to have quite a staff of permanent officials of their own, and to take a large part not only in the financial but in the general administration of the country. Finally, the assumption sometimes made that the English Parliament alone combined the functions of a legislative and tax-granting body with those of a high court of justice is by no means true: many Continental assemblies of estates present the same combination of functions (e.g., in Aragon, Poland, and universally among the German states).

The Word 'Parliament'

At the same time as 'parliaments' developed out of great councils, the very word 'parliament' underwent a parallel evolution. From the general meaning of 'conversation' it came to be a technical description of the new institution. In this passage Professor Treharne, heavily relying on the earlier work of H. G. Richardson, describes this evolution.

2 R. F. TREHARNE

When, beginning in the 1240s we find chroniclers, king's clerks, magnates and the king himself speaking and writing of 'the king's parliament', it slowly becomes apparent that they are thinking of something new, in the sense that the old word, 'council', '*conseil*', '*concilium*', does not adequately express their meaning any longer. A new word is being used, if not for a totally new thing, then at least for a new way of looking at something familiar. The purpose of this enquiry is to discover as closely as possible, what those who were active in politics and in government – the king, the prelates and nobles, the officials, the king's clerks – had in mind when they used the new word 'parliament' in any of its several forms. The result of such an investigation should prove relevant to the recent discussions of the origin and nature of parliament in England.

Mr H. G. Richardson summarized conveniently the early history of the word in its French, Italian, Latin and English forms.[1] Before 1240 it was much better known on the Continent than in England. In its primary sense of 'conversation' or 'talk' it occurs as early as the latter half of the eleventh century, and it long kept this meaning, so that Joinville could describe as '*leur parlement*' the secret meetings of Louis IX and his queen on the private staircase where they sought refuge from the strict and jealous eye of Louis' mother, Blanche of Castile. By a natural extension, the word came to be used for formal discussions between responsible persons or their accredited agents – 'parleys', 'talks', both in war and in peace; and this meaning took firm root, so

[1] 'The Origins of Parliament', *Trans. Roy. Hist. Soc.*, 4th Ser., xi (1928), 137–49.

that in 1262, Llywelyn ap Gruffydd, complaining of breaches of the truce by various Marchers, says that these occurred on the very day which both sides had agreed upon 'ad habendum parliamentum', when the Welsh had assembled 'ad dictum parliamentum'. Simultaneously, apparently beginning in Italy in the form parlamento, the word was also being used to describe a formal business assembly of townsmen, and during the twelfth century this meaning spread to cover the more formal meetings of the courts of kings and emperors, whether for business or for social purposes, or assemblies of his vassals called by a great baron, or a council of war held by a body of crusaders. The business sessions of a craft gild, and even secret meetings of a conspiratorial character, could be styled 'parliaments' in the thirteenth century.

For England, Baxter and Johnson's Medieval Latin Word-List notes parliamentum, in the sense of 'colloquy, council, parliament', as early as 1189, but does not give the context or the source.[1] The first use of the word in this sense in England, reported by Mr H. G. Richardson and tentatively dated by him in 1217, should be treated with the greatest reserve until we know at what date the passage he cites was in fact written. It was used in England, and particularly in the Welsh Marches, before 1220, occurring in private charters to describe meetings of a lord's court and military assemblies of his feudal service. The chroniclers and the king's clerks were slower to take it up, preferring older words like concilium and colloquium until after 1240. Matthew Paris, for instance, does not use the word parliamentum, in the sense of an assembly of the king's council or court, until 1246. He introduces the new word with an impressive magniloquence which suggests self-concious innovation, which he seeks to justify by emphasizing the importance of the assembly so described: Edicto regio convocata, convenit ad PARLAMENTUM generalissimum regni Anglicani totalis nobilitas Londoniis, videlicet praelatorum tam abbatum et priorum quam episcoporum, comitum quoque et baronum, ut de statu regni jam vacillantis efficaciter prout exegit urgens necessitas contrectarent. In reprinting this passage in his Select Charters, Stubbs hailed this first appearance of the blessed word with a flourish of capitals. Thereafter the word, though by no means the only term now used for such assemblies, becomes rapidly more common in Matthew's chronicle, and in other contemporary works such as the Liber de Antiquis Legibus (1254), the Flores Historiarum (1253), and the Annals of Burton (1255). By 1255 it was clearly accepted, even by conservative chroniclers writing in Latin, as a useful means of distinguishing specially

[1] This has been altered to c. 1210 in the new revised edition.

large gatherings of the *curia regis* or the *magnum concilium*, to which the king had summoned unusually large numbers of magnates to transact important business. But it was far from being, even at this date, the only permissible or even the commonest way of describing such an assembly, however great the attendance and however important the occasion: it was still only one of several possible terms.

When Mr Richardson wrote in 1928, the word 'parliament' was thought to have been first used officially in England in 1242. The earliest reference now known to 'parliament' in English official records occurs in the roll of the court coram rege *(before the king) for 1236–7. It records the adjournment of a lawsuit, over the right of presentation to an ecclesiastical benefice, from a session of this court to the forthcoming parliament at Westminster.*

3 CORAM REGE ROLL 1236

Excuses for non-attendance [received by the court] before the Lord King at Woodstock on Friday before St Andrew's Day (i.e. 28 November 1236).

Wiltshire. Adam, sub-dean of Salisbury [sent his excuse for absence] by Richard de Esseby in a case of *darrein presentment* against Hubert Heose [and the case is adjourned] to the octave of the feast of St Hilary (i.e. 20 January 1237) at Westminster at parliament (*ad parliamentum*). [Richard] pledged his faith [for Adam's appearance]. The same day [for attendance] was given to the bishop of Salisbury through his attorney in Court. And similarly the same day was given to all the witnesses who came, that is to say Henry d'Aubigny, Henry de Bovill and all the others. And the sheriff is responsible for their appearance in person.

Parliament in the 1270s

A realistic impression of the nature of parliaments in the 1270s, or perhaps a little earlier, as seen through the eyes of a friar, is given by Humbert de Romans, a man who had travelled widely and moved in the highest circles. After running the Tuscan and French provinces of his order in turn, he became in 1254 the fifth general of the Dominicans. He resigned the headship of the order in 1263, and his prolific writings are mostly thought to date from the period between his retirement and his death in 1277. All his works bear the marks of an intensely practical man, writing with authority and from experience. His De Eruditione Praedicatorum *is designed for practical use, to give guidance to Dominicans who might be called upon to preach in a wide variety of circumstances. By including a chapter on parliaments he was acknowledging the likelihood of Dominicans being asked to preach the sermon which, it is clear from later evidence, usually opened a parliament. The chapter falls amongst a group of sermon outlines designed for use on a variety of other lay occasions such as tournaments, the conferment of knighthood and the making of treaties. The three most important functions which he attributes to parliaments include not only politics and legislation, but also the calling of royal officials to account for their actions. He makes no mention of taxation, but suggests that parliament is an appropriate occasion to preach against administrative and judicial abuses. It is also interesting to note that he assumes the universality of the practice of holding parliaments in the major kingdoms of western Europe, and the regularity of their meeting several times each year.*

4 HUMBERT DE ROMANS

Of the way to prepare sermons rapidly for all sorts of occasions
In the parliaments of kings
It is the custom for great kings to hold parliaments at fixed times in any year at which they assemble many counsellors, many lay magnates and many prelates. They hold this sort of parliament for three main reasons: namely so that major affairs of state which cannot easily be settled during the year, may then be more wisely dealt with, after consideration by the magnates, since, according to Exodus 18, greater matters are to be reserved for greater men; also, so that the king's

ministers may account for themselves, [for this preach on] *Therefore is the Kingdom of heaven likened to a King who would take an account of his servants* (Matthew 18 v. 23); and also so that legislation for the kingdom may be promulgated there, for this preach on *It lieth upon me to take order for the affairs of the Kingdom* (1 Maccabees 6 v. 57). Other material for sermons in parliament, when there is likely to be a suitable congregation, may be had by remembering that many things sometimes happen in parliaments, against which one ought to preach. One is the perversion of counsel, for there are some counsellors of kings, who sometimes, so as to curry favour, dishonestly give advice that they think will be favourably received. Sometimes on account of private malice, or friendship, or on similar grounds they will diverge from the truth, and give false counsel, and this is exceedingly dangerous in a kingdom. As a certain wise man has said: It is easier for a king to be influenced by his counsellors, than they by him, and therefore it is worse for a country to have evil counsellors about the king, than to have an evil king. Therefore Job said in his blessing [chapter 21 v. 16] *May the counsel of the wicked be far from me and blessed is the king who has not gone astray through the counsel of such wicked men*. Another [sermon topic] is the miscarriage of justice, for it sometimes happens in parliament that people with powerful support, either through friends or wealth, have prevailed in law suits, perverting the course of justice *Because the wicked prevaileth against the just, therefore wrong judgment goeth forth* (Habbakkuk 1 v. 4). Against this quote Psalm 67. Thou shalt judge the children of men with righteousness. Another [sermon topic] is the difficulty of obtaining justice, and how what ought to be obtained can only be achieved with difficulty, *Justice hath stood far off* (Isaiah 59 v. 14). On the contrary Isaiah, chapter 5 v. 5, wrote of the good king, that he is *quickly rendering that which is just*. Another topic is contempt for the poor, for they are excluded and held in contempt in the courts, so that they can scarcely obtain a hearing. Against which quote Deuteronomy 1 v. 17, *There shall be no difference of persons, you shall hear the little as well as the great*. Another [topic] is the prohibition of evil deeds, such as are done by wicked bailiffs who remain for a long time in office, since certain other people defend them. Use the example of Menelaus who, through the greed of those who were powerful remained in power, increasing in wickedness. On the other hand it is written of the unjust steward, in Luke 16 v. 2, that as soon as he was accused, his lord said to him immediately *Now thou canst be steward no longer*, that is, from now on. Another [subject] is corruption by bribes, by which almost all courts are corrupted today. *Thy princes all love bribes, they run after rewards* (Isaiah 1 v. 23), and against it *Thou shalt not accept gifts; for gifts blind the eyes of the wise, and change the words of the just* (Deuteronomy 16 v. 19). Another [subject] is the danger of judging by outward appearances, for it is because of this that the worst men are honoured and the good men condemned in these courts. Against this, quote Leviticus 19 v. 15, *Respect not the person of the poor, nor honour the countenance of the mighty.* Another [subject] is the carrying out of malicious intentions, for there are many who conceive a hatred for others, and pursue them here to procure evil for them, if they can, just as the Jews, in the court of Pilate, procured the death of Christ, as they had plotted. These things and many others happen in parliaments which ought to be purged away by the goodness of the king. For how shall this court be able to correct the evils of the whole kingdom, unless it is first corrected itself? The king would put down these abuses, more effectively than any preaching, if he showed himself to be such a man that everyone knew that this behaviour heartily displeased him. The substance for this theme is in Proverbs 20 v. 8., *The King that sitteth on the throne of judgment, scattereth away all evil with his look,* namely when all understand from his look, that evil displeases him.

Parliaments in Spain and Germany

In a volume of this size it is obviously impossible to print even one comparative document from each of the multitude of parliaments which were coming into existence throughout Europe at about the same time as the English parliament. Two documents relating to the origins of Spanish and German parliaments have been selected for printing here, and a writ of summons to a French assembly is printed later (no. 37). The earliest certain record of a Spanish cortes which contained clergy, nobility and citizens relates to a cortes at Leon as early as 1188. This is much earlier than any comparable assembly elsewhere in western Europe. Although representatives of the cities sat occasionally in the cortes of Leon and Castille in the late twelfth and early thirteenth centuries, there is no evidence that they did so frequently until after 1250, or regularly until the end of the thirteenth century. Nevertheless Spanish concepts of the nature and function of political assemblies were considerably in advance of those elsewhere. In Germany in the thirteenth century it is difficult to know at what level to look for an assembly to compare with the English parliament, for the Holy Roman Empire, which comprised most of what we today call Germany, and parts of northern Italy, was in a state of dissolution. The nascent imperial diet was a high sounding but basically ineffective institution like the emperor himself. The effective unit of government was ceasing to be the Empire as a whole, and was becoming the individual principality, for example the duchy of Bavaria or the archbishopric of Cologne. It was therefore at the level of the principality that parliaments, landtage or diets were to develop effectively. The document which follows was drawn up at an imperial diet, held at Worms in 1231 by Henry, titular King of the Romans, who was acting as viceroy in Germany for his father, the last great medieval Emperor, Frederick II, whilst the latter was in Italy. It makes clear that the territorial princes, even if effectively emancipated from imperial constraint, ought not to rule absolutely in their own territories. It recognizes the principle that lay behind the development of all medieval parliaments, that the princes ought only to rule with the consent of their subjects, or rather of the more powerful of them. It is however not possible to date the origins of the parliaments of the German principalities to this statement of principle, for it takes time to enshrine principles in practice in thoroughly institutional forms.

5 THE CORTES AT LEON 1188

Decree established by Alphonso king of Leon and Galicia in the cortes at Leon with the archbishop of Compostella and with all the bishops and magnates of his kingdom and with those chosen by the cities.

1. In the name of God. When I held a cortes at Leon with the archbishop and the bishops and magnates of my kingdom and with citizens chosen from every city, I Alphonso, king of Leon and Galicia, established and confirmed with an oath, that I would preserve for all the inhabitants of my kingdom, whether clergy or laity, the good customs which they enjoy, as established by my predecessors.

3. I promised also, that I would not make war or peace or treaties, except with the counsel of the bishops, the nobles and the 'good men' by whose counsel I ought to rule.

6 THE DIET OF THE EMPIRE 1231

Henry, by the grace of God, King of the Romans to all the faithful people of his empire, his grace and goodwill. We desire everyone to know that at a solemn diet held in our presence at Worms we were asked to define if any territorial lord could make any constitution or new law without any consultation with the better and greater men of his territory. When the agreement of the princes had been asked the matter was defined in this way: That neither princes nor others could make any constitutions or new laws unless the consent of the better and greater men of the territory had first been obtained. We have therefore caused these present letters to be written and furnished with our seal, to give this sentence the strength of perpetual validity.
Given at Worms: 1 May 1231.

Regional Assemblies – the English Shire Court

In most parts of Europe important assemblies grew up on a regional level at the same time as, or even earlier than, the corresponding national assemblies. England was too small and too centralized a country for semi-autonomous provincial governments to exist, and in consequence no provincial assemblies developed with any real political competence. The nearest approximation to a provincial assembly in England was the shire court. In this excerpt from a letter sent by Henry III's government to the sheriff of Yorkshire in 1231 the composition of the shire court is discernible. Some elements of representation were already clearly apparent at this level, and probably had been for a good many years previously. Although the more important part of the court's membership was non-representative, each of the rural townships was represented there not only by a village official, but also by four other men who could be held legally responsible for their actions, and each borough was represented by twelve burgesses. The shire court was thus the visible expression of the community of the shire, just as parliament was to be of the community of the realm. The shire court was for the county community the focus of administrative, legal, social and political life, and therefore, when knights of the shire came to be summoned to parliament to represent the shire communities, it was naturally in the shire courts that they were chosen.

7 WRIT OF 1231

The king to the sheriff of Yorkshire, greetings. Summon through good summoners, all the archbishops, bishops, abbots, priors, earls, barons, knights and all free-holders throughout your jurisdiction; and from each township (summon) the reeve and four responsible men, and from each borough throughout your jurisdiction (summon) twelve responsible burgesses; and (summon) all others who ought and are accustomed to come before the itinerant justices, to be at York a week after Trinity (1 June) . . . to hear and carry out our command.

Assemblies in Church and State

At about the same time as parliamentary types of assembly were developing in lay society, both at national and regional levels, similar representative assemblies were being called into existence in the church in western Europe. There has been much argument about the extent to which clerical assemblies influenced or were influenced by lay assemblies. Two extracts from this controversy are printed here, from Sir Ernest Barker and Professor Marongiu. The former, who was concerned with the growth of representation in the church, particularly in the Dominican order, during the thirteenth century, maintained that in England clerical representation preceded lay representation. His argument has been severely criticized by a number of authors. Professor Marongiu has recently summarized these criticisms whilst strongly endorsing his general contention that institutional developments in medieval Europe in church and state cannot safely be treated separately. Although differing in emphasis, the opinions of these authors provide a healthy corrective to any narrow study of the English parliament in isolation.

8 SIR ERNEST BARKER

There are two main ideas underlying the English representative system of the thirteenth century – indeed from the thirteenth to the nineteenth century. In the first place the representation is representation of communities. It is representation not of geographical constituencies containing some thousands of electoral units, but of organized and organic communities, that have a real and regular life of their own. The House of Commons is a federation of these communities through their representatives: it expresses the medieval conception of the State as a *communitas communitatum*. In the second place the representative is a full representative. He binds his constituents. He is a proxy with full powers of attorney; there is no room for a referendum to his constituents. The knights and burgesses, says Edward in 1295, shall have full and sufficient powers for themselves *and their communities*, and business shall in no wise remain undone for want of such power. Both of these ideas are at home with the clergy. Their chapters are real communities, which can federate in a joint assembly, and are conscious of the reasons and the need of such federation, as early as 1226. With the nature of a *procuratorium* they are well acquainted; their chapters and monasteries have to send proctors to Rome as a matter of ordinary legal business, and Rome will invite proctors, from chapters at any rate, to a general Council of the Church. The reinforcement of the baronage by shire and borough representatives, which makes a national parliament, finds its precedent in the reinforcement of the episcopate by the proctors of chapters. Representation in a clerical parliament in 1226 is nearly thirty years prior to representation in the lay assembly of 1254. We may repeat the saying of Viollet: 'Je suppose que ces réunions ecclésiastiques ont pu contribuer à faciliter le développement et la régularisation des grandes assemblées civiles, des réunions d'états. . . . En effet, le premier des trois états, le clergé, se trouva, du premier jour, habitué et comme rompu à ce que nous appellerions aujourd'hui les usages parlementaires. Circonstance heureuse qui a dû contribuer, dans l'Europe entière, sinon à former, du moins à régulariser la tenue des états.' Stubbs has remarked that the medieval procedure of parliament is like that of convocation. There is the same list of *gravamina*, the same petition for remedy. And so we may urge that the Church by its organization, its ideas, its procedure, was a model and a precedent for that parliamentary system, which, we must admit and indeed urge, in turn reacted on the Church; for the regular parliamentary system of Convocation would have been impossible, unless it had found a parallel and a support in a national parliament, and unless it had been part of a whole structure of society which was consonant with itself.

And what of the Dominicans? Well, they are a part of that development of representation in the General Councils of the Church, in the provincial synod, and even (in Germany) in the diocesan synod, which marks the thirteenth century. In that development they appear early, as early as 1221; of that development they are the highest expression, for the use of representation was regular and systematic through the whole Order. They are a new Order, and they have the attraction of novelty; they are an Order with a high prestige, and their prestige will make them a model. They found friends for themselves in great men, like Stephen Langton and Simon de Montfort; and great men can give a vogue to ideas and practices which would otherwise pass unregarded, making a commonplace original, and a fantasy a practical policy. They had communicated their organization to an Order which had a greater attraction, and certainly a far greater vogue, than their own: the Franciscans after 1239 reproduced many of the features of the statesmanship of St Dominic. These are all so many channels of indirect influence. Direct influence can hardly be proved. That Stephen Langton had felt their influence when he admitted representation as far as he did in 1226 is only conjecture. That de Montfort, who from early years had been connected with the Order, felt and expressed their influence is equally conjectural, if perhaps a little more possible. That Kilwardby, himself a Dominican and ex-prior of the English province, was translating their ideas into practice in 1273 and 1277 is, at least, very probable. But we may content ourselves with asserting as a certainty, that they are the highest expression of the development of the representative principle in the thirteenth-century Church, and that the indirect influence of that expression must have been felt in the Church and to some extent in the State.

One lesson which emerges from this study may be remarked in conclusion. The study of the institutional development of the Middle Ages is an organic whole. We cannot isolate Church and State; not only do they develop side by side, but they interact in their development. The development of representation in Church and State must not be figured in the mind as the advance of two parallel lines in two separate squares; it is the growth of one idea into an institution, in that one and single *republica Christiana* under two governments (the *regnum* and the *sacerdotium*) of which Dr Figgis has taught us to conceive. Further, we must not in our insular way isolate the institutional development of England from that of continental Europe. We have learned of late not to contrast English with continental feudalism, but to see in both the same plant growing under somewhat different conditions. We have been taught by recent historians to think of the municipal development of the Middle Ages in Western Europe as a single whole, and of its problems as not to be solved country by country, but rather to be treated on the same lines for all countries taken together. The development of representation must be treated in the same way; it is a general movement in all Western Europe in the thirteenth century, and it must be regarded as such if it is to be understood in its fullness.

9 ANTONIO MARONGIU

As we have suggested the thesis of this English historian [Sir Ernest Barker] is open to numerous criticisms. In the first place he has been attacked for the schematic nature of his writing, and for the oddness of the fact that although Dominican principles [of representation] were translated into practice [in the 'convocation' of 1226] only five years after their arrival in England, another fifty years elapsed before any other event of the same type occurred. In the second place, already in 1213 – that is before the statutes of the Dominican order were drawn up – King John had summoned (it makes no difference whether the project was ever put into effect) four knights from each shire to come with the magnates to a general assembly or great council. The same critics, especially Pasquet, have pointed out that although it is impossible to admit that the English parliament was in any way simply an imitation of ecclesiastical assemblies, nevertheless, the claims of the ecclesiastics may have had 'some influence' on the lay world.

Communities, like individuals, live and act under the pressure of the psychological motives or stimuli which their way of thinking and their state of mind permit to filter in from their surrounding circumstances. It is therefore very difficult to sever the two elements, the lay, the profane or the civil, however one likes to express it, from the ecclesiastical in the organization of communal life in the middle ages. The life of the church was a more integral part of the history of society than at any other period. The law of the church was one of the laws of society, the ecclesiastical hierarchy was also a social hierarchy and directly, or indirectly, also a political one. Its collaboration with the lay power was a part of the political formula of the regime. Ecclesiastical society and civil society are thus difficult to separate and distinguish. Far from being mutually antagonistic they were strictly bound together by the identity of their opinions, of their ultimate objectives and of their personnel. We must, of course, beware of suggesting that parliamentary institutions, and especially the parliamentary institutions of any particular country, developed as a counterfeit and imitation of ecclesiastical assemblies. We must also beware of confusing theories, most seductive when unproven, with facts, or of confusing suggestions with proofs. Civil society, of which the clergy formed an integral part, could not be unaware of, nor remain indifferent to, the examples so universally spread throughout ecclesiastical organizations of the separation and co-ordination of powers, of democratic forms, and of government partially carried out through assemblies. In return, ecclesiastical organization could not but feel the effects of the general trend towards greater democracy, or of the feeling that was in the air, that all individuals concerned should participate in making decisions which affected them. There is much evidence of such participation not only in, but also outside the parliamentary field, for example in the various political or economic patterns of association in towns or guilds.

Part Two

THE ECONOMIC AND SOCIAL BACKGROUND TO EARLY PARLIAMENTS

Society and its Institutions – The Corporatist Theory

Professor Lousse, now President of the International Commission for the History of Representative and Parliamentary Institutions, is perhaps the most distinguished exponent of the 'corporatist' approach to the parliaments of medieval Europe. In the passage quoted he defines this theory, and expresses a belief in the strict correspondence between the structure of society and the form of its political, and particularly representative, institutions. Corporatist views have, however, been far from unchallenged. In an article on the Estates of Flanders, Professor Dhondt strenuously attacked the views of Professor Lousse.

10 EMILE LOUSSE

La théorie constitutionnelle et corporative peut être résumée en quatre propositions. La première de ces propositions est relative aux cadres dans lesquels les corps et les ordres se sont insérés. La *ständische Verfassung*, dans ce qu'elle a de plus universel, se compose d'une triple hiérarchie: territoriale, administrative et politique. La hiérarchie territoriale se confond avec le *Territorialstaat*: l'agglomération, sous la *potestas* d'un même prince, de plusieurs *pagi*, seigneuries et principautés antérieurement indépendants les uns des autres. Dans ce territoire formé par lui, le prince établit, de propos délibéré et par la vertu d'une volonté opiniâtre, une hiérarchie de plus en plus compliquée de fonctionnaires nommés par lui, commandés par lui, et strictement responsables envers lui de l'exercice de compétences déléguées (*das Beamtentum, der Beamtenstaat*). La hiérarchie sociale et politique des individus et des corps (*der Ständestaat*, au sens étroit) se constitue dans le même cadre, mais d'une manière plus autonome. Les distinctions entre les habitants d'un même État territorial se fondent sur la diversité naturelle des fonctions; par concession du prince, elles s'enrobent de catégories juridiques strictement correspondantes. Les personnes accomplissant les mêmes fonctions, ayant des intérêts communs, dotées du même statut d'orde privé, se groupent d'initiative en associations,

43

et certaines associations, dotées par le prince d'un statut propre, deviennent des corps privilégiés. Les corps se groupent en ordres, les ordres en pays, et les pays, le cas échéant, en unions permanentes de pays. La solidarité sociale se manifeste et s'exprime *'per gradus'*.

L'organisation corporative proprement dite (*das Ständewesen*) est fondée sur une correspondance de fonctions et de droits, de services et de privilèges: les fonctions accomplies appelant en retour l'octroi de privilèges, et les libertés concédées limitant les services à rendre dans l'avenir. La structure de la société ne repose pas sur l'égalité de nature, d'ailleurs reconnue, entre les individus. Le domaine du droit commun est réduit; celui des droits spéciaux par contre, extrêmement étendu. Les clercs sont régis par le droit canonique; les nobles, par le droit féodal; les bourgeois des villes et les manants du plat pays, par des coutumes et des chartes. Le statut de chaque personne physique est adapté à la place que celle-ci occupe dans la société, au rang qu'elle y détient et, pour tout dire d'un mot, à la fonction d'utilité générale qu'elle y remplit; les droits et privilèges, qui lui sont reconnus ou concédés, ont précisément pour but de lui faciliter l'accomplissement des services sociaux qu'elle est appelée à rendre et, subsidiairement, de l'en récompenser. Il en est de même pour les corps. Si l'autorité qui gouverne, leur octroie des statuts privilégiés, c'est qu'elle a pu reconnaître au préalable qu'ils remplissent des fonctions d'intérêt général et qu'elle veut sanctionner officiellement la situation qu'ils se sont acquise en fait, tout en les contenant dans de justes limites. Elle agit de même à l'égard des ordres, des pays, des unions de pays. Tous les contrats qu'elle passe, toutes les chartes qu'elle concède trahissent son unique souci ,traduisent la même conception: point de privilèges, si ce n'est pour définir le statut d'une fonction particulière; point de droits, à moins qu'il ne s'agisse de sanctionner des devoirs préalablement accomplis dans l'intérêt supérieur de la communauté. Le service à rendre est limité par le privilège; la *libertas* concédée au sujet individuel ou collectif constitue un obstacle à l'exercice arbitraire de la *potestas* du prince. C'est une double correspondance dont on ne peut se dispenser de tenir compte, ainsi que de la limitation du statut du *gradus* supérieur par ceux de tous les *gradus* subordonnés.

Une correspondance non moins stricte existe entre l'organisation et la représentation corporatives: entre le *Ständewesen* et la *Ständevertretung*. Puisque les services à rendre sont limités par les privilèges concédés, il importe que les titulaires puissent disposer de moyens légaux pour défendre l'intégrité de ceux-ci, chaque fois que le pouvoir essaie d'augmenter arbitrairement ceux-là. Les personnes physiques individuelles, du moins quand elles sont *sui juris*, agissent ou refusent d'agir *viritim*, c'est-à-dire par elles-mêmes et en leur propre nom; la représentation n'existe pour elles que dans l'ordre privé: par tuteur ou par mandataire. Les personnes morales, au contraire, les entités corporatives de tout ordre et tout grade opèrent rarement *'per communitatem'*, c'est-à-dire en généralité ou en assemblée plénière, mais plutôt par représentants ou députés. La représentation politique, analogue à celle que nous connaissons aujourd'hui, n'est pas antérieure aux sujets collectifs de droit, et elle s'établit naturellement à tous les degrés de l'organisation: pour les corps, les ordres, les pays, les unions de pays. Pour elle, comme pour l'organisation proprement dite, le statut de l'entité inférieure détermine et limite le statut de celle qui lui est immédiatement superposée. Et c'est finalement l'assemblée régulière des ordres qui assume la représentation des intérêts et la défense des privilèges des individus, des corps, des ordres, des pays et des unions de pays contre les abus possibles de la *potestas* du *dominus*.

Cette forme corporative de la société politique, nantie de sa triple hiérarchie, organisée et représentée par fonctions, privilèges et degrés, a existé dans tous les pays de l'Europe chrétienne depuis le déclin de la féodalité jusqu'à l'avènement du libéralisme politique. . . . Il faut traiter en un seul cycle toute l'histoire de ces pays, depuis l'époque féodale jusqu'aux révolutions qui ont détruit l'ancien régime. . . . L'ordre corporatif, tel qu'il vient d'être défini, n'a pas existé dans d'autres parties du monde, ni en Europe même à d'autres époques. Mais, durant le moyen âge et les temps modernes, il a été établi chez tous les peuples de l'Occident chrétien, sans exception: sur un fonds doctrinal unique, dans des institutions qui présentaient entre elles de frappantes analogies, et diversement accommodé toutefois aux contingences de temps et de lieu, à l'opportunité sociale et à la conjoncture économique, au tempérament des chefs et des peuples qui l'adoptaient.

11 J. DHONDT

L'école corporative donne une autre réponse. Pour elle, la société d'ancien régime était un monde organisé selon la raison, un ensemble harmonieux d'organismes qui tous avaient des droits et des devoirs bien définis, déterminés par le caractère fonctionnel de chaque groupe social, par le besoin d'assurer à chaque groupe le plein déploiement de son activité constructive. L'assemblée d'États faisant trait d'union entre le prince et le pays, assure le contact entre prince et sujets dans l'exercice du pouvoir suprême.

L'école corporative ferme consciemment les yeux à la réalité: elle admet une évolution, mais une seule, celle qui tend vers, et aboutit, à l'établissement des rapports politico-sociaux qu'elle postule, et se termine là. Autrement dit, cette école proclame expressément que, au début de l'évolution, des groupements se constituent à l'intérieur des grands ordres sociaux (clergé, noblesse, tiers), lesquels arrachent au prince la reconnaissance de leurs droits et devoirs. Ce but attient, tout est dit. Chacun (chaque groupe) ayant acquis une situation juridique qui lui permet de librement remplir la fonction juridique, économique, sociale qui est sienne, se contente dès lors de veiller à ce que cet état de chose ne soit plus modifié.

Système absurde: il méconnaît à la fois la réalité historique et la réalité humaine. La réalité humaine, c'est que l'homme ne s'étant encore jamais vu, au cours de son évolution, à l'abri du besoin et du danger, ne s'est jamais encore tenu pour satisfait de manière permanente d'une organisation politique quelle qu'elle fût. Il n'a donc jamais cessé de s'appliquer à transformer la société dans laquelle il vit. La réalité historique, sur laquelle nous insisterons au cours de cet exposé, c'est qu'il n'est pas vrai que la société d'ancien régime ait été ainsi idylliquement organisée. Dans toute société humaine, jusqu'à nos jours, l'organisation politique a été façonnée par et pour les forts; l'assemblée d'États du moyen âge et de l'époque moderne est une pure et simple application de cette maxime. On ne l'a guère montré jusqu'à présent – les juristes qui écrivent l'histoire des assemblées d'États ayant horreur des réalités.

Feudal Society

Parliaments were institutions characteristic of a post-feudal society. Their origins however are to be sought in the period of the dissolution of feudal society, and it therefore seems important to consider the nature of this. The two standard works on feudal society, by Professor Ganshof and the late Marc Bloch, translated into English as Feudalism *and* Feudal Society *respectively, present slightly different, but complementary, definitions.*

12 F. L. GANSHOF

The word 'feudalism' (Germ. *Lehnswesen* or *Feudalismus*; Fr. *féodalité*) is one to which many different meanings have been attached. During the French Revolution, it was virtually adopted as a generic description covering the many abuses of the *Ancien Régime*, and it is still in popular use in this sense today. Even if this quite illegitimate extension of its meaning be ignored, there exist many attempts at its analysis and definition which do not seem to be very closely related to one another. But if we limit ourselves to essentials and are prepared to overlook the subtle nuances of meaning which scholars, and particularly legal scholars, delight in, it will be found that the word is used by historians in two more or less distinct senses.

Feudalism may be conceived of as a form of society possessing well-marked features which can be defined without difficulty. They may be summarized as follows: a development pushed to extremes of the element of personal dependence in society, with a specialized military class occupying the higher levels in the social scale; an extreme subdivision of the rights of real property; a graded system of rights over land created by this subdivision and corresponding in broad outline to the grades of personal dependence just referred to; and a dispersal of political authority amongst a hierarchy of persons who exercise in their own interest powers normally attributed to the State and which are often in fact, derived from its break-up.

This type of society, whether one calls it 'feudalism' or the 'feudal régime', was that of western Europe in the tenth, eleventh and twelfth centuries. It came into existence in France, Germany, the kingdom of

Burgundy-Arles and Italy, all of them states deriving from the Carolingian empire, and in other countries – England, certain of the Christian kingdoms of Spain, the Latin principalities of the Near East – which passed under their influence. In other places and at other times, types of society have existed which show many analogies with the feudalism which one finds in France, Germany, the kingdom of Burgundy-Arles and Italy during the Middle Ages, so that scholars have been led to speak of 'feudalism' in ancient Egypt, in India, in the Arab world, in the Turkish empire, in Russia, in Japan, and elsewhere. In making these comparisons, historians have sometimes drawn parallels which a closer examination of the sources has failed to justify, though in some instances, as in that of Japan, the parallelism is very close.

Professor Calmette and the late Marc Bloch, in writing on feudalism in this sense, preferred to speak of 'feudal society'. Such a practice, if it were generally accepted, would have the advantage of allowing one to use the word 'feudalism' only in the second sense that can be attached to it.

In this second sense of the word, 'feudalism' may be regarded as a body of institutions creating and regulating the obligations of obedience and service – mainly military service – on the part of a free man (the vassal) towards another free man (the lord), and the obligations of protection and maintenance on the part of the lord with regard to his vassal. The obligation of maintenance had usually as one of its effects the grant by the lord to his vassal of a unit of real property known as a fief. This sense of the word feudalism is obviously more restricted and more technical than the other. We can perhaps regard it as the legal sense of the word, while the first use covers mainly the social and political senses.

These two meanings of the word feudalism are not unrelated to each other, since the society which we have described above is known as feudal because in it the fief, if not the corner-stone, was at least the most important element in the graded system of rights over land which this type of society involved.

13 MARC BLOCH

Let us therefore try to bring together in broad outline what we have learned about European feudalism, in the strict sense of the word, from its history.

The simplest way will be to begin by saying what feudal society was not. Although the obligations arising from blood-relationship played a very active part in it, it did not rely on kinship alone. More precisely, feudal ties proper were developed when those of kinship proved inadequate. Again, despite the persistence of the idea of a public authority superimposed on the multitude of petty powers, feudalism coincided with a profound weakening of the State, particularly in its protective capacity. But much as feudal society differed from societies based on kinship as well as from those dominated by the power of the State, it was their successor and bore their imprint. For while the characteristic relationships of personal subjection retained something of the quasi-family character of the original companionage, a considerable part of the political authority exercised by innumerable petty chiefs had the appearance of a usurpation of 'regalian' rights.

European feudalism should therefore be seen as the outcome of the violent dissolution of older societies. It would in fact be unintelligible without the great upheaval of the Germanic invasions which, by forcibly uniting two societies originally at very different stages of development, disrupted both of them and brought to the surface a great many modes of thought and social practices of an extremely primitive character. It finally developed in the atmosphere of the last barbarian raids. It involved a far-reaching restriction of social intercourse, a circulation of money too sluggish to admit of a salaried officialdom, and a mentality attached to things tangible and local. When these conditions began to change, feudalism began to wane.

It was an unequal society, rather than a hierarchical one – with chiefs rather than nobles; and with serfs, not slaves. If slavery had not played so small a part, there would have been no need for the characteristically feudal forms of dependence, as applied to the lower orders of society. In an age of disorder, the place of the adventurer was too important, the memory of men too short, the regularity of social classifications too uncertain, to admit of the strict formation of regular castes.

Nevertheless the feudal system meant the rigorous economic subjection of a host of humble folk to a few powerful men. Having received from earlier ages the Roman *villa* (which in some respects anticipated the manor) and the German village chiefdom, it extended and consolidated these methods whereby men exploited men, and combining inextricably the right to revenues from the land with the right to exercise authority, it fashioned from all this the true manor of medieval times. And this it did partly for the benefit of an oligarchy of priests and monks whose task it was to propitiate Heaven, but chiefly for the benefit of an oligarchy of warriors.

As even the most perfunctory comparative study will show, one of the most distinctive characteristics of feudal societies was the virtual identity of the class of chiefs with the class of professional warriors serving in the only way that then seemed effective, that is as heavily armed horsemen. As we have seen, of the societies where an armed peasantry survived, some knew neither vassalage nor the manor, while others knew them only in very imperfect forms – as in Scandinavia for example, or the kingdoms of north-western Spain. The case of the Byzantine Empire is perhaps even more significant because its institutions bore the stamp of a much more conscious directing thought. There, after the anti-aristocratic reaction of the eighth century, a government which had preserved the great administrative traditions of the Roman period, and which was furthermore concerned to provide itself with a strong army, created tenements charged with military obligations to the State – true fiefs in one sense, but differing from those of the West in that they were peasant fiefs, each consisting of a small farm. Thenceforth it was a paramount concern of the imperial government to protect these 'soldiers' properties', as well as small-holdings in general, against the encroachments of the rich and powerful. Nevertheless there came a time towards the end of the eleventh century when the Empire, overwhelmed by economic conditions which made independence more and more difficult for a peasantry constantly in debt, and further weakened by internal discords, ceased to extend any useful protection to the free farmers. In this way it not only lost precious fiscal resources, but found itself at the mercy of the magnates, who alone were capable thereafter of raising the necessary troops from among their own dependants.

In feudal society the characteristic human bond was the subordinate's link with a nearby chief. From one level to another the ties thus formed – like so many chains branching out indefinitely – joined the smallest to the greatest. Land itself was valued above all because it enabled a lord to provide himself with 'men' by supplying the remuneration for them. We want lands, said in effect the Norman lords who refused the gifts of jewels, arms, and horses offered by their duke. And they added among themselves: 'It will thus be possible for us to maintain many knights, and the duke will no longer be able to do so.'

The Breakdown of Feudal Society

Marc Bloch was killed in 1943 under tragic circumstances before he was able to write anything further on the transformation of feudal society. He only hinted at what he might have written on the economic causes for those fundamental changes in society which had come about by the mid-thirteenth century. Professor Painter, in concluding his study of the English feudal barony, interpreted the particular English situation in the light of these general economic and social changes. He demonstrated how they affected the baronage, which was the most important element both in society and in parliament. At an earlier point in the book he had already strongly expressed his own views on the disappearance of feudalism.

14 MARC BLOCH

We shall endeavour, in another work, to describe the intensive movement of repopulation which, from approximately 1050 to 1250, transformed the face of Europe: on the confines of the Western world, the colonization of the Iberian plateaux and of the great plain beyond the Elbe; in the heart of the old territories, the incessant gnawing of the plough at forest and wasteland; in the glades opened amidst the trees or the brushwood, completely new villages clutching at the virgin soil; elsewhere, round sites inhabited for centuries, the extension of the agricultural lands through the exertions of the assarters. It will be advisable then to distinguish between the stages of the process and to describe the regional variations. For the moment, we are concerned only with the phenomenon itself and its principal effects.

The most immediately apparent of these was undoubtedly the closer association of the human groups. Between the different settlements, except in some particularly neglected regions, the vast empty spaces thenceforth disappeared. Such distances as still separated the settlements became, in any case, easier to traverse. For powers now arose or were consolidated – their rise being favoured by current demographic trends – whose enlarged horizons brought them new responsibilities. Such were the urban middle classes, which owed everything to trade. Such also were the kings and princes; they too were interested in the prosperity of commerce because they derived large sums of money from it in the form of duties and tolls; moreover they were aware – much more so than in the past – of the vital importance to them of the free transmission of orders and the free movement of armies. The activity of the Capetians towards that decisive turning-point marked by the reign of Louis VI, their aggressions, their domanial policy, their part in the organization of the movement of repopulation, were in large measure the reflection of considerations of this kind – the need to retain control of communications between the two capitals, Paris and Orleans, and beyond the Loire or the Seine to maintain contact with Berry or with the valleys of the Oise and the Aisne. It would seem that while the security of the roads had increased, there was no very notable improvement in their condition; but at least the provision of bridges had been carried much farther. In the course of the twelfth century, how many were thrown over all the rivers of Europe! Finally, a fortunate advance in harnessing methods had the effect, about the same time, of increasing very substantially the efficiency of horse-transport.

The links with neighbouring civilizations underwent a similar transformation. Ships in ever greater numbers ploughed the Tyrrhenian Sea, and its ports, from the rock of Amalfi to Catalonia, rose to the rank of great commercial centres; the sphere of Venetian trade continually expanded; the heavy wagons of the merchant caravans now followed the route of the Danubian plains. These advances were important enough. But relations with the East had not only become easier and more intimate. The most important fact is that they had changed their character. Formerly almost exclusively an importer, the West had become a great supplier of manufactured goods. The merchandise which it thus shipped in quantity to the Byzantine world, to the Latin or Islamic Levant and even – though in smaller amounts – to the Maghreb, belonged to very diverse categories. One commodity, however, easily dominated all the rest. In the expansion of the European economy in the Middle Ages, cloth played the same vital rôle as did metal and cotton goods in that of nineteenth-century England. If in Flanders, in Picardy, at Bourges, in Languedoc, in Lombardy, and yet other places – for the cloth centres were to be found almost everywhere – the noise of the looms and the throbbing of the fullers' mills resounded, it was at least as much for the sake of foreign markets as for local requirements. And undoubtedly this revolution, which saw our Western countries embarking on the economic conquest of the world by way of the East, is to be explained by a multiplicity of causes and by looking – as far as possible – towards the East as well as towards the West. It is none the less true that it could not have occurred without the demographic changes mentioned above. If the population had not been more numerous than before and the cultivated area more extensive; if the fields – their quality improved by augmented manpower and in particular by more intensive ploughing – had not become capable of yielding bigger and more frequent harvests, how could so many weavers, dyers or cloth-shearers have been brought together in the towns and provided with a livelihood?

The North was conquered, like the East. From the end of the eleventh century Flemish cloth was sold at Novgorod. Little by little, the route of the Russian plains became hazardous and was finally closed. Thenceforward Scandinavia and the Baltic countries turned towards the West. The process of change which was thus set in motion was completed when, in the course of the twelfth century, German merchants took over the Baltic. From that time onwards the ports of the Low Countries, especially Bruges, became the centres where northern products were exchanged not only for those of the West itself but also for merchandise from the East. Strong international links united the two frontiers of feudal Europe by way of Germany and especially through the fairs of Champagne.

Such a well-balanced external trade could not fail to bring a flow of coin and precious metals into Europe and so add substantially to its monetary resources. This relative easing of the currency situation was reinforced – and its effects multiplied – by the accelerated rhythm of circulation. For in the very heart of the West the progress of repopulation, the greater ease of communications, the cessation of the invasions which had spread such an atmosphere of confusion and panic over the Western world, and still other causes which it would take too long to examine here, had led to a revival of commerce.

Let us avoid exaggeration, however. The picture would have to be carefully shaded – by regions and by classes. To live on their own resources remained for long centuries the ideal – though one that was rarely attained – of many peasants and most villages. Moreover, the profound transformations of the economy took place only very gradually. It is significant that of the two essential developments in the sphere of currency, one, the minting of larger pieces of silver much heavier than the *denarius*, appeared only at the beginning of the thirteenth century (and even at that date in Italy alone) and the other, the resumption of the minting of gold coins of an indigenous type, was delayed till the second half of the same century. In many respects, what the second feudal age witnessed was less the disappearance of earlier conditions than their modification. This observation applies to the part played by distance as well as to commerce. But the fact that the kings, the great nobles, and the manorial lords should have been able to begin once more to amass substantial wealth, that wage-earning, sometimes under legal forms clumsily adapted from ancient practices, should have increasingly supplanted other methods of remunerating services – these signs of an economy in process of revival affected in their turn, from the twelfth century onwards, the whole fabric of human relations.

Furthermore, the evolution of the economy involved a genuine revision of social values. There had always been artisans and merchants; individuals belonging to the latter class had even been able, here and there, to play an important rôle, though collectively neither group counted for much. But from the end of the eleventh century the artisan class and the merchant class, having become much more numerous and much more indispensable to the life of the community, made themselves felt more and more vigorously in the urban setting. This applies especially to the merchant class, for the medieval economy, after the revival of these decisive years, was always dominated, not by the producer, but by the trader. It was not for the latter class that the legal machinery of the previous age – founded on an economic system in which they occupied only an inferior place – had been set up. But now their practical needs and their mental attitude were bound to imbue it with a new spirit. Born in the midst of a very loosely-knit society, in which commerce was insignificant and money a rarity, European feudalism underwent a fundamental change as soon as the meshes of the human network had been drawn closer together and the circulation of goods and coin intensified.

15 SIDNEY PAINTER

The reigns of Richard, John, and Henry III were a period of transition. The relations between king and barons and between barons and mesne tenants were adjusted to changing circumstances and in the process gradually lost their feudal nature. The fundamental developments which eventually destroyed feudalism were economic. The increase in the volume of trade led to the growth of the towns which in turn enlarged the market for agricultural produce. A greater demand for Flemish and Lombard cloth made its makers seek more English wool. The actual production of the land in England increased. Moreover the expanding market brought a rise in the price level.

Perhaps the most important result of a higher price level was the increase in the cost of waging war. Rising prices combined with improvements in military equipment made knights more expensive. The king could no longer expect the barons to furnish their full quotas of fully armed men. At the same time he ceased to be satisfied with scutage payments at the traditional rates. Hence from 1190 to 1240 the service performed or the commutation paid by a baron was arrived at by separate bargains for each campaign. Fortunately for the barons the system was stabilized by the mutual acceptance of new quotas at a time when the crown was weak. As a result while the barons continued to owe personal service, the contingents of knights which they led to the host were reduced enormously. During this same period the barons resisted vigorously all attempts by the crown to increase their feudal financial obligations to correspond with changed economic conditions. I suspect that this was one of the chief reasons for John's quarrels with his barons. Henry II, Richard, and John had seriously depleted the royal demesne by generous grants to servants and favorites, and hence the crown profited comparatively little from increasing agricultural income. John knew that the revenues of most of his barons were expanding rapidly and he wanted a share. The result was his attempt to collect very high reliefs and to demand heavy fines on every possible occasion. Certainly *Magna Carta* indicates that the king's financial exactions were the barons' major grievance.

The reign of Henry III saw the barons victorious in the struggle to limit their feudal financial obligations to the traditional amounts. The £100 relief, which had been customary under Henry II and Richard and which was definitely established by *Magna Carta*, was actually reduced to 100 marcs. While the barons were not entirely successful in their claim that feudal aids could not exceed twenty shillings a fee, they never rose over forty shillings. With the exception of the profits from wardship and marriage the feudal revenues of the crown rapidly lost their importance. Customs duties and non-feudal levies supplied the crown with money – feudal aids were a mere pleasant windfall. Edward I and Edward II made some attempt to revive the feudal sources of revenue. The former for a time restored relief to the £100 level. Both monarchs tried to force the barons to pay scutage in addition to serving in the host or offering a fine, but the attempt was unsuccessful. While feudal aids continued to be collected occasionally, the feudal relationship between king and barons practically came to an end with the abandonment of the feudal host.

While the most significant developments in the history of the English barony during the thirteenth century stemmed from economic change, other factors played a part. Henry II had fundamentally altered the very bases of the English judicial and police systems. The popular courts of the shires and hundreds and the feudal courts of the barons were rapidly losing all important functions. The enormous extension of the judicial business of the royal courts upset the established balance of power between crown and barons. Hence a general readjustment was necessary. Throughout the reigns of John and Henry III the barons strove to limit as much as possible the encroachment of the royal courts on their authority and to gain what power they could at the expense of the local courts. A few very great lords obtained private justices and assizes. Others were able to hamper the royal justices by means of the privilege of return of writ. The provision of *Magna Carta* limiting the use of the writ *praecipe* was an attempt at a general restriction of the royal courts. This struggle terminated in a baronial victory when the crown was forced to acknowledge that additions to the powers of its courts could come only through statutes passed by a Parliament dominated by barons. . . .

The economic and political developments described in the preceding few paragraphs had extremely important effects on the internal history of the barony. The rise in the cost of knights modified greatly the relations between the baron and his vassals. In most cases it was not practical for the baron to apportion his reduced quota among his men. It was far simpler to take their scutage payments and hire knights to perform the service. Thus for a mesne tenant tenure by knight service became in reality tenure by scutage. At the same time the royal courts were rapidly depriving the baron's feudal courts of all business of any significance, and the barons summoned these bodies largely so that they could collect fines from those who failed to appear. Moreover the barons were replacing the hereditary officers drawn from their mesne tenants with paid officials. In short the personal relationship between lord and vassal disappeared. The lord simply collected certain money revenues from his tenants by knight service.

As the price level rose, the feudal revenues received by the barons from their vassals became comparatively less important. Scutages, aids, and reliefs were fixed in amount and could not be increased as incomes from land grew larger. While the evidence is by no means conclusive, I am inclined to believe that the same was true of the profits from franchises. The revenue that built strong castles, hired well-armed retainers, and supported luxurious living came more and more from the demesne manors. But in this respect many a baron could hardly equal, much less be superior to, his more prosperous mesne tenants. In short, tenure by barony soon had little meaning in terms of wealth, power, and prestige and rapidly became obsolete.

A friend and former colleague who has been kind enough to read this manuscript questions my conclusion that the feudal barony came to an end in the fourteenth century. Obviously this depends to a great extent on what one means by feudal. By 1350 the king no longer summoned the feudal host. Reliefs and feudal aids were an unimportant part of the royal revenue. When the king held a meeting of the Great Council or of Parliament, he did not restrict his individual summonses to men holding baronies by tenure. The barons' relations to their vassals were almost entirely financial. Their officials and soldiers were paid retainers. Finally the possession of a tenurial barony did not make a man a baron in the eyes of his contemporaries. There were still barons and baronies, but I cannot call them feudal.

The disappearance of feudalism

Political and economic conditions obliged the English kings to make some reduction in the number of knights they demanded from their barons. The cost of a knight had increased threefold [in the thirteenth century]. While the returns from land had been rising as well, the barons benefited only in respect to their demesne as they were unable to exact heavier service from their tenants. Thus a reduction of service quotas by two-thirds may have been necessary. But as Morris points out the service owed in Edward I's day was only one-eighteenth of that due to his great-grandfather Henry II. The only explanation that I can offer for this is that it represented a magnificent baronial victory in a struggle the details of which have been lost to us. The barons obtained the reduction of their military obligations to the crown to a point where they entailed some personal inconvenience but no financial burden. As the king still obtained his heavy cavalry through the feudal levy, the barons retained their control over his military policy. The money which would supply him with an adequate army had to be raised through other means. The fact that types of soldiers other than heavy cavalry were becoming increasingly important does not lessen the triumph of the barons in sliding out of their obligations. It may, however, be part of the explanation of their success.

It is important to notice the effect of these developments on fundamental feudal relationships. In the eleventh century the baron as the king's vassal was bound to follow his lord to war, and the resources of his fief were primarily devoted to furnishing the contingent of knights that he led to the host. As long as the feudal levy was used, that is until 1327, the personal obligation of the baron remained intact, but the reduction in service quotas that marked the late twelfth and early thirteenth century meant that the cost of furnishing his contingent would be a comparatively light tax on his barony. Once the feudal levy had lapsed, the obligation of the barons to perform feudal military service to the crown was at an end. As military service was the fundamental element of feudalism, it seems to me that after its disappearance the relationship between king and barons cannot be called feudal.

The Rise of a New Class — Buzones and Knights

Mysterious 'buzones' crop up intermittently in various thirteenth-century documents, and are obviously important people. For example, Henry III's great lawyer Bracton, who died in 1268, referred to them incidentally in his famous treatise on the laws of England when he was describing how itinerant justices should order their proceedings. In 1932 Gaillard Lapsley resolved the puzzle of the 'buzones' in an article which concluded with a description of them as forming the groups which dominated the shire communities and consequently provided the shire representatives in parliament. Professor Treharne has gone so far as to call these men a 'new class', and justified this by contrasting them with their ancestors and predecessors. The break-down of feudalism thus meant a much greater freedom of action and an enlarged sphere of activity for men of knightly and near-knightly status. Dr Hunnisett, working on the office of coroner in the middle ages, illustrates something of this enlarged sphere of activity, and Professor Holt suggests that their freedom of action must be dated back at least to the beginning of the thirteenth century.

16 HENRY DE BRACTON

The justices ought to transfer themselves to some retired place, and having called to themselves four or six or more of the greater men of the county, who are called the 'buzones' of the county, and upon whose nod depends the votes of the others, the justices should thereupon have a consultation with them in turns, and explain to them how it has been provided by the king and by his counsel.

17 GAILLARD LAPSLEY

Maitland thought of the *buzones* as active business-loving men who led the county court and were its mouthpieces and would when the time came be justices of the peace. This definition would treat the *buzones* as a group of country gentlemen actively concerned indeed with the business of the county court but having duties and capacities extending beyond it, men who from position, business capacity, and experience were influential in local affairs. The existence of such a group in any local community is antecedently probable, and I conceive that to-day any member of a Borough or County Council or an Academic Senate could name without difficulty, if not without indiscretion, the *buzones* of his time. A strong central government committed as deeply as the Angevin government was to a policy of local self-agency would naturally take account of such a group when it came to select persons to do its work in the counties. Bracton's direction to the judges is proof of this. Such a body from whatever point of view it is observed shows itself as representative. If the county court is in the habit of selecting the same men to verify essoins or make a record and speak for the community when it is accused of wrong, it is more than likely that these are the men it will choose when the king sends for knights of the shire to speak with him of the affairs of the realm. Such a group of men on the other hand will naturally be treated as representatives of the county by the central government, and this becomes apparent in proportion as commissions for local administrative work begin to multiply. Some years ago an investigation of the parliamentary representation of five of the Eastern Counties in the reign of Edward II led me to the conclusion that in those counties, at least, there was a smallish group of gentlemen of moderate position and no national importance who were constantly occupied with local affairs and local administration, and were recognized by the central government, which put one task after another upon them, as particularly fitted for this work. Further, that it was from this group that knights sent to the king's parliaments were usually drawn, and that it was not uncommon for them to be returned several times so that the task of representing the county in the king's court was treated as just another aspect of the day's work to which they and their forbears had been accustomed. One would be prepared to find a similar group in any other English county at that time. I suggest now that the existence of just such a group, chiefly occupied, it is true, with judicial and police work, in all counties in the thirteenth century is implied in Bracton's words. If this is the case, our inquiry will have resulted in fitting Bracton's *buzones* into the texture of English legal and administrative history at a point where it is beginning to be connected with the history of parliament.

18 R. F. TREHARNE

Need we, then, wonder if, in the two centuries which followed the introduction of knight service to England, the meaning of the title (of 'knight') changed so much that its bearers in 1258 may be considered, in comparison with the knights of William I, a new class? It is significant that the word by which the conquered English designated the mass of their conquerors was one which, on contemporary English lips, implied no social distinction, leadership, wealth or nobility whatsoever. It meant one who served in person as a humble dependent in the household of some great man, with, occasionally, a further specialised meaning of a servant trained in the use of weapons and in horsemanship. In the eyes of the subject English, the Norman knight was thus not a lord, but a servant, not noble or wealthy, but undistinguished by anything save his proficiency in the art of fighting on horseback. This, Professor Stenton has told us, was all that the word 'knighthood' denoted in the eleventh and early twelfth centuries – 'a skill which could be acquired by any able-bodied youth brought up in a military household,' and which could be exercised by any man who had undergone the necessary training and possessed, whether in his own right or by his lord's provision, the horse, the weapons and the simple armour required for his work. He was not, usually, a landholder, but simply a member of the bodyguard of some great man. These knights were, in the art of war, highly trained: the quarrel between William II and Anselm shows that the King and his barons did not regard as knights mere farmhands mounted on cart-horses, bearing weapons which they could not wield, and wearing armour with the uncomfortable air of new recruits on parade for the first time. Of the arts of peace William's knights knew little, for they had no lands of their own to manage, and no place in the government of either shire or hundred – 'their only experience was war', and even in military matters, their counsel was likely to be 'short-sighted and rash'. They were the rank and file, not the officers of the Norman army, and according to the plans of William I, there must have been at least 5000 and perhaps nearly 7000 of them in England when Domesday Book was compiled – specialized soldiers, good for little else but war, and sometimes so undistinguished that the Domesday scribes did not always trouble to record their names, but referred to them anonymously as 'quidam miles', much as though some humble socman or villein too unimportant to name, were being described.

But by 1258 a great change has come about. The status of the thirteenth-century knight, from whatever angle it is viewed, whether
military, social, economic, administrative or political, is such that he
can no longer be regarded on any lower plane than that of the nobility,
even though we must qualify his class as 'the lesser nobility'. In status
he is nobly born, often able to trace his descent back to one of the
original Norman invaders, and being himself quite often connected,
both by blood relationships and by marriage ties, with one or more of
the great baronial families. Economically, he is a landowner on a substantial scale, with at least one knight's fee, and probably more, often
held in scattered estates which may easily transcend the limits of a
single shire: he has peasant-farmers, free and unfree, as his tenants: he
holds one or more manorial courts to adjust their disputes and to punish
their petty crimes, and he may even hold more considerable liberties
of jurisdiction whereby he exercises functions which are otherwise
those of the local officers of the Crown. Since the management of his
own estates and the exercise of his own rights of jurisdiction often do
not fully satisfy his ambition and absorb his time, he is frequently
found as bailiff, steward, or 'sheriff' of some large honour, where he
works as a professional estate-agent and local judge for some great
lord. From such an office, after long experience and faithful service,
he may pass to the employ of the King himself, as steward, escheator,
or even sheriff, making this his life's profession and his chief interest:
the great majority of the sheriffs of the thirteenth-century were knights,
often serving in the very counties where their own principal holdings
lay. Or if they were less active-minded or ambitious, public administration still claimed much of their time, willy-nilly, for on their shoulders
lay the burden, and in their hands rested the privilege, of running the
shire court.

The great barons, between the claims of the Curia Regis and the
needs of their own estates, courts and councils, had now ceased to concern themselves with the regular work of the shire courts, while all
save the most substantial of the peasantry had neither the opportunity
nor the status to rival the knights, who were thus, as suitors, left in
effective control of that toughest and most vital of English institutions.
In the ordinary monthly meetings of the shire court, the knights are
the effective suitors and judges; the sheriff pronounces no judgement
on his own authority, but should be the mouthpiece of the knights,
who can, by obstruction or abstention, prevent any business whatsoever
from being done if they are so minded. Here they discuss royal demands

for taxes, both as to incidence and as to amount, as well as the manner of collection: they hear the king's instructions, orders and proclamations published; they choose the electors of the hundred juries for the general eyre; they elect coroners; they all serve as jurors alike in lawsuits and the many administrative enquiries, both general and particular, which the Crown requires the shire court to conduct. If there are royal forests in the shire, the functioning of the entire forest system, both courts and administration, depends upon them in exactly the same way and to much the same degree as does the working of ordinary local government. Moreover, even if a knight holds no office in the shire court, he may still be one of the unofficial but indispensable group of *buzones*, the body of leading, non-official knights who assist the sheriff to arrange the business of the shire, whom the sheriff consults when he needs advice, and from whose numbers sheriffs, escheators, coroners and forest officials are generally drawn. Indeed, the knight's public duties are by no means confined to the shire: since the time of Henry II, the verdicts of juries, both legal and administrative, if not reported to the royal justices or commissioners visiting the shire court, must be taken to the king's court by four of the knights who are specially sworn to answer before the king's court any questions arising from the verdict which they bear. And, ever since John, in 1213, summoned four knights from each shire to come and speak with him about the affairs of the realm, the central government has from time to time summoned the shire court to send two, three, or four knights to come as plenipotentiaries to the King's court, to discuss and grant proposed taxes, to report on local government, or even to bring the political and moral support of their shires to the aid of the Crown in difficult times.

19 R. F. HUNNISETT

Although not usually occupying other offices during or immediately before or after their tenure of a coronership, coroners were nevertheless of that knightly or near-knightly class which has been called *buzones* and which undertook all the tasks of local administration. Of the sixty-six Sussex county coroners who are known, thirty-seven definitely had at least one other office before or after their coronerships. One was a member of the royal household and five represented Sussex or one of its boroughs in Parliament. The activities of the rest were confined to

Sussex and the three neighbouring counties. One was an escheator, two sub-escheators, one a J.P., one an under-sheriff, one constable of a castle, one bailiff of a rape and one a village constable. Eleven were assessors and collectors of taxes, some on many separate occasions, one surveyor of the array of arms and thirteen acted at least once on various commissions of inquiry, gaol delivery, assize, oyer and terminer and *de walliis et fossatis*. Others were active in liberties, eight being stewards or bailiffs, one an under-bailiff, two feodaries and two keepers of gaols. Two were keepers of manors and one a keeper of the temporalities of the bishopric of Chichester. These figures produce a picture which is true for the whole country. In the fourteenth and fifteenth centuries grants of exemption were usually obtained not from the office of coroner alone but from a large number of local offices. But the *buzones*, although a small class, had their hierarchy. Those at the top became sheriffs, escheators and J.P.s. Coroners were generally of a slightly lower social stratum, although often from rising families. Thus, although comparatively few coroners either had been or became sheriffs, escheators or J.P.s, their descendants often did. Many of the medieval Sussex coroners helped to found families which were pre-eminent in the county for centuries, and the two Pelhams were ancestors of peers of the realm and Prime Ministers.

In the early thirteenth century the county coroners were almost invariably knights, but the percentage of knights gradually declined as the century wore on. Two reasons account for this. The office of coroner was unpaid and therefore unpopular with many. The first recorded purchase of a grant of exemption from the office is under the year 1202, and such grants became very numerous later. Secondly, while the number of eligible knights thus declined, there was a steadily increasing number of offices for them to fill and duties for them to perform. They had to be sheriffs, escheators, collectors and assessors of subsidies, commissioners of array, keepers of the peace and M.P.s, to name but a few, and by the late thirteenth century it was clear that there were not enough knights to go round.

20 J. C. HOLT

The society in which the battle for Magna Carta was fought and won was not one in which the great tenants-in-chief of the Crown dominated the political scene completely. When the barons promised to give their own men the privileges which they had received from the King, this was not just a matter of pious words, nor even just a skilful move to win the gentry to their side. It was an act recognizing social facts, and especially the impossibility of ignoring these men. A Simon of Kyme or a Thomas of Moulton could obviously not be ignored, neither could the mass of smaller men who made up the society of the English counties and provided the voluntary service on which the whole scheme of local administration depended. When Roger de Montbegon's pretensions were challenged in the county court of Nottingham in 1220, the challenge came from such a man, John of Leek, who instructed Roger with some firmness in the proper processes of waging his law. When the knights of Lincolnshire made a notable appeal to Magna Carta against the operations of their sheriff in 1225, the word was given to Theobald Hautein, who proceeded to lecture the sheriff and the court on the terms of the Great Charter and claim special knowledge of what was in the mind of the King and the great men who advised him. Only when Theobald was driven to bring pressure on his fellows did he point out that some of them were stewards who would have to account for their actions in this matter to their lords. Men like Theobald often were stewards; this must have added to their influence; but they were men of substance first and foremost, and sometimes their operations, as, for example, in the purchase of privileges from the King, specifically excluded the county magnates. The social and political independence which Mr McFarlane has seen these men enjoying in the fifteenth century, and Professor Treharne and Mr Denholm-Young in the middle years of the thirteenth century, was not new at these dates. It was already developing in 1215 and at this point it owed much to the way in which the knights had been called increasingly into the King's government under Henry II and his sons. Its more distant origins are not our immediate concern, but it is not perhaps necessary to derive them from some new Rise of the Gentry. Gentry were always rising; it is their habit.

Bastard Feudalism

The economic basis for the prosperity of the gentry class was shattered in the fourteenth century by a series of catastrophes, of which the Black Death was only the greatest. The gentry saw their rent-rolls shrink, their wage bills increase, the prices for their agricultural produce drop, and the proceeds from their manorial perquisites decline. It is hardly surprising that in such a situation of economic distress, which was at the same time one of political insecurity, many of them should barter their political independence for the benefits to be gained from the patronage of the great. This new type of patron–client relationship has become known by historians as 'bastard feudalism' since that term was popularized by Professor McFarlane some twenty years ago. McFarlane here defines what he intended the term 'bastard feudalism' to mean, and describes its beginnings. His description is further illustrated by one of the earliest known 'bastard feudal' indentures.

21 K. B. McFARLANE

Feudalism, if it is to have any recognizable meaning, implies the organization of society upon a basis of tenure. In a feudal society the principal unit is the fief, 'an estate in land (in England always a heritable estate) held on condition of homage and service to a superior lord'. Whether in England service, even military service, was ever wholly or indeed mainly a matter of tenure, I leave to others to decide. But by the fourteenth century it had largely ceased to be so, at any rate for the free man. In every direction the incidents of service were being commuted for money payments or rents. And by the end of the fifteenth century even servile tenures were rapidly disappearing. Feudalism still existed formally intact, but was becoming for all practical purposes a complex network of marketable privileges and duties attached to the ownership of land, with little or no importance as a social force. It was there, and indeed remained so for centuries to come – all-pervasive but inactive – in the background, while the new order of patronage, liveries and affinities occupied the front of the stage, as it was to do in England throughout the fourteenth and fifteenth centuries, with an epilogue which far outran so-called medieval times. It is this new order that we call 'bastard feudalism'. Its quintessence was payment for service. The idea of lordship was retained, but because it was divorced from tenure it was a lordship which had undergone a scarcely visible process of transubstantiation, leaving all but a few of its accidents unchanged.

The origin of the practice of substituting paid for unpaid service still remains untraced in detail. But its most significant stage was reached when the need was felt for an army more efficient and more durable than the feudal host. Already in the eleventh and twelfth centuries it had been found necessary to supplement the native levies with hired foreign mercenaries; and although their employment was contrary to Magna Carta the presence of continental adventurers in the royal pay can be found under both Henry III and Edward I. It was the latter king, however, who seems first to have extended the practice systematically to his English troops. According to J. E. Morris, who was the pioneer in this still neglected field, the earliest cases of the mobilization of native soldiers for service in return for wages, 'contract being reasonably inferred from the details, occur in 1277'. These novel arrangements seem to have been settled verbally and 'wages were issued for 40 days at a time, clearly in imitation of the feudal forty'. Edward made his contracts with a number of his greater barons, those evidently whose abilities and loyalty he trusted, and left them to make sub-contracts with the members of their respective contingents. The oldest known example of such a sub-contract in writing, one between Edmund Mortimer and Peter Maulay, was sealed at Wigmore in the summer of 1287;[1] and a very few more have survived from the last years of the thirteenth century.

Considering how grudgingly the old military service had been performed, it was not to be expected that much reluctance would be shown at accepting the king's pay and the transformation was rapid and complete. Only a small number of the greater feudatories, most of them earls, seem to have thought it beneath their dignity to receive money for what they owed gratuitously and to have stood out for the scrupulous performance of their tenurial obligations. But this was only a temporary stand, prompted perhaps by the fear of losing their pre-eminence in the common ruck of mercenary captains, and was soon abandoned. Feudal conservatism so disadvantageous to its upholders had no future and already in the Welsh and Scottish campaigns of the 1280s and 1290s we find most of them quite contentedly drawing pay. In little more than a generation they had all succumbed. The summons

[1] See below no. 22.

of the feudal host for the last time in 1327 caused so much irritation and administrative inconvenience that it was generally recognized that this method of raising an army was obsolete. Scutage followed it into disuse; the poor yield from this 'antiquated and detested due', compared with that derived from lavish parliamentary subsidies, made it not worth the trouble of collection.

22 INDENTURE OF MILITARY SERVICE 1287

This is the agreement made at Worcester on Sunday after the feast of St James the Apostle in the fifteenth year of king Edward, between the noble man lord Edmund Mortimer on the one hand and lord Peter de Maulay on the other – namely, that the said lord Peter shall remain with the said lord Edmund in the expedition of the Welsh war against Rhys son of Mareddud and his accomplices, hostile and rebellious against the lord king. He shall have ten covered horses . . . [these are individually described and priced] . . . and if it happens that the said lord Peter, by any accident should lose the said horses or any one of them in the service of lord Edmund, . . . [then he will be repaid on terms laid down]. . . . And as a greater security in this matter, the following is to be done: both lord Edmund and lord Peter have placed their seals alternately on this writing made in the manner of a cyrograph, and Edmund has made a recognizance in chancery that he owes lord Peter the said money on the stated conditions, as in the form above; and he has caused the recognition to be enrolled in the chancery; and he has conceded that if the said money, at the prescribed terms, is not paid, it may be levied from his lands, goods and chattels in the county of Hereford and elsewhere by bailiffs of the lord king, and paid to the lord Peter according to the above form. Given at Wigmore on the day and year above. . . .

The Wealth and Independence of the Towns

Starting from fundamental demographic and agricultural changes, Professor Miller has traced the economic causes of the increase in the number, size and prosperity of towns and townsmen in the thirteenth century. In the passage which precedes the extract quoted here he discussed the violent increase in population and the considerable consequent extension and intensification of agriculture, which in its turn brought about a very sharp increase in the incomes of the landholding classes, and the appearance within the peasantry of a group of proto-yeomen.

23 EDWARD MILLER

These trends in agricultural income have a further significance. Landlords like the bishops of Winchester or Ralf Camoys obviously sold agricultural produce on a considerable scale and thriving peasants were not less obviously farming for the market; but even the great mass of smaller peasants were also under some compulsion to do so, if only to raise cash for rents and seignorial charges. At the same time there is much other evidence for expanding exchanges. Thirteenth-century England exported grain, hides, dairy produce, tin and above all wool. It could be alleged at the end of the century that 'the wool of England is almost half the value of the whole land'[1] and, if this is an exaggeration, there can be no question that the wool trade was a massive and probably an expanding trade. Exports of wool, which were running at about 25,600 sacks yearly in the 1280s, averaged some 35,000 sacks in the first decade of the fourteenth century. A comparable increase in imports is also likely, for by the beginning of the fourteenth century England was absorbing from one fifth to a quarter of all the wine sent out from Bordeaux and providing a market for some 12,000 cloths each year brought in by foreign merchants alone.[2] This country, in

[1] W. Stubbs, *Select Charters*, 9th edn. (Oxford, 1929), p. 435.
[2] E. M. Carus-Wilson and O. Coleman, *England's Export Trade, 1275–1547* (Oxford, 1963), pp. 36–41; E. M. Carus-Wilson, *Medieval Merchant Venturers* (London, 1954), p. 242 n; M. K. James, 'Fluctuations of the Anglo-Gascon Wine Trade', *Econ. Hist. Rev.*, 2nd ser., iv (1951), p. 176.

brief, had been integrated into the international economy of thirteenth-century Europe. It was an important market for Gascon vineyards, Flemish clothiers and Baltic woodsmen and trappers. It helped to remedy the food deficits of Flanders and Gascony. It was the essential supplier of wool for the looms of industrial Flanders.

These external exchanges, moreover, were served and supplemented by increasingly active internal exchanges. During the twelfth and thirteenth centuries England was covered by a network of markets, so that by 1300 almost every village of any size and many that were very small had each their own. Transcending the markets were the fairs, some of which (like that at St Ives) had a regional or even an international repute. The period was also one of urban growth, and towns were the markets *par excellence* of the medieval world. The population of old towns increased; fifty-two new towns were created in the twelfth century and fifty-seven in the thirteenth;[1] and many villages, without attaining burghal status, developed some urban characteristics. Towns, too, were more than markets. They were the homes of crafts, of more concentrated and diversified industrial production than any village. This concentration, in fact, was becoming dense enough to establish a rough division of labour between town and country, between the sphere of industry and commerce on the one hand and that of agriculture on the other. More than that, there were signs of a more advanced division of labour within at least some towns, and in particular its organized expression in the form of craft gilds. These gilds were not quite unknown before the opening of the thirteenth century. They had already appeared in London, though we must remember that London was *sui generis* in its size and precocity of economic development; and also in the textile industry, though this again was an industry precocious in its organization and in the extent of its market. It is significant that at Norwich gilds (presumably including craft gilds) were prohibited as detrimental to the city in 1256 and 1285:[2] perhaps it is a fair deduction that they were still regarded as unofficial novelties. Even in London the crafts had to wait until the shadow of Edward I was lifted before they gained their place in the sunshine of the civic constitution.[3] In the thirteenth century, however, the crafts were making their appearance in

[1] Provisional figures of Professor Beresford's quoted in A. R. Bridbury, *Economic Growth* (London, 1962), p. 70.

[2] *British Borough Charters, 1216–1307*, ed. A. Ballard and J. Tait (Cambridge, 1923), p. 283.

[3] G. A. Williams, *Medieval London: From Commune to Capital* (London, 1963). pp. 264 sqq.

most towns of any size. The way was being prepared for the part they played in urban economic and political life during the later middle ages.

At the same time, we will underrate the scale of industrial development if we fix our eyes only on the towns. Indeed, the urban textile industry of the eastern plains seems to have fallen on evil days during the thirteenth century; but there may have been some compensation in the growth of a rural textile industry, especially in the west and in East Anglia. Tin production in the south-west seems also to have been rising at the beginning of the century and again in the early decades of the fourteenth century; and lead mining was being developed on a fair scale in the Mendips, the Peak district and on Alston moor. Iron-smelting was more widely dispersed and mainly directed to the supply of local needs, but two centres had a wider reputation. The Forest of Dean could supply Richard I with 50,000 horseshoes for the Third Crusade; and the Sussex Weald developed progressively during the thirteenth century until, by the mid-fourteenth, it had virtually captured the crucial London market. There was also a good deal of coal mining on a small scale and Tyneside was already emerging as a principal centre of this industry. Sea-coals, probably from the Tyne, were creating a smoke nuisance in London in 1307; they were used by lime burners, smiths, brewers and bakers; and in the mid-fourteenth century the bishop of Durham had five mines at Whickham, admittedly exceptional in their scale, which he was able to lease at an annual rental of £333 6s 8d.[1]

Agrarian expansion, the growth of markets and towns, some development of industry form a background to the activities of merchants. Many of them, of course, were foreigners whose utility Edward I commended to his subjects: Flemings, Gascons, Germans and, by the end of the century, above all Italians. This last group made their appearance in England early in the century; and the scale of their activities by the end of it is indirectly attested by the fact that Edward I borrowed over £100,000 from them to finance his Gascon visit in 1286-9 and that the Frescobaldi alone were able to lend another £122,000 to the English crown between 1289 and 1310.[2] More directly significant is the fact that, in 1273, Italians exported wool worth some

[1] E. M. Carus-Wilson, *Medieval Merchant Venturers*, pp. 183 sqq.; L. F. Salzman, *Medieval English Industries* (Oxford, 1923), pp. 17–18.
[2] A. Sapori, *Studi di Storia Economica Medievale* (Florence, 1946), p. 591, E. von Roon-Bassermann, 'Die erste Florentiner Handelsgesellschaften in England', *Vierteljahrschrift für Sozial- und Wirtschaftsgeschichte*, xxxix (1952), pp. 97 sqq.

£50,000, about a quarter of all the English wool going overseas.[1] At the same time, we have been warned not to underrate the rôle of the English merchant even in the wool trade and still less in other trades.[2] In 1273 English merchants bought licences to export wool worth nearly £75,000 (more than one third of the total exported); while at the beginning of the fourteenth century the English share was more like one half and it continued to increase during the ensuing decades.[3] The history of the merchant class of medieval England has still to be written but, even ignoring the giants of London, it contained men of enterprise and considerable wealth. Hugh Selby of York was descended from a family already engaged in the grain and wine trades in the twelfth century and himself exported wool to Flanders and imported wine from Anjou in the early decades of the thirteenth. He was mayor of York six times or more, the owner of many city properties and he acquired a country estate in at least three villages in the East and North Ridings.[4] He solidly established a dynasty which continued to be prominent in the affairs of York for the rest of the century. Not many men had quite so successful a story to tell; but the history of thirteenth-century towns suggests that there existed a far from insignificant class of traders whose enterprise had won them solid substance.

The prosperity of England's only major city, London, is illustrated by the strong views attributed to Henry III by the chronicler Matthew Paris in his rather colourful account of the crisis of 1248.

24 MATTHEW PARIS

When he had seen this the king became exceedingly angry and said to his counsellors 'Look how your advice has turned my magnates against me. I am about to lose Gascony. I have been robbed of Poitou.

---

[1] A. Schaube, 'Die Wollausfuhr Englands vom Jahre 1273', *ibid.*, vi (1908), pp. 68, 83; it has of course to be remembered that Schaube's figures relate to licences to export and not the amount of wool actually exported: Carus-Wilson and Coleman, *op. cit.*, p. 12n.

[2] E. Power, *The Wool Trade in Medieval English History* (Oxford, 1941), pp. 57 sqq.

[3] Schaube, *loc. cit.*; Carus-Wilson and Coleman, *op. cit.*, p. 12.

[4] *Victoria County Histories: the City of York* (London, 1961), pp. 34, 42, 45–6; and for similar families at Lincoln, see J. W. F. Hill, *Medieval Lincoln* (Cambridge, 1948), pp. 187, 195–6, 294–5, 385–91.

And now that I have come to the end of my funds, what am I to do?' Therefore they entered on a faint-hearted plan and without looking ahead made arrangements that the plate and jewels in the royal treasury should be sold by weight, without consideration for the value of the gold with which the silver gleamed, or of its skilled and laborious craftsmanship, so that at least some ready money should be acquired in this way, although 'the value of the workmanship even surpassed that of the material'. And the royal counsellors added a further shameful consolation to mollify the king, whispering to him 'Just as all the rivers flow back to the sea, so everything that is sold will surely come back to you in the end in the form of gifts presented to you, and on this account the king ought not to be upset'. After the sale the king inquired where his plate was sold and to whom. 'London' was the reply, to which the king said 'I know, I know, if the treasure of Augustus were sold, the city of London would absorb it completely by buying it up, for those rustic Londoners who call themselves barons are disgustingly rich. That city is a well that has never been exhausted.'

Part Three
THE COMPOSITION OF EARLY PARLIAMENTS

The General Composition of
Parliament

The Modus tenendi parliamentum, *which was written about 1321–4, is not a description of how parliaments were actually held but of how they ought to be held. It purports to record the way in which parliaments were held in a mythical past golden age – the reign of Edward the Confessor. Despite the partisan bias of its author, and his proneness to moralize and arrange his subject in symmetrical categories, the* Modus *gives some most useful insights into the actual characteristics of parliament in the latter part of the reign of Edward II. The clauses which have been selected here deal with the composition of parliament. They are followed by a commentary by Miss Maud Clarke from her* Medieval Representation and Consent, *which was primarily a detailed exposition of the* Modus. *Much of what she wrote was directed towards establishing the date at which the* Modus *was composed, and this preoccupation sometimes obscures the very considerable contribution that she made to the understanding of early parliaments in England.*

25 THE MODUS TENENDI PARLIAMENTUM

Here is described the way in which the parliament of the king of England and of his English [people] was held in the times of king Edward son of king Ethelred. It was declared by the more discreet men of the kingdom before William Duke of Normandy, conqueror and king of England. The Conqueror himself commanded this to be done; what is here was approved by him; and it was observed in his time and in that of his successors, kings of England.

I. *Summons of Parliament*

The summons of a parliament ought to precede the first day of parliament by forty days.

II. *Concerning the Clergy*

The archbishops, bishops, abbots, priors and other greater clergy who hold (land) by earldom or barony should be summoned (individually)

77

and should come to parliament on account of holding (land) in this way. None of the lesser (clergy should be summoned individually) unless their presence and attendance is required otherwise than for their lands, for example if they are of the king's council, or if their presence is thought necessary or useful to parliament, and the king is obliged to supply them with maintenance and their expenses in coming to and remaining in parliament.

The lesser clergy ought not to be summoned in this way, but . . . the king was accustomed to order his archbishops, bishops, etc. . . . to arrange for each deanery and archdeaconry to choose two skilled and suitable representatives . . . to come and be present at parliament. . . .

And thus all the clergy ought to be summoned to the parliament of the king under these two types of summons.

III. *Concerning the Laity*

All the earls and barons and their peers should be summoned and should come (to parliament), that is those who have lands and revenues to the value of a whole earldom, namely twenty knight's fees, with each fee reckoned at twenty librates (i.e. land worth twenty pounds a year), which makes four hundred librates in all, or to the value of a whole barony, namely thirteen and a third knight's fees. . . . None of the lesser laity should be summoned or should come to parliament by reason of their lands, unless their presence should be useful or necessary to parliament for other purposes.

IV. *Concerning the Barons of the Cinque Ports*

Also the king was accustomed to send his writs to the warden of the Cinque Ports ordering him to cause to be elected by each port two suitable and skilled barons from that port, to come and be present in his parliament, to reply, submit, urge and do in the same way as his baronies, as if each and every one from those baronies were themselves personally present there: and that each of these barons should come with his warrants in duplicate, signed with the common seals of his port, to the effect that they themselves had been duly elected and empowered for this and were sent on behalf of their own baronies, of which one copy should be delivered to the clerks of parliament, and the other remain in the possession of the baron himself. And when these barons of the ports were on the point of leaving parliament, with permission to do so, they were accustomed to have a writ under the great seal addressed to the warden of the ports, that he should cause each of these barons to have from the community of his port reasonable maintenance allowance and expenses, from the first day when they set out for parliament to the day on which they returned home. The writs specifically mentioned their length of stay in parliament, the day on which they came, and that on which they had permission to depart; and sometimes the writs used to mention how much these barons ought to take from their communities for each day, that is to say some more and some less according to the ability and standing of the individual, but it was not customary to rate two barons at more than twenty shillings a day, taking account of their stay, their labour and their expenses, nor was it usual for the court to allow these expenses automatically to any persons elected and sent by the communities, unless the individuals had behaved honourably and well in parliament.

V. *Concerning the Knights of the Shires*

The king was wont to send his writs to all the sheriffs of England, bidding each to cause to be elected by the shire two suitable knights, honest and skilled, from his shire, . . . [the summons is like that of members for the Cinque Ports, but the expenses are less] it is not usual to give more than one mark per day for the expenses of the two knights from a shire.

VI. *Concerning the Citizens*

[Cities are to] . . . elect two suitable honest and skilled citizens to come to and be present at parliament. . . . And the custom was for the citizens to be the peers and equals of the knights of the shire in expenses, in coming, staying and returning.

VII. *Concerning the Burgesses*

[In the same way, burgesses are to be chosen] . . . in the same manner as has been prescribed for the citizens. But the two burgesses were not wont to receive for their expenses per day more than ten shillings and sometimes not more than half a mark; and this used to be rated by the court according to the size and power of the borough and according to the honourable reputation of the persons sent.

VIII. *Concerning the Manner of Parliament*

First the form has been shown, in what terms, to whom, and at what time summons ought to be made to Parliament, and who ought to come by summons and who not; and secondly it must be said who should come by reason of their office, and are obliged to be present, without summons, through the whole parliament; on which point it must be noted that the two principal clerks of parliament, chosen by the king and his council, and the other secondary clerks, of whom and of whose office more will be said later in detail, and the principal crier of England with his sub-criers, and the principal door-keeper of England . . . are obliged to be present from the first day; the chancellor of England, the treasurer, the chamberlains and barons of the Exchequer, the justices and all clerks and knights of the king, together with serjeants at law, who are of the king's council, are obliged to be present from the second day, unless they have reasonable excuse why they cannot be present, and they should then send good excuses.

XIII. *Concerning the Absence of the King from Parliament*

The king is held in every way to be present personally in parliament, unless he is prevented by bodily illness. In that case he may remain in his chamber, but he must not remain outside the manor, or at least the vill, where the parliament is being held. And then he ought to send for twelve persons of the highest and best who have been summoned to parliament, namely for two bishops, two earls, two barons, two knights of the shire, two citizens and two burgesses, to regard his person and to testify regarding his condition. In their presence, he ought to commission the archbishop of the province, the steward and the chief justice separately and together to begin and to continue parliament in his name. There ought to be express mention in the commission of the cause of his absence, which ought to be sufficient. . . . The reason for this is that there was wont to be clamour and murmur in parliament on account of the absence of the king, because it is damaging and dangerous to all the community of parliament and of the realm when the king is absent from parliament. Nor ought he or can he absent himself unless only in the above case.

XIV. *Concerning the Places and Sessions in Parliament*

First as aforesaid the king will sit in the middle place of the greater bench, and on his right hand there will sit the Archbishop of Canterbury, the bishops of London and Winchester and after them, in order, the other bishops, abbots and priors in rows. On the king's left there will sit the Archbishop of York, the bishops of Durham and Carlisle and after them in order the earls, barons and lords. There shall always be such division between the aforesaid orders and their location that nobody shall sit except amongst his peers. The steward of England is responsible for providing for this, unless the king shall wish to assign another to the task. At the king's feet, on his right, there will sit the chancellor of England and the chief justice of England and his colleagues, and those of their clerks who are concerned with parliament. On the left, at the king's feet, there will sit the treasurer, chamberlains and barons of the exchequer, justices of the bench and those of their clerks who are concerned with parliament.

XV. Concerning the Principal Clerks of Parliaments

Also the two principal clerks of parliaments should sit in the middle of the justices, and are to enrol all the pleas and business of parliament. . . .

XVI. Concerning the Five Clerks of Parliaments

The king shall designate five skilled and experienced clerks, of whom the first shall serve and minister to the bishops, the second to the proctors of the clergy, the third to the earls and barons, the fourth to the knights of the shires, and the fifth to the citizens and burgesses . . . and the clerks shall write down the questions and replies which they shall make to the king and the parliament, and they shall go in to their several councils whenever they wish to have them, and when they have time free, they shall help the principal clerks with the enrolment.

XXVI. Concerning the Grades of the Peers of Parliament

The king is the head, the beginning and the end of Parliament. Thus he has no peer in his grade, and thus the first estate consists of the king alone. The second grade consists of archbishops, bishops, abbots and priors who hold by barony. The third grade consists of the proctors of the clergy. The fourth grade consists of earls, barons and other magnates and lords, who hold at the value of an earldom and barony, as is said above, in the section on the laity. The fifth grade consists of knights of the shires. The sixth estate consists of citizens and burgesses. Thus parliament has six orders. But it is to be understood that if any of the five grades below the king should be absent, so long as all have been given a reasonable summons to the parliament, it shall be nevertheless considered to be full.

26 MAUD CLARKE

The composition of Parliament as described in the *Modus* is based upon two simple principles. Members are summoned for two reasons and two reasons only; either they come for reasons of tenure as individuals (*pro sua propria persona*) or else they come as representatives of communities. Other persons come to Parliament by reason of office or service; though the king requires their presence, they are said to attend *sine summonitione* (VIII). These persons are the great officers of state – the chancellor, the treasurer, the chamberlains and barons of the Exchequer and the judges; serjeants at pleas and those of the lower clergy who belong to the king's council or whose presence is deemed useful; and the ushers, criers and clerks who are the officials of Parliament itself (II and VIII). The inclusion of lesser servants, like the usher and the crier, in the same category as the chancellor and treasurer serves to bring out the sharp distinction between the king's council or royal executive, and Parliament as the political assembly of the nation. Before considering this general distinction it is necessary to examine the constituent details of each group of persons who come to Parliament for any reason whatsoever.

The lay magnates summoned by special writ are '*omnes et singuli comites et barones et eorum pares*' (III). The omission of dukes is significant and at once points to a date [of composition of the *Modus*] before the creation of the duchy of Cornwall for the king's son in 1337. The only general titles of rank named are earls and barons, but their status is put so definitely on a tenurial basis that the right of attendance is extended to the *pares* or men of the same condition. The qualification for an earl is lands and rents to the value of twenty knight's fees, each worth £20 and making a total value of £400; for a baron, thirteen and a third fees, amounting to a total value of 400 marks (III). These figures give us a clue to the date of the classification. They derive ultimately from Magna Carta (§ 2), where the relief paid for a knight's fee is fixed at 100 shillings and that for an earldom or barony at £100. This ratio carried with it the implication that twenty fees made up an earldom or a barony and, when the baron's relief was reduced to 100 marks at the end of the thirteenth century, it was natural to conclude that a barony consisted of thirteen and a third fees. The rate of 100 marks for a baron appeared in the new relief clause in Edward I's re-issue of Magna Carta (1297) and, though the practice was certainly earlier, the valuation in the *Modus* seems to be based upon it. On the other hand, the value of an earldom went up in the first half of the fourteenth century and, at least from 1337, was reckoned at 1000 marks. The change seems to have begun in 1322 when Andrew Harclay was granted 1000 marks in land and rents to maintain his dignity as earl of Carlisle. That the new value was not then fixed is indicated by the absence of reference to it in the charter, granted at the same time, by which the elder Despenser was made earl of Winchester. Before Mortimer was made earl of March in 1328, he was given land and rent worth £1000, which, while in France before his succession, the king had promised him as soon as he should obtain the realm. It seems reasonable to suppose that Mortimer had been promised an earldom and £1000 to maintain the dignity. We may conclude that the valuation of an earldom went up at some time between 1322 and 1337, a conclusion which seems to make it impossible that the omission of dukes from the category of lay magnates was accidental.

The phrase *et eorum pares* obviously refers to the tenurial qualification and points to a time when a magnate might be summoned to Parliament who was not styled either earl or baron. The term peer, used generally throughout the *Modus* to mean any member of Parliament, bears here the special sense of an equal in tenure and thus corresponds closely to its later use to denote a peer of the realm. The beginning of this modern use cannot be traced beyond the reign of Edward II.

Earls, barons and their peers, according to the *Modus*, came to Parliament by reason of their tenures, that is, they were *piers de la terre*, summoned by right and not by the king's grace. There is no suggestion that the king could issue or withhold summons at his pleasure, or that the status of a baron depended on his writ rather than on tenure. We may suspect that emphasis on the form of special summons and on the exclusively tenurial basis on which it rested, was no more accidental than the emphatic treatment of the summons of the proctors through the prelates. We know that the leaders of the baronage were concerned about the mode of summons early in Edward II's reign. In 1312 the earls of Lancaster, Hereford and Warwick protested that they had not been cited to a Parliament at Westminster on February 27, in accordance with the ordinary formula in the register of the chancellor and, therefore, that they had neither gone in person nor sent proxies. The grounds of complaint are obscure. The earls were summoned in the usual way to a Parliament at Westminster on February 13, but this assembly was postponed because of the king's absence; no earls were summoned to a council held at York on February 27. Possibly the earls were aggrieved because the king had not held a Parliament at West-minster on February 27 instead of a council at York. However, for our purposes the main point is the form of the complaint and it shows clear-ly that the magnates in the reign of Edward II maintained their right to be summoned to Parliament, according to the formularies of the Chan-cery. They were, in short, determined that control of the composition of Parliament should not lie with the king.

The chapters relating to the lay commons (IV–VII), like that on the commons of the clergy, are written altogether from the point of view of the central assembly and are not concerned with details of elections or of constituencies. The core of each section is the writ of summons, ex-panded or paraphrased to emphasize the need of sending to Parliament competent persons with full authority to act for the communities that they represent. The descriptive formula of the writs – 'milites de discretioribus et ad laborandum potentioribus' – is replaced by the adjectives 'idoneos, honestos et peritos' and 'ad faciendum' is expanded into 'ad respondendum, subeundum, allegandum, et faciendum'. The elected members are even described as attorneys (*attornati*), so strong is the emphasis on their appointment with full power to act for others. The idea was not a novelty at any time in the fourteenth century; it had been developed in the reigns of Henry III and Edward I and was formulated definitely in the writs of summons to the Parliament of 1294. For purposes of dating, we can say no more than that the emphatic expression of the principle of representation suggests an early rather than a late stage in parliamentary development. . . .

Turning from the members of Parliament, both magnates and com-mons, we find opposed to them in the *Modus* the heterogeneous group of officials and servants enumerated in Chapter VIII. It will be con-venient to discuss them separately before considering the general interest of the hard line drawn between Parliament and the executive. In addition to the obvious division between councillors and servants, the council itself may be divided into the great officers of state, the judges and the ordinary councillors, either permanent or summoned for a special purpose. Each category will require separate treatment in order to bring out the significance of their appearance in the *Modus*.

The great officers of state named are the chancellor, the treasurer, the chamberlain and barons of the Exchequer and the judges (VIII, XIV). This selection is interesting in itself, as defining a particular period. The 'public, ministerial character' of the chancellor and treasurer was well established in the first half of the thirteenth century and as such had special treatment in the Provisions of Oxford. From early in Edward III's reign the keeper of the Privy Seal was regarded as the third minister of state. An exact date can hardly be assigned to his public association with the chancellor and treasurer: Tout puts it in the keepership of Richard of Bury (1329–31); Baldwin cites a statute of 1340 in which the officers to take oaths are enumerated as the chancellor, the treasurer, the keeper of the Privy Seal and the judges, as an indication that by that time the keeper was 'regularly given a rank in the council next to the chancellor and the treasurer'. His omission from the list in the *Modus* is a definite indication of an early date.

After the treasurer, the best manuscripts name the *camerarii et barones de scaccario* (XIV), but others, including the text hitherto printed, read *camerarius*, meaning the king's chamberlain. It is tempting to adopt the less authoritative reading, as the king's chamberlain was a household officer who never officially came 'out of court' and his appearance as third in the council would point to a time when he was unusually important. The work of Tout has made it easy to see in the younger Despenser the only chamberlain whose use of his office and personal authority would account for this remarkable elevation of a lay officer of the Household. Despenser was chamberlain from 1318 and, except during his brief exile in 1321, continued to act until his death in 1326. However, it is difficult to press this interpretation against the better reading, even though to name the chamberlains before the barons of the Exchequer and the judges may surprise us. The two chamberlains of the Exchequer were 'jointly second in command over the receipt, ranking immediately after the treasurer'. Apparently an order of association rather than an order of precedence was followed in the *Modus*. Their inclusion among the great officers of state must belong to a time when the distinction between ministers and technical officials was not fully understood; in the reign of Edward II the chamberlains and the re-membrancers were sometimes summoned to serve on the king's council. It is possible that the variations in the manuscripts may arise out of some original confusion between the two kinds of chamberlain, since in the Sherburn indenture (1321) the same alternative readings occur. However, the interest of the problem is mainly technical, as neither the king's chamberlain nor the chamberlains of the Exchequer would appear in the place of the keeper of the Privy Seal, except at an early period of the fourteenth century.

The barons of the Exchequer and the judges are named after the great officers of state. Their position as mere assistants or assessors is made explicit by the statement that the clerks are not subject to them and that no judge of England is judge in Parliament, nor is able to have his own records there (XV). It has been suggested that the judges lost their right to share in the functions of Parliament because they could not try peers of the realm, but it seems more probable that their disability arose, as the *Modus* indicates, from the fact that they had no right to membership, either by tenure or as representatives of communities. Stubbs noted that the omission of the word *ceteris* before *prelatis, magnatibus et proceribus* in the writs of summons had 'the great legal force' of excluding them from claiming peerage. Hence their remarkable position as 'assistants' with a voice but not a vote, a position which is a warning against over-emphasis on the judicial functions of the Parliament of estates.

The other members of the council are described as king's clerks and knights and serjeants at pleas. The king's clerks and knights were men in close personal attendance on the king, members of the royal household. The clerical element in the council was strongest under Edward II, though already under Edward I there were frequent references to 'clerks of the council'. To the Model Parliament were summoned the judges, *decanis, iuratis de consilio*, the barons of the Exchequer, *et aliis clericis de consilio*; the summons to the council of September 1297 was issued to eight persons called *clerici de consilio*, as well as to the archdeacons of Chester and East Riding and to two friars. Under Edward II much administrative work was carried on by the king's clerks and they were summoned steadily with the judges to the council. The king's knights are less often specifically named in the councillor's summons. In 1297 nine knights were summoned of whom eight were judges; the ninth, Bogo de Knovil, was constable of the castle of Montgomery. Maitland has noticed the presence of twenty-four knights, as councillors at the Parliament of 1305; of these ten had received the baronial summons, eight were judges and had received the councillor's summons and the rest were for the most part constables and captains in the service of the crown. The more important lay members of the royal household, like the chamberlain, Peter de Champvent, who was summoned to Parliament in 1300 and 1301, were probably reckoned among the king's knights. Under Edward II few persons specifically described as knights were summoned, though the term certainly covered those judges who were knights and also the chamberlains and steward of the Household. There seems no doubt that laymen were in a substantial majority among the professional councillors. The king's serjeants, judges in the making, were necessarily few in number, but at least three lawyers of some eminence, Herle, Stonor and Geoffrey le Scrope, were Edward II's councillors before they were raised to the Bench. We know also that serjeants at law acted as advocates for the king in Parliament in 1316 and 1320.

Baldwin has noted that the list of councillors in the *Modus* 'bears the stamp of the earlier part of the century', the time when, as Maitland puts it, 'we have to picture to ourselves the council as being in the main a body of officers, of ministers, of men who in one capacity or another are doing the king's work and receiving the king's pay'. By the reign of Richard II, at latest, most of this strong professional element had been excluded from the council. Even the judges ceased to be sworn councillors before the middle of the reign of Edward III.

Under Edward I and Edward II it was characteristic of the king's council, both within Parliament and without, to contain all the categories enumerated in the *Modus*. Though what may be called the professional element – judges and civil servants – remained in the council until the minority of Richard II, it declined both in strength and in importance under Edward III. The evidence of the councillors' writs of summons may be taken as a rough indication of the way in which the size of the professional council was reduced. In the last years of Edward I the number of officials specially summoned varied between thirty-nine and fifteen (1295–1307). Under Edward II the largest number thus summoned was forty-three in 1313, thirty-eight in 1318 and 1321, thirty-seven in 1308 and 1318, thirty-five in 1308, and thirty and thirty-two in 1307, 1312, 1318 and 1320; in 1315, 1316 and 1322 thirty-three councillors' summonses were issued. In the first decade of Edward III the highest numbers reached were twenty-one and twenty-three in 1333–35 and in the second decade the average number cannot be put much higher than a dozen. There seems no doubt that the large professional council was an outstanding feature of Edward II's government, and it cannot be found at full strength after that date.

The Council in Parliament

The very strong stress laid by Maud Clarke on the place of the council in early parliaments cannot be dismissed on the ground that her base in the Modus was only a theoretical one, for F. W. Maitland reached a similar conclusion starting from the very concrete foundation of the roll of the Lenten parliament of 1305 which he published. Maitland's introduction to this parliament roll has become a classic of parliamentary history and has been repeatedly reprinted. In the introduction he surveyed the composition of this particular parliament, and then proceeded to emphasize the importance of the council in parliament.

27 F. W. MAITLAND

[The Lenten parliament of 1305] was a full parliament in our sense of that term. The three estates of the realm met the king and his council. The great precedent of 1295 had been followed and, if the writs of summons were punctually obeyed, the assembly was a large one. By rights there should have been present some ninety-five prelates, about a hundred and forty-five representatives of the inferior clergy, nine earls (if we include the Prince of Wales and the Earl of Angus), ninety-four barons, seventy-four knights of the shires, and about two hundred citizens and burgesses; altogether some six hundred men. Besides these we must take account of thirty-three members of the king's council to whom writs were sent, and, as we shall see hereafter, there were yet other men present and performing important duties, men who had a special knowledge of Scotland and Gascony.

This assembly was kept together for just three weeks. On the 21st of March a proclamation was made[1] telling the archbishops, bishops and other prelates, earls, barons, knights, citizens and burgesses in general that they might go home, but must be ready to appear again if the king summoned them. Those bishops, earls, barons, justices and others who were members of the council were to remain behind and so were all those who had still any business to transact. But the 'parliament' was not at an end. Many of its doings that are recorded on our roll were done after the estates had been sent home. The king remained at Westminster,

[1] See below no. 28.

surrounded by his councillors, and his parliament was still in session as a 'full' and 'general' parliament as late as the 5th and 6th of April....

Now if we are to frame any exact conception of the body or various bodies of men by whom the business that is recorded on our roll was transacted, and of the mode in which they dealt with that business, it seems necessary that we should understand the composition of the king's council. Unfortunately, as is well known, the council of Edward I is still for us an ill-defined group of men. Writs of summons and writs for wages will often teach us the names of all the barons who were called to a parliament and enable us to know who it was that represented the pettiest boroughs, and yet we cannot enumerate with any certainty the members of the council. We can indeed make a list of those of its members who, not being prelates or barons, were summoned by name to be present at a given parliament. On the present occasion no less than thirty-three men were thus summoned. The list included Phillip Willoughby the chancellor of the exchequer, the justices of the two benches and the barons of the exchequer, several men who were being employed as justices in eyre and thirteen masters of the chancery or clerks of the council. The title 'masters in chancery' is one which may lead us astray by suggesting that those who bear it are, like their successors in later days, principally engaged in performing certain subordinate functions in a great court of law and equity. But this is not so. If, with Dr Stubbs, we say that at this time the chancellor is 'the principal secretary of state for all departments', we may call these masters the 'under-secretaries of state'. Though already a keeper of the privy seal is beginning to intervene between the king and his chancellor, though already the king, at least at times, seems to have one yet more intimate clerk who is known as his secretary, the chancery is still the great secretarial department; it does nearly all the king's writing for him, whether such writing concerns foreign affairs or the government of England. If for a moment we may use such modern terms, we may say that the chancery is Home Office, Foreign Office, Board of Trade, Local Government Board all in one; in short it is a general secretarial bureau, which exercises a certain control even over the only other great official 'department' that there is, namely the exchequer. Thus when the king is surrounded by the masters or principal clerks of the chancery, he has at his side the men who know most about the way in which England is governed and foreign affairs are managed, 'permanent' or fairly permanent, 'under-secretaries of state', and yet men who are on their promotion, for some of them may well look to being chancellors or treasurers before they die. It is among them also that the king finds his diplomatists. The thirty-three names therefore upon our list represent almost all that England has to show in the way of legal learning, official experience and administrative ability.

But then of course it is certain that there are members of the council who are not upon this list. They have been otherwise summoned. In the first place there are the two great ministers. The treasurer, Walter Langton, has been summoned as bishop of Lichfield; he is king Edward's right hand man. The chancellor, William Hamilton, who, when compared with Langton, seems an insignificant person, can appear as dean of York. But there must be other prelates and there must be lay nobles who are members of the council. On the other hand it is difficult, if not impossible, to believe that every prelate or baron is a member of the council. We see this from that proclamation of the 21st of March which has already been mentioned. On that day the mass of prelates and nobles is sent home; but the members of the council are to remain behind. Now it would be a hard task were we to seek to recover the names of all those who in any given year were king Edward's sworn councillors. . . .

When, however, all due allowance has been made for all our doubts and mistakes, we have to picture to ourselves the council as being in the main a body of officers, of ministers, of men who in one capacity or another are doing the king's work and receiving the king's pay. Even those prelates and barons who remain at Westminster, when their fellows have gone home, are hardly mere prelates and barons. The Bishops of Durham and Carlisle are not just two bishops; the magnificent Anthony Beck, the strenuous John Halton, we might almost call provincial governors, the military governors of districts which are exposed to invasion. Clifford and Despenser are not just two powerful barons; they are the two forest justices, and as such they are at this moment two very important ministers. Valence and Britanny are the king's best generals. The Earl of Lincoln, the faithful Henry Lacy, is as near to being a prime minister as a layman can be. And then the council embraces all the great courts and all the great boards. A full meeting of the council is a full meeting of the king's bench, of the common bench, of the chancery, of the exchequer: it is this and more than this.

Maitland's argument is illustrated here by two examples. The Lenten parliament of 1305 was still in session when only the members of the council remained, and even as late as 1332 the Lenten parliament was still called 'parliament' when the representatives of shires, towns and lower clergy had gone home.

28 PARLIAMENT ROLL 1305

And afterwards, on the 21st of March, it was proclaimed by commandment of the king, in the following words:

To archbishops, bishops and other prelates, earls, barons, knights of the shires, citizens and burgesses and other members of the commonalty, who have come here, to this parliament, at the command of our lord the king, the king thanks them very much for their attendance. He wishes that for the present (*quant a ore*) they will go back to their districts, so that they may return quickly and without delay at the moment when they are again summoned, except the bishops, earls and barons, justices and others who are [members] of the council of our lord the king. These shall not depart without special leave of the king. And those who have business still to do shall remain to pursue their business. And the knights who have come on behalf of (*pur*) the shires, and the others who have come for the cities and boroughs, shall apply to Sire John de Kirkby, and he will let them have writs of expenses for their districts. . . .

29 PARLIAMENT ROLL 1332

Let it also be recalled that on the Saturday following the first day of parliament, the knights of the shires, and the citizens and burgesses who had been summoned to the parliament, and also the clergy, were given leave to return home, whilst the prelates, earls and barons, and the members of the king's council remained there.

The same conclusion about the importance of the council in parliament arrived at by Maitland and Miss Clarke was also reached from yet another angle by Professor Tout. As the greatest historian of the administrators of medieval England, he was naturally concerned with the place of royal officials in parliament. He emphasized their preponderant part in its activities even more than Maitland or Miss Clarke.

30 T. F. TOUT

The history of administration has up to now run through channels parallel to, yet independent of, the ordinary courses of constitutional history. We have, accordingly, been able to study in detail the administrative history of the reign of Edward I without in the least troubling ourselves with what is to most scholars the central fact of the period, the development of parliamentary institutions. The essential point of the great councils, and of the parliaments which grew out of them, is that they were occasional and intermittent phenomena. The essence of the administrative machinery is that it is always in existence, continually at work. Even in modern times parliaments, whose chief ostensible function is to pass new laws, may perhaps in the long run exercise less influence on national development than does the administrative machinery by which this legislation is executed. In medieval days, when the idea of novel legislation was repulsive to the common mind, this was still more emphatically the case. What availed the parliament, which met at the best for a few weeks in the year, as compared with chancery, wardrobe and exchequer which were always at work?

The popular parliaments of Edward I grew out of the feudal great councils, of which they were an 'afforced' and representative development. The great council of magnates in its turn was but an aspect of the *curia regis*, the royal household strengthened and enlarged by the magnates who went to court on great occasions or at seasons of special necessity. The root, then, of the popular parliament was the household, just as much as the household was the source of all the offices of the administration. The primary business of councils and parliaments was to give the king advice; the fundamental duty of the administrative offices was to embody in action the will of the king. But in practice the advisory and the executive functions must necessarily overlap; most of all must they overlap in a political system so fluid as that of the middle ages. We are bound, however, to make distinctions that come to little in practice. It is only by such a process we can make any distinctions at all in medieval institutional history.

The advisory and the executive functions approach most nearly in the permanent king's council which was always at his side to help him in dealing with problems of government as they arose. The royal council, the privy council as later ages called it, is often treated as itself an executive body. This view is true enough of the last century or so of the middle ages when everything was preparing the way for the system of 'government by council' perfected in Tudor times. It is unfortunate, however, that even the latest and best of the historians of the council has to some extent followed the fashion of the lawyers, who see history as a plane surface, subjected for all time to the legal system in which they have been brought up. They have read the Tudor conditions into the history of the thirteenth- or fourteenth-century council, just as peerage lawyers have read the hereditary house of lords and the ridiculous doctrine of abeyance into the history of the reign of Edward I. They cannot help regarding the council as an executive office, as a branch of the administration. But the real function of the council was to give advice. If the king took the advice, he generally associated the council with him in responsibility for the resulting action. But the decision was the king's alone, and any consequent executive acts came, not from the king in council, but from the ordinary administrative machinery. Such an act might be embodied in a writ of great seal, and so become an act of chancery. It might be translated into a writ of privy seal and thus become a function of the wardrobe. If it mainly concerned finance, it was very likely to result in a writ under the seal of the exchequer, and accordingly the executive agent was the exchequer. But in no case did the council, as such, act, though often enough the council figures in the marginal annotations of the chancery rolls as the sole source of warranty of an executive act embodied in a chancery writ. There was also, as time went on, an increasing tendency for the council's advice to materialize into writs of privy seal; but it is quite wrong to regard the privy seal as in any special sense the seal of the council. . . .

The executive offices and the council are, then, different in kind, and the only real problem for us is the extent to which the former had influence on the latter. This means in effect the extent to which the officers, forming the staff of the administrative departments, participated personally in the councils and parliaments of their time, and also the degree to which they influenced the deliberations of these assemblies. Naturally their influence was more intimate on the smaller ring of permanent councillors than on the great councils, which were essentially aristocratic in their origin, and ultimately also became widely representative in character. But the early Edwardian parliament was not composed of the 'three estates', the lords, commons and clergy of later times. It was essentially a single body, in which the initiative and power rested with a limited circle of men, accustomed to politics and affairs.

It was an assembly which, save when moved by great gusts of passionate opposition, was content to be guided by the king and his advisers. We must not be satisfied, therefore, in stressing the well-known facts that all the chief officers of the crown, clerical and lay, were sworn in the king's council, and that, parliament being an enlarged council, they naturally took their places in every parliamentary gathering, whether specially summoned or not. It is more to the purpose that a large proportion of the initiative and the discussion in all parliaments lay with them, and that the magnates only could withstand their influence. They had, therefore, a weight quite out of proportion to their numbers. But numbers in a medieval assembly mattered little. We have not yet got to the stage where decisions were arrived at in large bodies by a counting up of votes for and against a measure.

The Magnates in Parliament

In theory the opposing side with which the crown parleyed in early parliaments was the community. If in practice the 'crown' meant the royal councillors, so the 'community' could be held effectively to mean the magnates. Professor Roskell has however shown that many magnates frequently failed to turn up. This not only allowed the council yet further to dominate parliament, but also, in Professor Roskell's opinion, suggests that at least by the end of the fourteenth century, the commons were not merely ancillaries, but the main body to be encountered by the council in parliament.

31 J. S. ROSKELL

Whether in the Old English witan, or in the *curia regis* or *commune concilium* of the Norman and Angevin kings, or in the later medieval parliament, archbishops, bishops, abbots, and lay magnates had a long tradition of obligatory service. In the post-Conquest, feudal period, counsel was an immaterial form of aid due to the king from the great men of the land, prelates and *proceres* alike, in virtue of their fealty or homage. The lords spiritual and temporal, when summoned to parliament, were expected to attend. Formally granted exonerations from personal appearance, whether for a special occasion or for life, were never more than a few at any one time. Appearance by proxies or attorneys was in constant use, at least among the churchmen: this was in a sense inevitable, being a common phenomenon in all kinds of medieval assemblies and courts. But such a practice was the object of royal disapproval on occasion, certainly in the fourteenth century, and the whole emphasis of the language of the writs of summons was on the needfulness of personal attendance. That frequent attendance in parliaments was likely to be found burdensome by the many might be deduced even as early as 1258, for when in the Provisions of Oxford it was laid down that parliament should meet at fixed intervals three times a year it was agreed that no more than twelve magnates, additional to those appointed as members of the baronial council of fifteen, need come together, 'pur esparnier le cust del commun'. Certainly in the fourteenth century there is no shortage of evidence that the lords' attendance was frequently spasmodic, and at times so embarrassingly scanty as to have a very deleterious effect on parliament's capacity to proceed with its business: in fact, now and then, parliament had to be abandoned altogether on this account. The heavy fines for failure to attend, proposed in the *Modus tenendi parliamentum*, a treatise which is to be attributed to this century, confirm the seriousness of the problem. And perhaps the recurrent petitions (fourteen in the century between 1344 and 1444) against the exoneration of the free tenants of peers of parliament from contributions to the wages of the knights of the shire have some bearing on the subject: if many of those peers were not attending parliament, any such exemption of their tenants was likely to be regarded as even more unjustifiable. However this may be, at the end of the fourteenth century there was one occasion when even the commons felt called upon to complain of a poor 'turn-up' on the part of the lords. The fifteenth century was to witness instances of claims on the part of individual magnates for precedence over one or more of their compeers, but in this there is probably more of a recognition that the lay lords were hardening into a parliamentary peerage based on the hereditary principle, than a suggestion that they were generally finding their parliamentary occupation more congenial and less of a burden than before. Although, for the most part, the clerks who made up the rolls of the parliaments of the fifteenth century were not so ready to reveal the king's dissatisfaction with abstentions from parliamentary attendance as had been their predecessors of the previous century, there is evidence in the rolls and elsewhere of a different kind to suggest that the attitude of the ecclesiastical and lay baronage to parliamentary service had undergone no important change for the better. The attendance of the parliamentary abbots was evidently throughout the medieval period even normally deplorable; so much so, that the theory that 'during the middle ages the spiritual peers . . . always outnumbered their temporal colleagues', and that the Tudor period (with its monastic dissolutions) saw 'the reduction of the spiritual peers from more than half to less than a third of the whole house', is a myth if we think in terms of actual attendance and not merely of the chancery lists of those individually summoned. At some times of great political stress, when clearly it was to their interest to do so, certainly the secular prelates and the lords temporal turned up in great force (as in 1388, 1397, 1399, 1426, and 1433). On the other hand in the very difficult circumstances of the later years of Henry VI's reign, abstention from attendance in some parliaments was even at the time regarded as serious, and this led to the first recorded fines for absence levied by parliamentary authority. The attendance of the secular prelates, by and large, was relatively satisfactory. But, though so many of the bishops were ex-civil servants, to whom Westminster was in a sense always a 'home from home', even their attendance was dependent for its fullness on the circumstances of the moment. The dutifulness of the lay nobility was very much conditioned by political interest and also by status: members of its upper ranks attended very well on the whole, but the barons and bannerets, so it would appear, only very indifferently even as a regular thing.

What all this meant, from the time when, in the later fourteenth century, the royal council began to contain a substantial and generally increasing number of prelates and magnates, was that the Upper House of parliament was frequently no more than an ample session of the continual council afforced by a comparatively not very significant number of other peers. And the fact that there was seemingly no very material difference between the attendance of the lords at great councils and their attendance in parliaments, suggests that parliaments rather than great councils were summoned for purposes to the pursuance of which the presence of the elected commons was deemed to be, and indeed really was, most needful. In fact, it would perhaps not be going too far to say that, in practice, parliaments were called in order to get together a full meeting of the ordinary council, afforced by as large a number of other lords as possible, and so that they should meet the elected commons.

The absence of both lay and ecclesiastical magnates may be seen in practice as early as 1306 in a memorandum of the Trinity parliament in that year. It lists three bishops as present in person, but fourteen as only represented by proxy. It lists five earls as present in person, but three as absent. A surviving writ indicates that a fourth earl, Oxford, also sent a substitute. The memorandum of the parliament lists eleven barons as present, and merely says largely that quamplures alii magnates et proceres *only sent proxies. The close rolls show that, apart from the earls, no less than sixty-three lay people received individual writs of summons. Returned writs, nominating substitutes in much the same terms as the Earl of Oxford, survive from a handful of the fifty-two absentees.*

32 MEMORANDA ROLL 1306

There came *in person* before the King and his council at Westminster on that day; Anthony Bek, Patriarch of Jerusalem and Bishop of Durham, W(alter) Langton, Bishop of Coventry and Lichfield, Ralph Baldock, Bishop of London; H(enry) de Lacy, Earl of Lincoln, J(ohn) de Warenne, Earl of Surrey, R(alph) de Monthermer, Earl of Gloucester and Hertford, H(umphrey) de Bohun, Earl of Hereford, G(uy) Beauchamp, Earl of Warwick; Robert Fitz Walter, Hugh le Despenser, John de Hastings, Hugh de Vere, William Martin, Henry le Tyeys, John Lavel, Roger de Mortimer, John de Mohun, Alan de la Zouche, William Leyburn, and Robert de Burghersh, the Warden of the Cinque Ports with certain barons of those ports. And also *by proxies and attorneys* Archbishops Robert of Canterbury and William of York; Bishops Thomas of Exeter, Richard of Hereford, John of Winchester, John of Chichester, Thomas of Rochester, Robert of Ely, John of Norwich, John of Lincoln, Simon of Salisbury, William of Worcester, Walter of Bath and Wells and John of Carlisle; the Abbots of Westminster, St Edmunds, St Augustines at Canterbury, St Albans, Glastonbury, Peterborough, Ramsey, Thorney, Selby, Malmesbury and St Peters at Gloucester; Roger Earl of Norfolk and Marshal of England, Thomas Earl of Lancaster, Edmund Earl of Arundel and very many other prelates, magnates and great men, and also from each county of the realm two knights and from each city two citizens and from each borough two burgesses chosen by the communities of the counties, cities and boroughs to treat, ordain and consent to the aforesaid demands in the name of the said communities.

33 WRIT OF SUMMONS 1306

Edward by the grace of God King of England, Lord of Ireland and Duke of Aquitaine to his beloved and faithful Robert de Vere, Earl of Oxford, greeting. Since we have decided that our eldest son Edward shall be girded with the belt of knighthood at Whitsun next, God willing, and since an aid is due to us on such an occasion according to the rights of our crown, we command you, and firmly enjoin you by the fealty and homage which you hold towards us, that you should be present in your own person before us and our council at Westminster, on the day after

Trinity Sunday, to discuss with the prelates and other magnates and great men of our kingdom and to decide what should be done about the aid to us in this case, and to consent to whatever shall be decided in this matter. Alternatively you may send your attorneys, having sufficient authority and instructions from you, to do the same. And send this writ back. Witness myself at Winchester the 5th April in the thirty-fourth year of our reign.

On the back of the writ has been written:

Robert de Vere, Earl of Oxford, has deputed to act in his place John de Wascoyl and John de Bouser.

On the back of the similar writ sent to Geoffrey de Camville has been written:

Geoffrey de Camville by his letters patent has deputed to act in his place Thomas de Ralegh, Robert de Stokhaye and Simon Belde or any one of them who shall happen to be present.

The Commons in Parliament

Professor Roskell suggested that by the late fourteenth century parliaments were called essentially in order that the council should meet the elected commons. In the period of parliamentary origins, however, the commons were of far less significance. In Dr Pasquet's view the early representatives came out of duty and to serve the king's convenience. They were called not because their presence was necessary, even for granting taxation, but because it was useful. It may, however, be suggested that the line between utility and necessity is a very fine one, and that Pasquet perhaps over-argued his case.

34 D. PASQUET

Our investigation has shown us that the convening of representatives of the counties and towns in parliament was essentially the work of the crown. This convening is to be traced to remote origins. The custom of summoning four knights, on behalf of the county, before the king's court appeared to us to have been firmly established in the reign of Richard I. And parliament is only an amplified form of the king's court. In the thirteenth century the kings gradually adopted the custom of summoning several counties at once, and even all the counties of England together. Through the sheriffs they summoned before themselves and their council two, three or four discreet knights to represent a county and to speak in its name. Sometimes, when the circumstances seemed to demand it, they particularly ordered that these knights should be elected by the county court. On other occasions the sheriffs were merely commanded to provide for the attendance of four knights, as in the case of an ordinary judicial citation. The purpose of the summons was not always the same. The knights might be required to give evidence in an inquest on the administration of the sheriffs. Or their assent might be required for an aid, the collection of which would be difficult without their co-operation. Lastly, in its struggles against the magnates, the crown was not above seeking the help of the numerous and powerful class of gentry, who held a large portion of the land of England and in the county courts administered the countryside.

At a moment of crisis, when nearly all the magnates were opposed to him, Simon de Montfort, then ruling in the king's name, summoned to parliament not only representatives of the county communities, but also representatives of the town communities.

For the counties and towns, as for the prelates and barons, the summons was in the nature of a feudal obligation. Attendance at the king's parliament was not a right, but a duty or, to adopt the contemporary expression, a service – the service, or suit, of court. As regards the knights and burgesses, the compulsory character of the summons is very clearly shown by the practice of demanding security for their appearance; a practice which was in use from the beginning of Edward I's reign and does not seem to have been then an innovation. We never find the counties and towns claiming to be summoned to parliament as of right. The knights and burgesses were by no means anxious to repair to London, York or Shrewsbury in order to waste valuable time over the king's business and to play a part of but small importance in the king's assembly. Even if the knights, long accustomed to such summons, discharged their service without much grumbling, the towns offered a passive resistance which in the end often defeated the perseverance of the sheriffs and the wishes of the king.

The formation of the house of commons has long been represented as the last step in a development which began with the Great Charter, was continued by the Provisions of Oxford and the great parliament of 1265, and ended in the 'model' parliament of 1295. This development was held to have been caused by the alliance of the magnates, gentry and bourgeoisie, who all united to oppose the excessive power of the crown and succeeded in limiting the royal authority. But the study of the documents has led us to quite other conclusions. The nation did not demand representation in the king's parliament. It was the king who imposed on his subjects the duty of sending him their representatives.

Edward I changed an occasional expedient into a regular custom, not in order to associate the whole nation with himself in the work of government, but in order to strengthen the royal power. He only summoned the representatives of the commons when such a course seemed to him to serve his own interests; and often the most important agenda were discussed in their absence. If in the end he made a practice of summoning them almost regularly, this was because he perceived that the previous consent of the knights and burgesses greatly facilitated the collection of aids and even enabled the government to collect rather more than would otherwise have been possible. Another reason was that the petitions, in which the delegates of the communities begged him to redress wrongs irremediable by the ordinary processes of the law, gave him full information on the condition of his kingdom and enabled him to make all aware of the strength of the royal arm. Every abuse of power by a great lord, every injustice by a servant of the crown, every invasion of the royal rights was denounced before the king's court; and thus the sessions of the full parliaments carried on the grand inquests of the beginning of the reign. Lastly, the assemblies of representatives from counties and towns embodied one of the fundamental ideas of Edward's policy. In parliament, as formed by him, the old feudal distinction between tenants-in-chief and sub-vassals was entirely abolished. The king had before him only subjects. Despite its feudal form, the summoning of the commons was an essentially anti-feudal measure, the object of which was to strengthen the central power and to subject all the inhabitants of the realm, of whatever rank in the feudal hierarchy, to the direct authority of the monarch. In this respect Edward continued the policy of Henry II and emulated Philippe le Bel.

But Edward's plans did not succeed; or rather they succeeded only in part. The assembly of representatives from counties and towns did indeed rapidly achieve the destruction of the feudal system of society. But it did not result in an increase of the royal power, as Edward had hoped.

About the middle of the fourteenth century the house of commons, which existed only in embryo in the model parliaments of Edward I, assumed the character of an established and clearly defined institution. We may ask why the knights associated themselves with the burgesses. Between these two groups, which were elected by the communities of the realm and represented the 'poor folk of the land' and whose constituents paid the greater part of the royal taxes, was there any natural affinity drawing them together? Or were the knights excluded from the baronage by the growing tendency towards the constitution of an hereditary peerage? It is difficult to say. Anyhow, in the early years of Edward III's reign, we clearly see the two groups of representatives drawing together. It is uncertain whether the knights and burgesses united in one body at the parliaments of March and September 1332. It is almost certain that they did so at the parliaments of December 1332 and January 1333. Undeniably they did so in 1339 and 1341. At first the co-operation between the two elements, of which the new institution was formed, was not perfect. The bourgeoisie were an inferior class, subject to heavier charges than was the community of the realm. Sometimes the royal government still negotiated separately with them, as before. But the distinction between the knights and burgesses gradually became a mere question of their respective degrees of influence in parliament.

Parliament long retained the appearance of a single whole. As councillors of the king, the lords remained in the great hall of the council. They did not form a separate chamber; and the term 'house of lords' does not appear till the sixteenth century. Even the deputies of the commons, although they established themselves in the chapter-house of Westminster Abbey and there deliberated apart, formed a committee of parliament (as Professor Pollard has pointed out) rather than a real 'house'. From time to time they crossed the road to appear 'in parliament', their speaker at their head. It was only very slowly that the original unity of parliament ceased to have any real existence and was reduced to a mere form; and even more slowly did the commons come at last to play a decisive part in the English constitution.

Our knowledge of the composition of the 'commons', that is of those who represented the 'communities' of the shires and boroughs in parliament, is largely derived from the writs of summons which were sent out by the king's orders to the sheriffs of the various counties. This is because the sheriffs, when they had seen that elections had been made, returned the writs with the names of the elected knights and burgesses written on the back. The following example relates to the parliament of February 1305. Lists of those attending parliament have been built up from such material, but it is often difficult to identify the men concerned, such as Theobald de Nevill and Robert de Flixthorp. It needs a great deal of patient research to create biographies of the individuals elected in sufficient detail to make generalizations about the sort of men who actually represented the shire or town communities in parliament, their wealth and the extent of their lands, and their administrative or military experience.

35 WRIT OF SUMMONS, ENDORSEMENT AND WRIT OF EXPENSES 1305

Summons

Edward, by the grace of God, king of England, lord of Ireland, and duke of Aquitaine, to the sheriff of Rutland, greeting. We propose, God willing, to hold parliament at Westminster on Tuesday 16 February, to decide and discuss certain matters which specially concern our realm of

England and the establishment of our land of Scotland, and also various other matters, and we wish to have special discussion and deliberation on this business with the prelates, magnates and leading men of this realm. We therefore firmly enjoin and order you without delay to elect from among the more discreet men and those more fitted to the task, two knights from the shire and two citizens from each city in the shire and two burgesses from each borough, and cause them to come to us at the said time and place. Also that the said knights should then have full and sufficient authority on behalf of themselves and the community of the county, and the citizens and burgesses on behalf of themselves and the communities of each city and borough, to do whatever shall then be decided by common counsel in the foregoing matters, lest the business remain unfinished for lack of sufficient authority. And return here the names of the knights, citizens and burgesses and this writ. Witnessed by the king at Burstwick 12 November [1304]

Endorsement

Two knights were elected in the full county (court) of Rutland, and full and sufficient authority was given and conceded to them by the county to act (for it) and commit (it) in all things as shall be ordained by the council of the king, namely: Theobald de Nevill, knight, whose coming to you at the time and place specified in the writ is guaranteed by Ralf de Bella Fago, Hugh de Swafeld, Peter le Venour and Robert ad Aulam; also Robert de Flixthorp guaranteed by Thomas son of Alice de Wyssenden, Roger son of John (de Wyssenden), Richard le Freman (of Wyssenden) and Richard le Hert. And there is no city or borough within the county of Rutland and therefore no citizens or burgesses were chosen by me in this county.

After the parliament was over, the sheriff received a further writ telling him to make the county pay the expenses of its representatives.

Expenses

The king to the sheriff of Rutland greeting. We order you to collect from the community of your county, both within liberties and without, for our beloved and faithful Theobald de Nevill and Robert de Flixthorp, knights, who recently, by our command, came, on behalf of the community, to Westminster to deliberate with us on various matters specially concerning us and the state of our kingdom, and (let them have) their reasonable expenses for coming to us, staying here, and returning home from here, as has customarily been done on other similar occasions.

Witnessed by the king at Westminster 20 March.

The evidence for the way in which knights or burgesses were chosen for early parliaments is extremely meagre. The following extract from one of the letter books of the corporation of the city of London is one of the most illuminating pieces of evidence. Even this is ambiguous, and various, unproven, hypotheses have been put forward to explain the double election which it describes.

36 LONDON LETTER BOOK

On Wednesday before the Feast of Saint Michael in the twenty fourth year of the reign of King Edward [26 September 1296], a royal writ was sent in these words:

Edward by the grace of God etc. to theWarden and Sheriffs of London. We wish to have 'colloquy' and 'treaty' with the earls, barons and other magnates of our kingdom to provide remedies against the dangers which menace this kingdom in these days. We have therefore ordered them to be with us on the morrow of All Souls next [3 November] at Bury St Edmunds to 'treat', 'order' and do whatever is advisable for avoiding the dangers, and for the greater safety and utility of the kingdom. We firmly enjoin and order you that you cause two citizens to be chosen without delay from among the more discreet of the city and to come to us at the said time and place. Also that the said citizens should then have full and sufficient authority on behalf of themselves and the community of the city, to do whatever shall then be decided by common counsel in the foregoing matters, lest the business remain unfinished for lack of sufficient authority. And return here the names of the citizens and this writ. Witness myself at Berwick upon Tweed 25 August in the twenty fourth year of our reign [1296].

Because of this order all the aldermen of the city were summoned and four men from each ward of the city who, with unanimous assent and consent, all chose Stephen Eswy and William de Hereford to go to the King's parliament at Bury St Edmunds for the community etc. And with unanimous assent, they offered them 20s a day for their expenses [including] going and returning.

So as to carry out the above command of the King, the community, that is to say six of the better and more discreet men of each ward, were summoned on the Monday before the feast of St Edward the King in the twenty fourth year of the reign of King Edward [8 October 1296] into the presence of John Bretun, Warden, Stephen Eswy, William de Hereford, William le Mazeliner, Walter de Finchingfeud, Nicholas de Farndone, Thomas Remein, Salomon le Cotiller, John of Dunstaple, William de Bettoyne and Henry le Bele, Aldermen. They then chose Stephen Eswy and William de Hereford, Citizens and Aldermen, to go to the king in his parliament at Bury Saint Edmunds. The commonality replied through Richer le Mercer, Richard Poterel, John le Coffrer and Gilbert de la March.

It is interesting to compare the form of English writs of summons with continental ones. This French example exhibits many of the same characteristics. It is a writ summoning town representatives to an assembly in October 1318.

37 FRENCH WRIT OF SUMMONS 1318

Philip . . . to our beloved échevins of the town, greeting. Since we have to discuss and decide certain matters concerning the good estate of our realm, the peace, and the well being of you and all our other subjects, we require, order and command you by this [writ] to delegate three or four good men, from among the wisest in your town, who shall have sufficient authority from you to agree, do and undertake all that shall be decided. Send them to us a fortnight after the coming feast of St Remy to Paris, where we then propose to be, God willing, and do not fail in this in any way, and write back to us by the bearer on the same day that you shall receive this writ. Given at our royal abbey at Pontoise in the year of grace 1318 on the 29th day of June.

It will have been noticed that the English writs of summons of 1304 and 1296, and also the French writ of 1318, were very insistent on representatives of shires and boroughs having sufficient authority to bind their constituents. This may be used as an argument that the representatives were something more than merely bringers of petitions or agents for focusing public opinion, as some historians have suggested. It would appear to imply that consent, to taxation for example, binding on the communities, was actually necessary to the government, and not merely useful as Pasquet thought (above no. 34). It is therefore fascinating to have the draft of a blank form of authority for burgesses coming to an assembly in April 1268. It was sent out by Henry III's government with the summons, and was designed to be filled up and returned with the representatives, perhaps even in duplicate as the Modus *later suggested (above no. 25, section IV).*

38. FORM OF AUTHORITY 1268

The mayor or bailiff and the whole community of the city of —— to all the faithful in Christ to whom these present letters shall come, greetings in the lord. We decided that —— our mayor and —— our bailiffs and —— our co-citizens or co-burgesses should be appointed to the council called by the legate in London a fortnight after Easter about the affairs of our lord H., illustrious king of England, and of the kingdom and community of England, and of ourselves, that they, full faith being placed in them, may speak on our behalf upon the aforesaid affairs in the council or on the occasion of the council. And we shall ratify and accept whatsoever they shall do in our name.

The Function of Burgesses in Parliament

Although the knights of the shires were the dominant element in the 'commons', they were greatly outnumbered by the burgesses. Miss McKisack here discusses what is known of the function of the borough representatives in parliament.

39 MAY McKISACK

To the student of the parliament rolls it is easily apparent that it was the knights of the shire, and not the citizens or burgesses, that were the leaders of the Commons in the medieval parliament. The rolls have remarkably little to tell us of the activities of the burgesses. It would appear that despite their numerical superiority the part played by them in parliament was, if not insignificant, at least inconspicuous. No burgess was appointed Speaker before the reign of Henry VIII; and it is a rare exception for the name of an individual burgess to find its way into the official records of parliament. The education and traditions of the knights undoubtedly gave them advantages which few of the burgesses could hope to share, and it was natural that both king and magnates should look to the knightly class for advice on matters of general policy. Yet it is possible to lay too much emphasis on the argument *ex silentio*. The parliament rolls are not, and do not profess to be, an exhaustive record of all parliamentary transactions. Still less are they concerned to report those private deliberations of the commons which were not recognized as forming part of the official proceedings of parliament. The presence, in every parliament, of a group of men concerned in their daily lives with trade and finance must have been of inestimable advantage to the rulers of medieval England, harassed as they were by constant financial anxiety. As will be shown, it is hardly possible to doubt that the part played by the townsmen in parliament must have been of much greater significance than a cursory reading of the printed rolls might lead us to suppose.

Moreover, the work of the parliamentary burgesses has a twofold aspect. Those who elected and paid them were not accustomed to think in terms of public service. For the electors, the chief function of their representatives was, in the words of a Norwich record, 'to increase our liberties as they may be able'. Faced with the necessity of electing representatives and of paying them for their services, the governing bodies of the towns were determined to obtain value for their money. Thus, the representatives often found themselves burdened with the responsibility of pursuing the town's advantage in parliament by seeking confirmation of charters or favourable responses to petitions, and with the necessity of undertaking private business for their constituents in or near London. From the point of view of the Crown, the burgess comes to parliament in order that the borough may be bound by the measures to which he there gives assent; but from the local point of view he is his town's attorney, and his summons to parliament affords an opportunity of laying local grievances before a central assembly. It is impossible to appreciate the importance of the parliamentary citizens and burgesses without considering both aspects of their work.

Direct evidence as to the activities of the burgesses in parliament is very scanty. The author of the *Anonimalle Chronicle*, for example, in his description of the deliberations of the commons in the Chapter-house of Westminster Abbey in 1376, tells us only of the speeches made by the knights. The author of the *Chronicon Angliae*, describing the same parliament, throughout uses *milites* as a synonym for the Commons. Rarely do we find burgesses among those appointed to serve on parliamentary committees or to perform any other special public service. None, even of the great London merchants, is elected Speaker. A few appointments to committees, a few famous privilege cases, afford the sum total of direct information to be deduced from the parliament rolls. It seems reasonable to deduce the subordination of the burgesses to the knights – a natural adjustment in view of the increasing tendency among modern scholars to see the Commons as the spokesmen of the Lords rather than as the initiators of an independent policy.

The direct evidence, such as it is, may conveniently be examined a little more closely. . . . These scattered instances do not, of course, represent the complete sum of the parliamentary activities of the burgesses.

That they acted with the knights, withdrew with them for deliberation in the Chapter-house or elsewhere, assisted at the election of the Speaker, advised as to the amount of the subsidy which the Commons could sustain, and helped to frame the common petitions, is sometimes stated and must generally be assumed. The great number of petitions relating to the franchises of the towns and to matters of trade and finance must have been, at least in part, the work of the merchant classes. Occasionally we find traces of the recognition of the burgesses as a separate entity. At the time of the re-establishment of the home Staple in 1353, one copy of the document containing the reasons for the change was given to the knights, another to the citizens and burgesses. Sometimes the term 'commons' is used to distinguish the citizens and burgesses from the knights. In April 1343 *the knights of the counties and the commons* were charged to assemble in the Painted Chamber and to consult among themselves as to the proposals for peace with France, and again, in January 1348, *the knights of the counties and others of the commons* were ordered to consult together on the conduct of the war. The author of the *Anonimalle Chronicle* writes of the assembling of the 'knights and commons' in the Chapter-house, during the parliament of 1376. Such instances serve to remind us of the presence, in the medieval parliament, of a body of well-to-do townspeople, but they do not give us much help in estimating the significance of their presence there.

From the very beginning of representative parliaments one of the main preoccupations of the burgesses must have been with finance. Recent historical criticism has shown itself sceptical of the belief held by Hallam, Gneist, Stubbs, and other nineteenth-century writers, that Edward I was led to summon representatives to parliament largely by his desire to obtain their consent to taxation. The emphasis now laid upon other aspects of parliament, judicial and administrative, has tended to divert attention from the financial aspect. It has been pointed out that what we know of Edward's autocratic temper accords ill with the view that he would willingly have sought the consent of his subjects to any tax which had hitherto been levied by kings at their own pleasure. The concessions granted by the *Confirmatio Cartarum* of 1297 are worded in general terms, and Edward's intention to evade them is shown by his appeal to Clement V to absolve him from his oath. Parliament was primarily and essentially the high court of justice, and the summoning of representatives might well justify itself on administrative grounds. Yet when due weight has been given to these considerations, neglected by an older generation of historians, the fact remains that one of the earliest functions of the Commons was to accede to money grants, and that it was in the sphere of taxation that they first won any appreciable degree of control over the Crown. When the King, in 1295, announces his intention to hold a colloquy with his earls, barons, and other magnates, *super remediis contra pericula quae eidem regno hiis diebus imminent providendum*, it is evident that the remedy which he has

in mind is financial; and when the sheriffs are commanded to obtain
the election of knights, citizens, and burgesses endowed with full and
sufficient powers for themselves and the communities they represent,
ad faciendum quod tunc de communi consilio ordinabitur in praemissis, it seems
hardly less evident that it is to money grants which the words refer.
Further, when the writ for the collection of the aid, issued in December
of the same year, states that the earls, barons, knights, and others
liberaliter fecerunt undecimam de omnibus bonis suis mobilibus, and that the
citizens, burgesses, and other good men of the demesne, *septimam de
omnibus bonis suis mobilibus . . . nobis curialiter concesserint et gratanter*, it
seems idle to dispute the importance of the financial motive or to deny
that consent to taxation, however formal, was intimately connected
with representation. Although the practice of Edward I shows that he
never admitted his inability to tax certain classes of his subjects at will,
yet the desirability of obtaining a general consent to taxation seems to
have been early recognized. In the course of the fourteenth century such
assent came to be regarded as an essential preliminary to direct taxation,
and throughout the later Middle Ages the voting of subsidies was
among the most important parliamentary duties which the Commons
had to perform. The King's need of money looms large in the opening
sermon of almost every parliament, and the main preoccupation of the
knights and burgesses is to secure that taxation shall not be intolerably
heavy, and that a due share of it shall be paid by all classes.

When we turn to the local aspect of the representatives' work we
become still more clearly aware of the responsibilities of their office.
The manifold duties with which many towns entrusted their representatives fall roughly into three groups. First, the representatives were
given the task of laying local grievances, in the form of petitions, before
the central assembly; secondly, they were asked to undertake general
business for the town; and, thirdly, they were often required to bring
back to their constituents a report of the progress of events in parliament
and of the liabilities to which the commons were committed. The
national records are not concerned with these aspects of the burgesses'
activities, but they may be fully illustrated from local sources.

Part Four

POLITICAL THEORY IN THE AGE OF PARLIAMENTARY ORIGINS

Medieval Attitudes to Government and Law

There is no agreement amongst historians of political thought on the essential basis of law and government in the Middle Ages. The Carlyles have emphasized a single, simple, underlying attitude, that all political authority in the Middle Ages was derived from the community. Professor Ullmann, on the other hand, has stressed the lack of agreement between medieval thinkers, and the complexity and changing nature of their views of political authority. One of the principal objects of the Carlyles was to link political theory and political practice together, and in this, the conclusion of the thirteenth-century volume of their vast work, they attempted to draw together the results of their examination both of the views of political theorists and of the origins of parliamentary institutions.

40 R. W. and A. J. CARLYLE

The political order of the Middle Ages, therefore, was not only built upon the principle of the supremacy of the law, but had developed a method by which this supremacy could be enforced even upon the prince. This is the real political meaning of the struggle over the question of taxation. The feudal prince was legally entitled not only to the various services of his vassals, but for certain purposes had the right to demand financial contributions. But his right was in this matter determined by custom and law; he had no arbitrary or unlimited rights over his vassals' property, any more than over their persons. Many even of the Bologna Civilians repudiated the opinion which was attributed to one of their number, Martinus, that the emperor had an absolute right over the property of his subjects, and as far as we have seen no other writer or jurist even suggests such a theory.

The authority of the prince was then, in the political system, as well as in the theory of the Middle Ages, founded upon law and limited by law. It is here that we find the foundation of that contractual principle which was sometimes expressed and always implied in mediæval political theory. The obligations of the prince and the people were mutual obligations, and these obligations were expressed in the law.

The mediæval thinkers were little, if at all, affected by the unhistorical and artificial theory of the seventeenth century, of an original contract by which the commonwealth was formed, but the conception of a mutual agreement between the ruler and the subjects was familiar to them. As we have pointed out, it was the foundation of all feudal relations, and was emphatically stated by the feudal jurists.

The conception was, however, as it seems to us, older and more deeply rooted than the developed feudalism. It appears to us that it can be traced to the forms of the coronation order as far back as the ninth century, and it survives in the English coronation order of to-day. For while the subjects swear to obey the prince, the prince swears to administer the law. The sharp and drastic terms in which this principle was stated by Manegold of Lautenbach may be abnormal, but the principle was normal; the prince held his authority on the understanding that he fulfilled his obligations. The prince who persistently violated them forfeited all claim to his position, and might properly be deposed. This is the constitutional principle not only of Manegold, but of St Thomas Aquinas, and the history of the Middle Ages illustrates sufficiently clearly that it was not a merely abstract principle.

It may, however, be said again that these principles and practices represent a somewhat undeveloped and even barbarous condition of society, and that would no doubt be true if they stood alone, if the Middle Ages had not advanced any further. This was, however, not the case; on the contrary, it is clear that we can see both in fact and in theory the development of a system of a limited and constitutional method of government. St Thomas Aquinas will furnish us with the best example of this theory. In the same passage which we have just cited, he sets out the general principle that it would be well that the authority of the king should be so tempered that he could not easily abuse it, and in the 'Summa Theologica' he expresses his own preference for a form of government in which authority should be shared by the king with others, who should represent the community. His opinion is restated by John of Paris. How far either St Thomas or John or Paris were aware of the actual tendencies of the constitutional development of the twelfth and thirteenth centuries does not appear; but their theories correspond with the actual facts.

We have in this volume endeavoured to give a summary account of some of the experiments by which in the course specially of the thirteenth century it was attempted to provide for some constant and effective control upon what we should call the administrative action of the Crown, but these, except in so far as they anticipated the later development of the principle of the responsibility of ministers, were in themselves abnormal and of comparatively little importance. It was not until the development of some method by which the community as a whole should be more or less effectively represented that this continuous control over the action of the crown could be properly created.

It was, therefore, in the creation of a system which could be conceived of as representing the whole community that the political development of the Middle Ages culminated, and that its political principles found their most complete expression. It is no doubt true that it was under the pressure of particular conditions and movements in various countries that the elective and representative bodies were created, but the principle which they embodied was the principle which lay behind the character of the whole political civilization of the Middle Ages, and it is only a grave misunderstanding which would separate between the development of the representative system and the general political principles of mediæval society.

We venture therefore to say, and we do it without hesitation, that the proper character of the political civilization of the Middle Ages is to be found in the principle that all political authority, whether that of the law or of the ruler, is derived from the whole community, that there is no other source of political authority, and that the ruler, whether emperor or king, not only held an authority which was derived from the community, but held this subject to his obedience to that law which was the embodiment of the life and will of the community, and that the development of the representation of the community in Cortes or Parliaments or States-General was the natural and intelligible form which that principle assumed. How it came about that in the course of the succeeding centuries these rational and intelligible principles of political society should have in some measure given place to the somewhat barbarous conception of the absolute monarchy, we hope to consider in the next volume; but we trust that we have succeeded in making it clear that, whatever may have been the circumstances which explain this, to the Middle Ages the conception of an absolute or arbitrary monarchy was practically unknown.

The life of the Middle Ages was turbulent, disorderly, often almost anarchical, but they found the remedy for this not in submission to an irrational despotism, but in the recognition of the supreme authority of law, a law not external or mechanical, but the expression and embodiment of the life of the community.

*Out of the variety and complexity of views expressed on government and law
in the middle ages, Professor Ullmann singled out two dominant and conflicting
attitudes, by which representative institutions on the one hand and absolute
monarchy on the other could be justified. He stressed the essential dichotomy in
the theoretical position of the medieval king which follows from these conflicting attitudes to government and law. He equally stressed the revolutionary
change in political thought brought about by the renewed knowledge of
Aristotle's* Politics *in western christendom in the second decade of the thirteenth
century, and by the writings of St Thomas Aquinas (c. 1225–74), who was
certainly the most influential writer of the thirteenth century, and was himself
strongly influenced by Aristotle. Professor Ullmann exemplified this revolution in thought by elaborating what he calls the ascending conception of government and law in terms of the idea of representation in fourteenth-century
England.*

41 WALTER ULLMANN

Medieval Conceptions of Government and Law

Confining ourselves to the medieval period, we can detect there two
conceptions of government and law diametrically opposed to each
other, in fact so much opposed that they were exclusive of each other.
Tertium non datur. Both were operative, though at one time the one
held sway and at other times the other had the upper hand.

There is the ascending conception of government and law according
to which law-creating power may be ascribed to the community or the
populus – the composition of the latter, who does, and who does not,
belong to it, is of no concern to us in this context – which makes law
through the appropriate machinery: power is concentrated in the
people itself, so that one can speak of law and governmental power as
rising or ascending. Governing authority and the law ascend from the
broad base in the shape of a pyramid. Whatever power is found in the
organs of the government, whatever power they have in creating law,
is in the last resort traceable to the people: it is they who have, for
reasons of practical efficiency, handed over specific power to specific
organs for a specified time. The organs remain responsible to the people.
The idea of representation, that is, the idea that public officers represent
the community and act on its behalf, is germane to this ascending theme.
This conception of government and law, because of its populist com-
plexion, may also be called populist.

Opposed to this ascending conception is the descending conception of government and law. Accordingly, governmental authority and law-creating competency descend from one supreme organ: power is distributed 'downwards', again in the shape of a pyramid, but so that whatever power is found 'down below' at the base of the pyramid, is not, as in the ascending theme, an original power, but one that is derived from 'above'. This one supreme organ, in whom all power is located and who hands it 'downwards', is God Himself who has appointed a vice-gerent on earth: in actual fact it is the vice-gerent who possesses the sum-total of power, having himself derived it from God. Strictly speaking, the idea of representation does not arise within this conceptual framework, but only that of delegated or derived power in the shape of the specific divinely conferred office. Just as the idea of representation is essential to the ascending theme of government and law, so is the concept of office essential to the descending theme: the office itself is of divine origin, because set up by God Himself. Consequently, since all power is anchored in divinity – 'There is no power but of God' – the descending conception can also be called theocratic. For the ascending theme the *voluntas populi*, for the descending counterpart the *voluntas principis*, is the hallmark. The one is the reverse of the other.

Feudal and Theocratic Kingship

Our discussion of medieval kingship has so far concentrated exclusively on its theocratic element. It is however only in conjunction with the feudal element in kingship that the full medieval kingship emerges. Just as it is true to say that the medieval king was theocratic, in the same way it is true to say that this same king was also a feudal overlord. For the feudal function in the king as feudal overlord must be separated conceptually from his theocratic function. The clear separation of the two functions is not only a demand of neat and tidy thinking, but also one imposed by the history of what is, perhaps a little too loosely, called constitutional development. We have had an opportunity of stating that on the level of theocratic kingship a constitutional development – by which I mean the establishment of controls, measures and checks on the exercise of theocratic monarchic functions – lay notionally beyond what was humanly possible. The development of a constitution in this sense could proceed only on the level of the other function in the king, on that of his feudal overlordship.

It is clear that the feudal function of the king was diametrically opposed to his theocratic function. Whether the feudal function came to be annexed to the theocratic one, or whether the reverse process was the case, is of no moment here: what is of moment is that the feudal function in the king created that *Zwitterding*, that curious amphibious being, with which so much constitutional history and legal development is intrinsically linked up. As ruler the medieval king harboured in his breast two irreconcilable functions: the theocratic one, according to which his own *voluntas* created law, and which he exercised on the strength of his own considerations, unimpeded and independent as they were, and the feudal one, according to which it was not his *voluntas* alone that constituted the material force of law, but the implicit or explicit consent of the feudal tenants-in-chief to the law. For purposes of government and making of the law the feudal king had to proceed by consultation and agreement with the other parties in the feudal contract, for brevity's sake with the barons. It is the contractual nature of the feudal nexus which puts the feudal king on a level fundamentally different from that of the theocratic king. Within this feudal framework there was no margin for the sovereign display of a *voluntas*. Seen thus, the medieval king presented an irreconcilable dichotomy within himself, a dichotomy that brooked no compromise. As so often in medieval history, we are here faced with a characteristic medieval feature, that is to say, a fundamental contradiction which affects the very basis of so vital an institution as kingship.

On Aristotle

It would perhaps be convenient to sketch very roughly the Aristotelian tenets as far as they concern our topic. The doctrine culminates in the view of the State, the supreme community, as a product of nature. The State is, according to him, an issue of the law of nature – and not an issue of any convention or agreement. This law of nature that brings forth the State is proper to man himself. Man is born with the natural law which determines him to live in the State; neither civilized life nor the attainment of man's aspirations is possible outside the State. The family, the village, the town and still greater communities are the necessary, because natural, pillars of the State. The State is therefore the consummation of all the natural communities and is the highest, because most natural, crowning of the lower-placed associations. One of the essential points at once emerges: the organic structure of the State, rising from below upwards. Another point is at hand: the naturalism of the State. This naturalist feature pervades the whole thinking of

Aristotle. 'Nature does nothing in vain'; 'Nature does nothing super-fluous'; 'Nature behaves as if it foresaw the future'; and so forth, state-ments of Aristotle which show the overriding importance he attaches to the working of nature in his system. What is behind these views is the attribution of a purpose, of an aim, of a telos to nature itself. . . .

The further essential feature of Aristotelian doctrine is that the think-ing and reasoning capacity of man is determined by the law of nature. Blind obedience to the natural proclivities is the hallmark of animalic creatures and their communities; the reasoned transformation of the laws of nature into a common will is the hallmark of man's State. Conscious willing, the reasoned *voluntas*, of man is the expression of the law of nature. The natural urge of animals to congregate, and the natural urge of men to form the State, stand in the same relation as the uncouth natural sound expressing pleasure and pain to language which expresses good or evil: the fixation of right and wrong is the result of human reasoning capacities, and right and wrong are determined by the human insight into, and understanding of, what nature itself de-mands. The *voluntas* of man is therefore intrinsically linked with the nature of man.

Being a product of nature and, according to Aristotle, willed by nature, the State as the supreme human association can not only not do anything against nature, but on the contrary is the supreme fulfilment of the dictates of nature. The knowledge of right (and of wrong) is an issue of the natural law of men: the knowledge of justice (and of in-justice) equally is an emanation of this law of nature. And since the social instinct is implanted in all men by nature, justice becomes the bond of men in the State: the administration of justice is the principle of order in political society. Nature working through the vehicle of human reasoning and willing not only brings forth the State, but also determines the path of the State, and this through the same natural law which was the original begetter of the State. Nature wills the 'good' and, since the State or the political community is the highest expression of human natural associations, it aims at the highest good. The attain-ment of the highest good for man is therefore conditioned by his living in the State.

The means to achieve this attainment is the law. It is the articulated will of nature, adapted to the State and pronounced by the citizens. As the bond of the State the law has the purpose, the aim or *finis* of enabling man to attain the highest good. The actual source of the law in the State Aristotle finds, logically enough, in the people itself or, as he terms it, in the multitude whose will determines what should be the law. The problem is none other than the seat of ultimate sovereignty:

> The principle that the multitude ought to be supreme rather than the few best is capable of a satisfactory explanation.

According to Aristotle the power of the popular assembly is rooted in natural law. Hence, since the creation and promotion of the common good, the *utilitas publica*, is the aim of the law, which in its turn is made by the citizens, the ultimate authority must consequently be the meeting of the citizens.

On Aquinas

The point of reference of this political science was the actual living together of the 'multitude of men' and their organization, their machinery, which existed in order to attain the aim of 'good living'. But this is not a speculative task at all – speculation concerns itself with ascertaining the truth – but an eminently practical one, concerned as it is with the actual activities of man in society, with man's operations to achieve his aim. Political science is primarily *operativa*, and not merely *cognoscitiva*. Its basis is human reason with which man is naturally endowed, and thus is made the pivotal point of political science. This also means the liberation and emancipation of human reason, certainly within the terms of reference of political science. This is the declaration of human reason – within this orbit – as self-sufficient, because it is natural.

Thomas not only introduced a new department of learning, but on the same basis also coined the new term *regimen politicum*. Its full meaning appears best when it is contrasted with the *regimen regale*: the latter is characterized by the ruler's having absolute power – *plenaria potestas* as Thomas calls it – that is, a ruler who is not bound by the laws: this ruler is, of course, nothing else but the old medieval king who stands above the law and cannot consequently be restricted by the laws, of which he himself is the source. Opposed to this is the *regimen politicum*:

> *Politicum autem regimen est, quando ille qui praeest, habet* potestatem coarctatam *secundum aliquas leges civitatis.*

This ruler who is, so to speak, hedged in by the laws of the State, has little in common with the familiar theocratic king. It is indeed not difficult to see that Thomas' exposition greatly helped the ascending thesis of government. In connexion with democracy he speaks of the *status popularis* and his definition of democracy leaves nothing to be desired: it is the people's power – the *potestas populi* – because

> *ex popularibus possunt eligi principes et* ad populum *pertinet electio* principum.

This view necessarily leads to the conception of representation: for it is the ruler who 'personifies the people': 'eius [scil. populi] personam gerit' and therefore it could also be maintained that 'what the ruler of a State does, the State itself is said to do'. Thomas' view on the capability of the people to legislate does not differ materially from that expressed in the fourteenth century.

The Idea of Representation

It might be worth while to point to one more important issue, namely the idea of representation, an idea which was strongly marked in fourteenth-century England. Now we shall see later that the doctrine of representation contained in its essence all the features of the ascending (populist) conception of government and law. Power resides with the *populus* and they elect or appoint officers who act on behalf of the people, execute its will and who embody in one form or another the principle that they are responsible to the people. This view is in fact the very antithesis of a correctly understood theocratic conception, the descending thesis of government and law. No reconciliation is possible. Within the ascending framework there are no subjects, because all members of the *populus* in their aggregate are *superiores*: the *populus* itself is sovereign. The implementation of these principles against a determined theocratic government must lead to revolution. It is perhaps one of the most remarkable features of the late medieval English constitutional development that the ideas of representation, in themselves the offshoots of the ascending thesis, found so easy and unimpeded an inlet. The reason for this – historically and ideologically – remarkable feature lay in the preparation of the soil by feudalism to which indeed the idea of representation was no strange bedfellow. The assimilation of the representative principle, its easy accommodation in the habitat of the *communitas regni*, can be explained without great effort by the preceding development. The smooth passage of the populist principle into the framework of 'representative' government was conditioned by the feudal past: because feudalism had been a reality of government, the principle of representation could be absorbed into the system of the 'constitution' without any of the reverberations which this would have otherwise caused. It is the king in parliament who possesses legislative sovereignty. Chief Justice Thorpe's statement in the year 1365 that 'parliament represents the body of all the realm' can be squared with the most advanced contemporary continental populist doctrines of the principle of representation. How easily in fact populist principles could merge with feudal principles, could be shown already in Bracton: we recall that in interpreting the *lex regia* he juxtaposed the *populus* of Rome with the baronage of his own time, a slight confusion, but one that was indicative of the receptivity of the feudal soil for the ascending themes.

These brief selections on law and government from the Summa Theologica *of St Thomas Aquinas clearly illustrate his attitude. Such statements as 'the consent of the whole community . . . has more value than the authority of the ruler', or 'all should in some respect participate in the government', show how the ascending conception of political authority was gaining ground under the influence of Aristotle whom Aquinas refers to as 'the Philosopher'.*

42 THOMAS AQUINAS

The Value of Custom

All law proceeds from the reason and will of a legislator: divine and natural law from the rational will of God; human law from man's will, regulated by reason. Now reason and will in man are manifested in action both by word and by deed: for the test of what one considers good is to be found in the way one acts. Now it is clear that by words, which are the expression of the interior motions and concepts of the human reason, law can be changed and also explained. In the same way law can be changed and explained by means of actions, many times repeated, such as result in custom: and it can thus happen that new customs arise, which have the validity of law; in the sense that such exterior actions, frequently verified, clearly manifest the interior move-ment of the will and the concept of reason. For whatever is done fre-quently would seem to result from a deliberate judgement of reason. In this sense custom has the power of law, it may annul law and it may act as the interpreter of law.

The Relationship between Custom and Law

The community within which a custom becomes established may be of two conditions. If it is a case of a free community possessing the right to enact its own laws, the consent of the whole community in the observance of a certain custom has more value than the authority of the ruler, whose power to enact laws derives from the fact that he represents the community. In this case it is open to the entire community, though not to single individuals, to establish a law. – If, on the other hand, it is a community which does not enjoy the right to establish its own laws or to abrogate a law emanating from some superior authority, a custom which becomes established in such a community may, nevertheless, attain the status of law if it continues to be tolerated by those whose duty it is to legislate for the community. For, from the fact that it is so tolerated, it follows that the legislator approves what is established by the custom.

The Various Forms of Government, and Their Fusion in the Government given by God to the Jews

With respect to the right ordering of power in a city or nation, two points must be considered: the first is that all should in some respect participate in the government. It is this, in fact, that ensures peace within the community, and, as we are told in the *Politics* (II, chaps. 1 and 2), all peoples prize and guard such a state of affairs. The other consideration refers to the form of government or of regulating affairs. Among the various forms of government which the Philosopher enumerates in the third book of the *Politics* (chaps. 5, 6, and 7) the more important are the *kingdom*, in which one alone governs according to virtue; and *aristocracy*, that is government by the best elements, in which a few hold office according to virtue. So the best ordering of power within a city or a kingdom is obtained when there is one virtuous head who commands over all; and who has under him others who govern virtuously; and when, furthermore, all participate in such government, both because all are eligible, and because all participate in the election of those who rule. This is the best form of constitution which results from a judicious admixture of the *kingdom*, in that there is one person at the head of it; of *aristocracy* in that many participate in the government according to virtue; and of *democracy* or popular rule, in that rulers may be elected from the people and the whole population has the right of electing its rulers. It was such a form of government which was established by the divine law. For Moses and his successors governed their people as sole heads over all: but they elected to their assistance seventy-two Elders according to virtue: as it is said (Deuteronomy 1 v. 15): 'And I took out of your tribes men, wise and honourable, and appointed them rulers.' And this was aristocracy. But it was democratic in the sense that they were elected from the whole people, for it is said in Exodus (18 v. 21): 'Seek out from the whole people wise men,' etc.; and also in the sense that the people elected them, for it is said in Deuteronomy (1 v. 13): 'Let me have from among you wise and understanding men,' etc. So it is clear that there was an excellent ordering of authority in the Law [of the Old Testament].

The influence of Aristotle is again apparent in the Defensor Pacis *of* Marsilius of Padua *(c. 1275–1342). Aristotle wrote in his* Politics *'that the people at large should be sovereign rather than the few best – would appear to be defensible, and while it presents some difficulty it perhaps also contains some truth'. Marsilius, probably writing with his experience of government-by-assembly in the Paduan city-state in mind, took over Aristotle's tentative statement of a possibility and made of it an assertion of fact.*

43 MARSILIUS OF PADUA

Let us say, then, in accordance with the truth and the counsel of Aristotle in the *Politics*, Book III, chapter 6, that the legislator, or the primary and proper efficient cause of the law, is the people or the whole body of citizens, or the weightier part thereof, through its election or will expressed by words in the general assembly of the citizens, commanding or determining that something be done or omitted with regard to human civil acts, under a temporal pain or punishment. By the 'weightier part' I mean to take into consideration the quantity and the quality of the persons in that community over which the law is made. The aforesaid whole body of citizens or the weightier part thereof is the legislator regardless of whether it makes the law directly by itself or entrusts the making of it to some person or persons, who are not and cannot be the legislator in the absolute sense, but only in a relative sense and for a particular time and in accordance with the authority of the primary legislator. And I say further that the laws and anything else established through election must receive their necessary approval by that same primary authority and no other, whatever be the case with regard to certain ceremonies or solemnities, which are required not for the being of the matters elected but for their well-being, since the election would be no less valid even if these ceremonies were not performed. Moreover, by the same authority must the laws and other things established through election undergo addition, subtraction, complete change, interpretation, or suspension, insofar as the exigencies of time or place or other circumstances make any such action opportune for the common benefit. And by the same authority, also, must the laws be promulgated or proclaimed after their enactment, so that no citizen or alien who is delinquent in observing them may be excused because of ignorance.

A citizen I define in accordance with Aristotle in the *Politics*, Book III, chapters 1, 3, and 7, as one who participates in the civil community in the government or the deliberative or judicial function according to his rank. By this definition, children, slaves, aliens, and women are distinguished from citizens, although in different ways. For the sons of citizens are citizens in proximate potentiality, lacking only in years. The weightier part of the citizens should be viewed in accordance with the honorable custom of polities, or else it should be determined in accordance with the doctrine of Aristotle in the *Politics*, Book VI, chapter 2.

Quod Omnes Tangit...

In a number of articles Professor Post has stressed the importance of legal theory in any discussion of medieval representation. Here he asserts that thirteenth-century kings were compelled to summon parliaments because of developments in legal theory.

44 GAINES POST

Of all the elements in Roman law that played a role in the rise of representation, the most important, I think, was the principle of consent stated by Justinian, *C.* 5, 59, 5: 'ut quod omnes similiter tangit, ab omnibus comprobetur' – 'what touches all (equally or similarly), shall be approved by all'. A familiar maxim in the thirteenth century, *quod omnes tangit*, was freely quoted both literally and in paraphrase by legists and canonists, and in the *Liber Sextus* issued by Boniface VIII it became a *regula iuris*. It was asserted by cathedral chapters and by Pope Honorius III in 1225–27 as a justification for the representation of the chapters in provincial councils. Matthew Paris stated it about 1240 as the basis of the right of archdeacons to be consulted before the higher prelates of England could grant a subsidy to the king. Edward I quoted it when ordering the Archbishop of Canterbury to summon representatives of the clergy to the famous Parliament of 1295[1] *Quod omnes tangit* was clearly the basis of Philip IV's summons for the Estates General of 1302, when the quarrel with Boniface VIII was called a serious business touching (*contingentia*) both king and kingdom.

Such, in general, was the legal interpretation of *quod omnes tangit* in the thirteenth century. A well established rule of law, recognized in Church and in state, in Roman-law and common-law countries alike, it caused new communities of free men and their rights to be recognized as clearly as the rights of the great. It caused representation to become that of the rights of free men who felt that their superiors did not adequately represent these rights *ex officio*. Thus the canons of cathedral chapters in the early part of the century asserted that their rights were touched by royal taxation, and that they as well as the prelates should

[1] See below no. 45.

be summoned to councils. Knights of the shire and burgesses demanded and obtained the right to represent their own interests in royal assemblies. At the same time prelates and magnates, finding that they could not legally respond for those beneath them, also asserted that the lower clergy and nobility and townsmen should be summoned. The kings, then, were compelled to summon representatives of communities to give the consent of lesser free men. They did not do this exclusively because, as some authorities have argued, they needed to persuade a larger public, by means of propaganda in great assemblies, to give taxes or assent to general legislation. They did it because the law and the new legal procedure made it compulsory for them to do so.

Nor did the kings have to summon representatives because of a rising theory of democracy. *Quod omnes tangit* expressed no idea of the democratic sovereignty of the people. The king was superior in authority by law and tradition. But since he must rule according to law and justice, he had to observe the new legal procedure. Consequently, when he wanted something not permitted by the private law, he was compelled to summon all who were touched and obtain their consent. If, however, he was acting for the public welfare, he had the right as head of the state, by public law, to decide in his high court and council that all must consent. This consent, then, was not voluntary, but procedural; consent established by legal rights but subordinate to the decision of the king and his court. In brief, *quod omnes tangit* was neither a constitutional principle of sovereignty of the people, nor a theoretical maxim. It was a principle of the fundamental medieval legal theory, that of government, by law, for the people, not government of and by the people.

In fact, *quod omnes tangit* as a legal rule did not apply to *all* the people in a kingdom. It applied only to those who had free status and enjoyed special rights or privileges and liberties. When a king wanted a subsidy, he was touching directly the rights of great barons, prelates, lesser nobles (knights of the shires), and the leading burgesses and citizens, and members of the clergy who were members of corporate communities. Therefore he summoned the great prelates and magnates as individuals, even though they lived in shires or towns; but the knights and townsmen as communities. Serfs and humble freemen of town and country were not concerned, and thus enjoyed no right of representation, however heavily taxes might ultimately fall on them. Nonetheless, as a result of the triumph of the Romano-canonical maxim, consent was far more widespread than it had been in the feudal age. Ultimately the same principle was to be enjoyed by all men, and all men were to be recognized as free. In the thirteenth century it is the basis of the same theory as that thundered by Patrick Henry in a later age: Taxation without representation is tyranny!

The views of Professor Post are illustrated by the famous writ of summons to the parliament of November 1295 issued by Edward I's chancery.

45 WRIT OF SUMMONS 1295

The King to the venerable father in Christ Robert, by the same grace Archbishop of Canterbury, primate of all England, greeting. As a most just law, established by the careful providence of sacred princes, exhorts and decrees that *'what affects all, by all should be approved'*, so also, very evidently should common danger be met by means provided in common. You know sufficiently well and it is now, as we believe, divulged through all regions of the world, how the king of France has fraudulently and craftily deprived us of our land of Gascony. . . . He has gathered together for the conquest of our kingdom a very great fleet and an abounding multitude of warriors . . . ; and he now proposes to destroy the English language altogether from the earth, if his power should correspond to the detestable proposition of the contemplated injustice, which God forbid. Because, therefore, 'darts seen beforehand do less injury', and your interest especially, as that of the rest of the citizens of the same realm, is concerned in this affair, we command you, strictly enjoining you in the fidelity and love in which you are bound to us, that on Sunday next after the feast of St Martin, in the approaching winter, you be present in person at Westminster; citing beforehand (*praemunientes*) the dean and chapter of your church; . . . [and the proctors of the lower clergy] to be present along with you, having full and sufficient power from the same chapter and clergy, to 'treat', ordain and do, along with us and with the rest of the prelates and principal men and other inhabitants of our kingdom, how the dangers and threatened evils of this kind are to be met. Witness the king at Wingham, the thirtieth day of September.

Changes in Theory in Thirteenth-century England

By the mid-thirteenth century there were two traditional views of authority in England. On the one hand there was the older, contractual, feudal tradition which had been considerably eroded and somewhat transformed, on the other hand there was the more recent tradition, assumed by monarchs since Henry II, that a king should not be limited in his actions by any human agency, but only by law, which could itself be interpreted either as custom, or as the king's own apprehension and application of the immutable tenets of natural law. These two traditions preceded the reception of Roman Law and of Aristotle in the course of the thirteenth century. Bracton (d. 1268), one of Henry III's judges, was still expressing traditional views in his De Legibus et Consuetudinibus Angliae. *For him the king was only under God, from whom his authority naturally derived.*

46 HENRY DE BRACTON

Moreover, the king has no peer in his kingdom, because thus he would lose his headship, since an equal has no command over his equal. Again, and all the more strongly, he ought not to have a superior, nor to have anyone more powerful, because thus he would be inferior to his own subjects, and inferiors cannot be equal to the more powerful. Moreover, the king ought not to be under man, but under God and under the law, because the law makes the king. Therefore let the king attribute to the law what the law has attributed to him, namely, domination and power. For there is no king where will rules and not law. And that he ought to be under the law, since he is the vicar of God, appears evidently through his likeness to Jesus Christ, Whose place he occupies on earth. Because the true mercy of God, when many ways were available to Him for the recovery of the human race, ineffably chose the most preferable way, by which He would use not the force of power but the reason of justice for the destruction of the devil's work. And thus He wished to be under the law, that He might redeem those who were under the law. For He did not wish to use force, but judgment. Likewise also the blessed bearer of God, the Virgin Mary, Mother of the Lord, who by a singular privilege was above the law, yet to show an example of humility did not refuse to be subject to legal institutes. Thus, therefore, the king, that his power may not remain unbridled. Therefore, there ought not to be anyone greater than he in his own kingdom in the administration of law; however, he ought to be the least, or as if he were the least, if he seeks to obtain judgment. But if judgment is sought from him, since no writ runs against him himself, there will be place for a supplication that he may correct his act and amend it, and if he does not do so it suffices for his punishment that he await the vengeance of God. Let no one, indeed, presume to dispute his deeds, much less to oppose his acts.

In this situation the doctrines of Roman Law had a two-edged effect. This passage from the early third-century lawyer, Ulpian, was much quoted in the thirteenth century. Although it strongly emphasized the authority of kings, it also stressed that this authority was derived from the people, not from God.

47 ULPIAN, as quoted by JUSTINIAN

What the Emperor has determined has the force of a statute; seeing that, by a *lex regia*, which was passed on the subject of his sovereignty the people transfer to him and confer upon him the whole of their own sovereignty and power.

Theory was applied to practice at one stage in the struggle between Henry III and a section of his baronage, when affairs reached an impasse and an appeal for arbitration was made to the king of France. In 1264 Louis IX gave his decision – for the king and against the magnates. In quashing the provisions of Oxford of 1258 he gave practical force to his authoritarian point of view. He attributed to kings, who for him derive their power from God, an untrammelled freedom of action, with unrestricted rule in their kingdoms.

48 ST LOUIS'S MISE OF AMIENS

. . . In the name of the Father and the Son and the Holy Spirit. By our [present] decision or ordinance we quash and annul all the aforesaid provisions, ordinances, statutes, and obligations, however called, and whatever has followed from them or by occasion of them, especially since it appears that the supreme pontiff by his letters has proclaimed them quashed and annulled; ordaining that as well the said king as all the barons and others who have consented to the present arbitration, and who in any way have bound themselves to observe the aforesaid [provisions], shall be utterly quit and absolved of the same. We likewise add that, by virtue or force of the aforesaid provisions or obligations or ordinances, or of any authority already granted by the king on that account, no one shall make new statutes or observe those already made; nor ought any one, through non-observance of the aforesaid [provisions], to be held the enemy, either principal or otherwise, of any one else, or for that reason incur any penalty. . . . We also decree and ordain that the aforesaid king at his own volition may freely appoint, dismiss, and remove the chief justice, chancellor, treasurer counsellors, lesser justices, sheriffs, and any other officials and ministers of his kingdom and his household, as he was used and able to do before the time of the provisions aforesaid. Furthermore, we repeal and quash the statute made to the effect that the kingdom of England should henceforth be governed by natives and that all aliens should leave the kingdom, never to return, except those whose residence the faithful men of the kingdom commonly agreed to, ordaining by our decisions that aliens may safely remain in the said kingdom, . . . the king may safely call to his counsel such aliens and natives as shall seem to him useful and loyal, just as he was able to do before the time aforesaid. Likewise we declare and ordain that the said king shall have full power and unrestricted rule within his kingdom and its appurtenances, and shall in all things and in every way enjoy such status and such full power as he enjoyed before the time aforesaid. By the present ordinance, however, we do not wish or intend in any way to derogate from royal privileges, charters, liberties, establishments and praiseworthy customs of the kingdom of England existing before the time of the same provisions. . . .

Now this our ordinance or decision we have promulgated at Amiens on the morrow of the blessed Vincent the Martyr, A.D. 1264, in the month of January [January 23]. In testimony whereof we have caused our seal to be attached to the present letters.

The Mise of Amiens was not to last. At the battle of Lewes later in the year, the baronial point of view was successfully vindicated, at least for the time being, by force of arms, and the anonymous contemporary poet who celebrated the occasion took care to summarize the two conflicting views of authority represented by the opposing armies.

49 THE SONG OF LEWES

See! we touch the root of the disturbance of the kingdom about which we are writing, and of the dissension of the parties who fought the said battle; to different *objects* did they turn their aim.

The King with his party wished to be thus free, and *urged that* he ought to be so, and was of necessity, or *that* deprived of a king's right he would cease to be king, unless he should do whatever he might wish; that the magnates of the realm had not to heed, whom he set over his own counties, or on whom he conferred the wardenship of castles, or whom he would have to show justice to his people; and he would have as chancellor and treasurer of his realm anyone soever at his own will, and counsellors of whatever nation, and various ministers at his own discretion, without the barons of England interfering in the King's acts, as 'the command of the prince has the force of law'; and that what he might command of his own will would bind each. For every earl also is thus his own master, giving aught of his own in what measure and to whom he will – castles, lands, and revenues, he entrusts to whom he will, and although he be a subject, the King permits it all. Wherein if he shall have done well, it is of profit to the doer, if not, he himself shall see to it; the King will not oppose him whilst injuring himself. Why is the prince made of worse condition, if the affairs of a baron, a knight, and a freeman are so managed? Wherefore they intrigue for the King to be made a servant, who wish to lessen his power, and to take away his dignity of prince; they wish to thrust down into wardship and subjection the royal power made captive through sedition, and to disinherit the King, that he may not have power to rule so fully as hitherto have done the kings who preceded him, who were in no wise subject to their own *people*, but managed their own affairs at their will, and conferred their own at their own pleasure. This is the King's pleading which seems true, and this allegation protects the right of the realm.

But now let *my* pen be turned to the opposite side. Let the proposal of the barons be subjoined to what has already been said; and when the parties have been heard let the statements be compared, and after comparison let them be closed by a definite termination, so that the truer part may be clear; the people are more prone to obey the more true. Therefore let the party of the barons now speak on its own behalf, and let it duly follow whither it is led by zeal. Which party in the first place openly makes protestation, that it devises naught against the royal honour, or seeks *anything* contrary to it; nay, is zealous to reform and magnify the kingly state; just as, if the kingdom were devastated by enemies, it would not then be reformed without the barons, to whom this would be proper and suitable; and he who should then falsify himself, him the law would punish as guilty of perjury, as a betrayer of the king. He who can contribute aught of aid to the king's honour, owes it to his lord when he is in peril, when the kingdom is deformed as it were in extremity.

The king's adversaries are enemies who make war, and counsellors who flatter the king, who by deceitful words mislead the prince, and with double tongues lead him into error; these are worse adversaries than the perverse, they make themselves *out to be* good, when they are misleaders, and they are procurers of their own honour; they deceive the unwary whom they render more careless through pleasant *words*, whence they are not guarded against but are looked on as speaking useful *things*. These can deceive more than *can* the open. . . . And if such *men* by their aims were to alter the realm, so as to supplant right by unright; and after trampling on the natives were to call in strangers, and were to subdue the kingdom to foreigners; were not to regard the magnates and nobles of the land, and were to put mean *men* in the highest *place*, and were to cast down and humble the great, were to pervert order and turn it upside down; were to abandon the best, be urgent on the worst; would not those who should do thus, lay waste the kingdom? . . . If thus or otherwise the kingdom be wasted, or the kingdom be made utterly destitute, then ought the magnates of the kingdom to take care, that the land be purged of all errors. And if to them belongs the purging of error, *and to them* belongs provision the governess of customs, how would it not be lawful for them to take foresight lest any evil happen which might be harmful; which, after it may have happened, they ought to remove, lest of a sudden it make the unwary to grieve. . . .

Since it is agreed that all this is lawful for the barons, it remains to reply to the reasonings of the king. The king wishes, by the removal of his guardians, to be free, and wishes not to be subject to his inferiors, but to be over them, to command his subjects and not to be commanded; nor does he wish to be humbled to those set in authority, for those, who are set in authority, are not set over the king, nay rather are men of distinction who support the right of the one; otherwise the king would not be without a rival (*lit.* unique) but they, whom the king was under, would reign equally. Yet this incongruity which seems so great, may, with God's assistance, be easily solved. . . .

The king says: 'I agree to thy reasoning, but the election of these men falls under my choice; I will associate with me whom I will, by whose defence I will govern all *things*; and if my own *men* be insufficient, have not understanding, or be not powerful, or if they be evil-wishers, and be not faithful, but may perchance be treacherous, I wish thee to make clear, why I ought to be constrained to certain persons, *and* from whom I have power to get better assistance.'

The reasoning on which matter is quickly declared, if it be considered what the constraining of the king is. All constraint does not deprive of liberty, nor does all restriction take away power. Those that are princes wish for free power, those that are lords wish not for wretched slavery. To what purpose does free law wish kings to be bound? That they may not be able to be stained by an adulterine law. And this constraining is not of slavery, but is the enlarging of kingly virtue. So is the king's child preserved that he may not be hurt, yet he becomes not a slave when he is so constrained. Yea thus also are the angel spirits constrained, who are confirmed that they be not apostate. For that the Author of all is not able to err, that the Beginning of all is not able to sin, is not impotence but the highest power, the great glory of God and His great majesty. Thus he who is able to fall, if he be guarded that he fall not, is aided by such guardianship to live freely; neither is such sustenance of slavery, but *is* the protectress of virtue. Therefore let the king like everything that is good, but let him not dare evil; this is the gift of God. They who guard the king, that he sin not when tempted, are themselves the servants of the king, to whom let him be truly grateful, because they free him from being made a slave, because they do not surpass him, by whom he is led. But whoever is truly king is truly free, if he rule himself and his kingdom rightly; let him know that all things are lawful for him which are fitted for ruling the kingdom, but not for destroying it. It is one thing to rule, which is the duty of a king, another to destroy by resisting the law. Law is so called from binding (*lex a ligando*), which is so perfectly described as *the law* of liberty, as it is freely served.

... It is *the part* of a prince not to crush, but to protect; it is *the part* of a prince not to oppress, but to earn by numerous benefits the favour of his own, even as Christ by His grace earned the love of all. If the prince has loved, he ought to be loved in return; if he has reigned rightly, he ought to be honoured; if the prince has erred, he ought to be called back, *yea* to be denied by those whom he has unjustly burdened, unless he is willing to be corrected; if he is willing to be improved, he ought at the same time to be raised up and assisted by them. Let a prince hold this rule of reigning, so that he may have no need of not calling his own *subjects*; ignorant princes, who confound those under them, will perceive that the unconquered refuse to be thus conquered. If the prince shall think that he alone has more of truth, and more of skill, *and* more knowledge than the commonalty, that he more abounds in grace and more in the gifts of God; if it be not presumption, nay be *so* in truth, then his own true instruction will shine through the hearts of his subjects with light, and will inform his own *people* with moderation.

We put forward Moses, David, Samuel; each of whom we know was a faithful prince. Who endured many things from their own subjects, yet did not for their deserts cast them off, nor set strangers over them, but ruled through those who were their own *men*. 'I will set thee over a greater people, and will slay this *people*,' says God. 'I would die rather than that this people should perish,' let the kindly Moses, worthy of his office of prince, reply. And thus the wise prince will never reject his own *men*, but the foolish one will disturb the kingdom. Whence if the king be less wise than he ought, what service is he for ruling the kingdom? Shall he of his own proper understanding seek by whom he may be supported, by whom his own lack may be supplied? If he alone choose, he will be easily deceived, who has no knowledge who may be useful. Therefore let the community of the realm take counsel, and let that be decreed which is the opinion of the commonalty, to whom their own laws are most known; nor are all *the men* of the province such fools as not to know better than others their own realm's customs, which those who are before bequeath to those who come after. Those, who are ruled by the laws, have more knowledge of them; those, in whose use they are, become more experienced. And because it is their own affair which is at stake, they will care more and will procure for themselves the means whereby peace is acquired. They can know little who are not experienced, they will profit the kingdom little except they are stedfast. From this it can be gathered that the kind of men, who ought rightly to be chosen for the service of the kingdom, touches the community . . .

If therefore the king has not the knowledge to choose by himself men who know how to counsel him, it is hence clear what ought then to be done; for it concerns the community that wretched *men* be not made guides of the royal dignity, but the best and chosen men, and the most approved who can be found. For since the governance of the realm is the safety or ruin of all, it matters much whose is the guardianship of the realm. . . . Therefore the king's pleading concerning his subjects carried whithersoever they will at their own pleasure, is through this sufficiently answered, sufficiently invalidated; while whoever is a subject is ruled by a greater, because we say that it is not lawful for any man *to do* whatever he wishes, but that each man has a lord to correct him in error, help him in well-doing, and raise him up whenever he falls. We give the first place to the commonalty. We say also that law rules the dignity of the king; for we believe that law is a light, without which we infer that the guide goes astray. . . . If the king be without this law, he will go astray; if he hold it not, he will err shamefully. Its presence gives right reigning, and its absence the disturbance of the realm. That law speaks thus: 'By me kings reign, by me is justice shewn to those who make laws.' That stable law shall no king alter, but through it shall he strengthen his changing self. If he conform to this law he shall stand, and if he disagree with it he will stagger. It is commonly said, 'As the king wills, the law goes'; truth wills otherwise, for the law stands, the king falls. . . . And let the king prefer nothing of his own to the common *weal*, as though the safety of all gave way to him *who is but* one; for he is not set over *them* to live for himself, but so that this people which is put under him may be secure. Thou wilt know that the name of king is relative; thou wilt also understand that his name is protective; whence it was not lawful *for him* to live for himself alone, who ought by living to protect many; he who wishes to live for himself ought not to be in command, but to dwell apart and be as one alone. It is the glory of a prince to save very many; with trouble to himself to relieve many; let him not therefore allege his own profit, but his regard for his subjects by whom he is trusted; if he shall have saved the kingdom, he has done what is *the duty* of a king; whatever he shall have done otherwise, in that he has failed. From this is the true theory of a king sufficiently plain, that the position of king is unknown to one who is at leisure for his individual interest. . . .

From all that has been said above, it will be clear that it is the duty of the magnates of the kingdom to see what things are convenient for the governance of the kingdom, and expedient for the preservation of peace; and that the king have natives at his side, whether as councillors or as the greater *men* of the realm, not strangers nor favourites who supplant others and the good customs. For such discord is the step-mother of peace, and brings in battles, devises treachery. For just as the envy of the devil brought in death, so does hate divide the court. The king shall keep the natives in their rank, and by this management shall rejoice in ruling. But if he have sought to degrade his own *men*, have overturned *their* rank, it is in vain that he will ask, why when so deranged they do not obey him; nay, they would be mad if they were to do so.

Even if the battle of Evesham in 1265 reversed the decision of Lewes in favour of the king, the political experience of the years between 1258 and 1265 left its mark on political theory. Later versions of Bracton's De Legibus et Consuetudinibus Angliae *included an interpolation utterly inimical to the original views expressed by Bracton himself (see above no. 46), who would no doubt have been horrified at the idea of law students imbibing from his book the notion that the king should be bridled by his earls and barons if necessary.*

50 INTERPOLATION IN BRACTON

Likewise, no one can judge the deed or charter of the king so that the king's act is made void. But someone will be able to say that the king might have done justly and well, and if, by the same reasoning, he has done this, that it is ill done; and will be able to impose upon him the obligation of amending the injustice, lest the king and his justiciars fall into the judgment of the living God on account of the injustice. The king has a superior, namely, God. Likewise the law, through which he was made king. Likewise his court, namely, the counts and barons, because the counts are called, as it were, the partners of the king, and he who has a partner has a master. And therefore, if the king be without a bridle, that is, without law, they ought to put a bridle on him, unless they themselves are, with the king, without a bridle.

The views of this interpolator were to be echoed in a number of legal treatises during the next few decades, including the somewhat eccentric and moralizing

Mirror of Justices. It was probably compiled about 1290, and was written in French. It was therefore presumably intended for lay members of the baronial and knightly class. The occasions on which the earls or counts (comites) *judged the actions of the king and acted as his companions or partners* (comites) *in legislation were now specifically assumed to be parliaments.*

51 THE MIRROR OF JUSTICES

And albeit that the king should have no peer in his land, nevertheless in order that if the king should by his fault sin against any of his people, in which case [neither he] nor any of his commissioners could be judge, he being also party, it was agreed as law that the king should have companions to hear and determine in the parliaments all the writs and plaints concerning wrongs done by the king, the queen, their children; and their special ministers, for which wrongs one could not otherwise have obtained common right. . . .

For the good estate of his realm King Alfred caused his counts to assemble, and ordained as a perpetual usage that twice a year or more often if need should be in time of peace, they should assemble at London to hold parliament touching the guidance of the people of God, how the folk should keep themselves from sin, and live in quiet and receive right according to fixed usages and holy judgments.

Under this statute divers ordinances were made by divers kings down to the present time, which ordinances are disused by those who are less wise and because they are not put in writing and published in definite terms. . . .

Abuses of the Law

There are some who say that, while other realms make use of written law, England along makes use of her customs and usages as law. But between right and wrongful usages there is a great difference; for wrongful usages, which are not warrantable by law nor allowable by holy writ, are not to be followed, e.g. the usage of thieves which is the usage to rob and steal. And to set forth certain abuses which are held for usages, and which are frauds on the law and repugnant to right and not avowable by holy writ, is the object of this chapter, which makes a collection of a part of the abuses of the law of persons as a supplement for the knowledge of right law and true usages.

Abuse is disuse or misuse of right usages, turning them into abuse, sometimes by contrariety and repugnance to right, sometimes by excessive use, sometimes by non-use or deficient use, and sometimes by extravagant use.

The first and sovereign abuse is that the king is beyond the law, whereas he ought to be subject to it, as is contained in his oath.

It is an abuse that whereas parliaments ought to be held for the salvation of the souls of trespassers, twice a year and at London, they are now held but rarely and at the king's will for the purpose of obtaining aids and collection of treasure. And whereas ordinances ought to be made by the common assent of the king and his earls, they are now made by the king and his clerks and by aliens and others who dare not oppose the king but desire to please him and to counsel him for his profit, albeit their counsel is not for the good of the community of the people, and this without any summons of the earls or any observance of the rules of right, so that divers ordinances are now founded rather upon will than upon right.

It is an abuse that the laws and usages of the realm with their occasions are not put in writing, so that they might be published and known to all.

Part Five

THE FUNCTIONS OF
EARLY PARLIAMENTS

The Many Functions of Early Parliaments

Maitland's introduction to the parliament roll of 1305 published in 1893 was of far greater importance than is usually the case with a scholarly introduction to a definitive text. In many ways it laid down the lines along which later research into the history of parliaments would run. A passage in which he emphasized the importance of the council rather than the 'estates' has already been quoted (above no. 27). In the following passage he neatly categorized the functions of all early parliaments, even though not every one of these types of business is thought to have taken place in the particular parliament which he was discussing. On the other hand the clarity of his categorization has obscured for later historians a proper comprehension of the very real lack of differentiation of function in these early parliaments (see below no. 68). Furthermore his emphasis on the judicial aspect of early parliaments, rather than the concern in these assemblies for political business and the taxation needed to carry it on, has bedevilled later consideration of their functions, and has excited the most lively discussion ever since.

52 F. W. MAITLAND

And now we may ask the question, what does our record tell us of the part played in this parliament by the king's council, and by those who constituted or represented the three estates of the realm? We may bring the business of a medieval parliament under five heads, namely – (1) the discussion of affairs of state, more especially foreign affairs; (2) legislation; (3) taxation or supply; (4) the audience of petitions; (5) judicial business, the determination of causes criminal and civil.

(1) The king had summoned the estates in order that he might treat 'of certain matters specially touching our realm of England and the establishment of our land of Scotland', and no doubt the state of Scotland was one of the main matters which required his attention and the advice of his councillors. Let us remember that just at this moment Edward was at the full height of his power. All looked well; it seemed as if the evening of his reign was to be peaceful and glorious. He had lately traversed Scotland from end to end hardly finding an enemy, save in the garrison of Stirling Castle, and now even Stirling was his.

Wallace, it is true, was in all probability still at large when our parliament was sitting at Westminster; but he was a hunted outlaw and his capture, when it took place soon afterwards, cannot have been an unlooked-for event. As for the young Earl of Carrick, Edward had no reason for suspecting him of a grand ambition; we see him taking part in the parliament as one whom the king trusts. The task in hand was to provide for Scotland a settled form of government, a task that might demand prolonged debates, but not, it would seem, a hopeless task. What Edward did at this parliament was to call upon the Bishop of Glasgow, the Earl of Carrick, and John Mowbray to say how Scotland should be represented at another parliament to be holden later in the year. They reported that two bishops, two abbots, two barons, and two men elected by the community of Scotland would be representatives enough. As to the place at which the parliament should meet, they left that to the king; as to the time, the Scots could hardly be ready before Midsummer. Thereupon the king fixed London and the 15th of July as the place and date for the assembly. Afterwards he postponed that date until the 15th of September, and then at Westminster the ten Scottish representatives and twenty members of the English council drew up the important 'Ordinatio super stabilitate terræ Scotiæ'. However, at the moment what should interest us most is this, that in our lenten parliament the three Scottish spokesmen did not answer the question that had been put to them until after the assembly of the English estates had been dissolved. Those who were not members of the council had been sent home on the 21st of March; not until the 26th did the Bishop of Glasgow, Robert Bruce, and John Mowbray bring in their report.

Whether Edward had sought advice in this matter from the mass of the clergy, baronage, and commoners, we cannot say; nor do we know that the affairs of Gascony afforded material for a general debate, though there was an enormous mass of Gascon business to be transacted. Edward had lately recovered his French provinces, and was just sending out a new set of representatives. John of Havering, who had been justiciar of Wales, was to be in supreme command as seneschal of the duchy; Richard of Havering, lately the escheator north of Trent, was to be constable of Bordeaux; William Dene, seneschal of the Agenais; Frisot de Montclar, treasurer of Agen. Vast quantities of writs had to be issued for the payment of arrears of many kinds.

To come nearer home, we have seen how the king expected that the clergy would make an attack upon him. He was now quite strong enough to meet, to forestall, such an attack. He had not forgotten the humiliation that he had suffered at the hands of Archbishop Winchelsea. With his very good will, as we may well suppose, a petition was presented by the barons and commons complaining that the monks, more especially the Cistercians, sent large sums of money out of the country to alien mother houses. Of this matter we must speak under another head, but it may have been discussed in many meetings by the assembled laity. The treatment of the offending archbishop, who had lately been giving a fresh cause of complaint by 'visiting' the king's free chapel in Hastings Castle, was a subject to be debated rather at the council board than before the estates of the realm.

(2) In the way of legislation this parliament did little. No statute was passed which at once found a place upon the statute roll; but there are several acts of a more or less legislative character which should be briefly mentioned.

In answer to the petition of the laity touching the revenues of the religious houses the following reply was given: – 'The king in his full parliament, by the consent of the prelates, earls, barons, and others of the realm, has ordained and established a certain statute about this matter.' Our roll, as will now be seen for the first time, goes on to add – 'in the form that follows'. But nothing follows; a blank space is left; the statute, if drawn up, was kept in abeyance. Two years afterwards it was formally enacted or re-enacted at another parliament and became the well-known Statute of Carlisle, 'De asportis religiosorum'. The reasons for this delay are not obvious; but we have to remember that at the date of our parliament the papacy was vacant, and that Edward may have had several reasons for keeping in suspense over the future pope a statute which might prevent the flow of money from England to Rome or Avignon.

There has passed into our collections of statutes out of the Vetus Codex an 'Ordinance for Inquests' made at this parliament. It is an answer to a petition presented by Simon Parker, and provides in general terms that an inquest to which the king is party, is not to be stayed merely because the king's pleaders assert that some of the jurors are not favourable to the king. This was agreed and ordained 'by the king and his whole council'. Such an ordinance was beneath the dignity of the statute roll, and we should have great difficulty in proving that it had the assent of the estates. But it was a concession by the king, and the king's ordaining power would easily cover the making of such a concession.

An Ordinatio Forestæ which is on our roll was placed also upon the close roll; it has been received into our printed statute books. It is the king's answer to certain petitions and does not purport upon its face to bear the authority of the assembled estates or even the authority of the council. . . . We can hardly treat this as an act of legislation; certainly we cannot treat it as an act in which the estates of the realm took part. But no doubt at their meetings there was much talk about the forests, and discussion of those grievances which in the next year were met by an ordinance of sufficient importance to be placed upon the statute roll.

Lastly, there is, or rather once was, on our roll what was called in the margin thereof 'Ordinatio de trailbastons'. The king has appointed justices to inquire of, hear and determine divers felonies and trespasses. Their commissions are upon the patent roll; the earliest is dated on the 6th of April. The king now gives them certain instructions as to their proceedings. These will be of some importance in later history, for 'a commission of trailbaston' becomes one of the known forms of commission with which justices can be equipped. But this again we can hardly regard as a legislative act. The king has always enjoyed and still enjoys a very large discretionary power of sending justices when and whither he pleases, and of defining the matters about which they are to inquire. Even were we to examine the new commission minutely, we might find in it little that was very new or to us very striking, nevertheless the issue of it was the one thing done in this parliament that all the chroniclers have thought worthy of note; indeed a certain annalist speaks of this year as the year of trailbaston. This vigorous attempt to free the land of vagabonds takes its place along with the execution of Wallace, the disgrace of the archbishop, and the coronation of a new pope; they are the memorable events of the year, at least so it strikes a contemporary.

(3) As to taxation, we have every reason to believe that on the present occasion no tax of any kind was imposed, and we have no evidence to show that the king asked for money. He seems to have been very poor. The salaries of his justices and his clerks were in arrear, and they had to be told that they must wait for better times. It is of course possible that some statement of his necessities was laid before the assembled magnates, clergy and commons, but we read nothing of any 'supply' or of any demand.

(4) But by far the greater part of our parliament roll is occupied by entries which concern the audience of petitions. Before we discuss any

of the many questions which such entries suggest we must remember that many of the original petitions exist, and the external form of a petition should be briefly described.

It will in general be a strip of parchment about five inches long, while its breadth will vary from three inches to a bare inch. On the front of this strip and along its length the petitioner's grievance and prayer will be written, usually in French, rarely in Latin, and will be addressed 'to our lord the king' or 'to our lord the king and his council'. On the back of this strip and across its breadth there will almost always be written some words, usually in Latin, rarely at this time in French, which either prescribe the relief which the petitioner is to have or send him away empty. Then below this endorsement there will very often occur the syllable *Irr̃*, while just now and again we find the full *Irrotulatur*. Then, if we are lucky enough to connect this document with an entry on the parliament roll, the relation between the two will be of this kind: – By means of the formula, *Ad petitionem A. de B. petentis quod, etc., Ita responsum est quod, etc.*, the roll will first state the substance of the petition, having turned its plaintive French into businesslike Latin and pruned away its immaterial details, and then it will give with absolute accuracy the words of that response which is endorsed on the petition.

And now we may glance at the grave question, How and by whom and when and where was this business, this long and laborious business, transacted? We know that for some time past the multitude of petitions presented at the king's parliaments had been giving trouble and had been met by various expedients. . . .

On the present occasion we obtain fuller information. Already on the 5th of February, three weeks before the day fixed for the parliament, Edward, who was then at Swaffham in Cambridgeshire, wrote to his chancellor about this matter. 'We bid you,' he said 'along with the treasurer, to whom we have issued a similar command, proclaim that all those who have petitions to deliver to us and our council at our forthcoming parliament, shall deliver them day by day to those who are assigned to receive them between now and the first Sunday of Lent [the 7th of March] at the latest. And do you and the others of our Council in London "deliver" as many of these petitions as you can before we come, so that no petitions shall come before us in person, save only those which cannot in anywise be "delivered" without us, and these last you are to have well tried and examined and set in good order. This proclamation should be made in the great hall at Westminster, in the chancery, before the justices of the bench, in the

Guildhall, and in Westcheap, and the names of those who are to receive petitions must be declared. You are to let me know without delay in what manner you have fulfilled this command and whom you have appointed to receive the petitions.' From this it would seem that the work of examining and even of answering the petitions – for to 'deliver' a petition is to answer it – was to be taken in hand by those members of the council who were in London some days before the date appointed for the parliament.

(5) We pass to judicial business, noticing that the line between this and the hearing of petitions is not very sharp. The *Placita* which came before this parliament were few but miscellaneous.

In the first place we have the very famous case of Nicholas Segrave. Segrave and Cromwell had been serving with the king in his Scottish campaign; Segrave had brought an accusation against Cromwell and a judicial combat had been waged between them in the king's court. Then, however, Segrave, perhaps because he knew that the king would stop the duel, challenged his adversary to fight him in the court of the king of France; he withdrew himself from the English host and was endeavouring to make his way to France when he was captured. He confessed this grave offence – it was nothing less than treason. Edward then asked his council what was the punishment meet for such a crime. Their answer was – Death. The king, however, of his special grace was content that Segrave should find seven manucaptors who would undertake that he would render himself to prison if ever the king should call upon him to do so.

As regards the tribunal before which Segrave stood we can say this much: – The sheriff of Northampton was told to bring him before the king in the forthcoming parliament at Westminster, so soon as the king should arrive there: – He made his appearance 'in full parliament in the presence of the king, the archbishop of Canterbury, and divers earls, barons and others of the king's council': – When sentence was to be pronounced the king asked the advice of 'the earls, barons' (not, it will be observed, the prelates, for there was like to be a judgment of blood), 'and others of his council': – It is said by a chronicler that they discussed the matter for three days: – Segrave's manucaptors appeared 'before the king and his council' on the 29th of March and executed their bond on the 31st in the presence of the treasurer, three other bishops, the two chief justices, and others. The assembly of the estates had been dissolved on the 21st. It is very possible, however, that the trial took place while all the magnates were still at Westminster;

Segrave was a baron and had been summoned as such to the parliament.

The citizens of Salisbury had refused to submit to a tallage set upon them by the bishop under the authority of a charter granted to one of his predecessors by Henry III. On the 5th of March a writ went to the sheriff of Wiltshire bidding him summon the mayor, citizens, and the whole community of the city to be 'before us and our council' at Westminster on Mid Lent Sunday (the 28th of March). On that day four men appeared bearing full powers from the civic community; two of them were, if we may already use such a phrase, the sitting members for Salisbury, a third had represented the town at a former parliament. They and the bishop pleaded, and then the matter having been discussed 'before the king and his council', a judgment was pronounced. 'The king wills and commands' that the citizens do pay the tallage on this occasion, while as to the future they must choose between submitting to tallage and abandoning their franchises. They take the latter course, and on the 6th of April 'before the whole council' the mayor surrendered the mayoralty into the king's hand. It is clear that in this case the trial did not take place until the assembly of the estates had been dissolved.

Such records as these – and many others of a like kind might be cited from other rolls – bring us within sight of an often debated and still debateable question. What in Edward I's day was the jurisdictional competence of the king's council, and in particular what was the relation in matters of judicature between the council and the nascent house of lords?

Perhaps some new light might fall upon this old question were we to view it from what might be called the archivist's standpoint, were we to say for the moment that every one of the high courts in England must have a separate set of rolls. If we take up this not indefensible position, and leave out of sight the chancery and the exchequer and also the courts of the itinerant justices, we shall then hold that Henry III during the last half of his reign has two, and only two, high courts of law. The one of these is 'the bench'; it has a separate set of records, 'the *de banco* rolls'. The other is professedly held before the king himself; it follows him in his movements; it has a separate set of records, 'the *coram rege* rolls'. For ordinary purposes this latter court consists of a few professional justices; later in the reign a chief justice is definitely appointed to hold 'the pleas *coram rege*; but at any moment this court can be afforced by the presence of the king, of his councillors, of numerous barons and prelates. Now and again its roll will bear as a title 'Pleas before the King and his Council'. It is superior to 'the bench', for it can correct the errors of 'the bench'. Then early in Edward I's reign a further differentiation takes place. The court held *coram rege* when it assumes its everyday shape – that of a tribunal consisting of a few professional justices – becomes 'the king's bench'; what has formerly been 'the bench', though it always preserves this title, becomes, in common parlance, 'the common bench'; at a later day it will be the court of common pleas. But there is a greater change than this. A new set, unfortunately a meagre, disjointed set, of plea rolls (which, however, are not pure plea rolls, for they deal also with petitions and other matters) begins to appear. A court which is to stand above king's bench is being evolved out of the old court held *coram rege*; its rolls are the 'parliament rolls'. But the process is slow. For a while this highest tribunal is hardly distinct from the king's bench. Every plea in the king's bench is in theory a plea *coram ipso domino rege*, and the rolls of the king's bench never cease to be the *coram rege* rolls. The superior tribunal is rather, if we may so speak, an afforced, an intensified form of the inferior tribunal than a separate court; a plea that is put upon the parliament roll may be put upon the king's bench roll also; the justices of the king's bench are members of the council, and a case heard at a full meeting, a parliament, of the council, is heard by, among others, the justices of the king's bench. A plea may be adjourned from a parliament to the king's bench or from the king's bench to a parliament without breach of continuity.

A new tribunal is evolved, or rather, two tribunals become three. We can see this development taking place in the pages of Bracton and Fleta. Bracton [d. 1268] knows but two of those courts of which we are speaking: there are justices resident at the bench; there are yet more exalted justices attending the king's person. Fleta [c. 1290–2] knows three: there are justices resident at the bench; there are other justices who fill the king's own place, but above even them there is another tribunal, 'for the king has his court in his council in his parliaments, in the presence of prelates, earls, barons, nobles, and other learned men, where judicial doubts are determined, and new remedies are established for new wrongs, and justice is done to every one according to his deserts'. Bracton has to account for two sets of rolls; Fleta for three. Whether we ought to say that the highest of the three tribunals is the new one, whether we ought to describe the process as the deposit of a middle tribunal between the lowest and the highest, whether both of these phrases are not too definite and too modern to describe the real facts – these are grave problems which must be left to others. Our imaginary archivist would perhaps say that he could not decide them until he had made up his mind on the humbler question whether many parliament rolls have been lost. Our present point must be that before the end of Edward's reign there are three courts each with its roll.

What is the nature of the highest of these three? Is it council, is it house of lords? Fleta will warn us that we are asking an almost un-answerable question. 'Habet enim Rex curiam suam in consilio suo in parliamentis suis, præsentibus prælatis, comitibus, baronibus, proceribus et aliis viris peritis', that is all that we can safely say. The highest tribunal of the realm is the king in council; it is the king in his council in his parliaments, in the presence of prelates, barons, and other learned men. To deny that it is the king in council is impossible; to deny that it is the king in parliament, or rather that its sessions are parliaments, is impossible.

Politics in Early Parliaments

Of the five categories into which Maitland divided the business of medieval parliaments, the first, the discussion of affairs of state, had previously attracted most attention from historians. A century ago Bishop Stubbs emphasized this political function of parliament when he summarized his views of its development in the thirteenth century in his justly famous Constitutional History *of England. He looked at the thirteenth century very much from a nineteenth-century standpoint and saw behind the development of parliament a conscious 'grand design' on the part of Edward I, directed towards the creation of a balanced constitution, in which king and people could cooperate together in parliament for political ends – the greatness of the country and the happiness of the people. Stubbs's 'whig' interpretation remained the acceptable orthodox view throughout the latter part of the nineteenth century, and even casts its shadow over historical scholarship today. Half a century after Stubbs had first published his* Constitutional History, *Dr Pasquet violently attacked his view that Edward I consciously designed parliament so that the whole nation should participate in the government of the realm. Pasquet, on the contrary, iconoclastically denied that the commons in Edwardian parliaments were summoned either to perform any political or legislative function, or even necessarily to consent to taxation.*

53 WILLIAM STUBBS

On a review of the circumstances of the great struggle which forms the history of England during the thirteenth century, and after realizing as well as we can the constitution that emerges when the struggle is over, a question naturally arises as to the comparative desert of the actors, their responsibility for the issue, and the character of their motives. It is not easy to assign to the several combatants, or the several workers, their due share in the result. The king occupies the first place in the annals; the clergy appear best in the documentary evidence, for they could tell their own tale; the barons take the lead in action; the people are chiefly conspicuous in suffering. Yet we cannot suppose either that the well-proportioned and well-defined system which we find in existence at the death of Edward I grew up without a conscious and intelligent design on the part of its creators, or that the many plans which, under his father, had been tried and failed, failed merely because of the political weakness or accidental ill-success of their promoters. Comparing the history of the following ages with that of the past, we can scarcely doubt that Edward had a definite idea of government before his eyes, or that that idea was successful because it approved itself to the genius and grew out of the habits of the people. Edward saw, in fact, what the nation was capable of, and adapted his constitutional reforms to that capacity. But, although we may not refuse him the credit of design, it may still be questioned whether the design was altogether voluntary, whether it was not forced upon him by circumstances and developed by a series of successful experiments. And in the same way we may question whether the clerical and baronial policy was a class policy, the result of selfish personal designs, or a great, benevolent, statesmanlike plan, directed towards securing the greatness of the country and the happiness of the people.

First, then, as to the king: and we may here state the conclusions before we recapitulate the premises, which are in fact contained in the last two chapters. The result of the royal action upon the constitution during the thirteenth century was to some extent the work of design; to some extent an undesigned development of the material which the design attempted to mould and of the objects to which it was directed; to some extent the result of compulsion, such as forced the author of the design to carry out his own principles of design even when they told against his momentary policy and threatened to thwart his own object in the maintenance of his design. Each of these factors may be illustrated by a date; the design of a national parliament is perfected in 1295; the period of development is the period of the organic laws, from 1275 to 1290; the date of the compulsion is 1297. The complete result appears in the joint action of the parliaments of Lincoln in 1301 and of Carlisle in 1307.

The design, as interpreted by the result, was the creation of a national parliament, composed of the three estates, organized on the principle of concentrating local agency and machinery in such a manner as to produce unity of national action, and thus to strengthen the hand of the king, who personified the nation.

This design was perfected in 1295. It was not the result of compulsion, but the consummation of a growing policy. Edward did not call his parliament, as Philip the Fair called the States General, on the spur of a momentary necessity, or as a new machinery invented for the occasion and to be thrown aside when the occasion was over, but as a perfected organization, the growth of which he had for twenty years been doing his best to guide. Granted that he had in view the strengthening of the royal power, it was the royal power in and through the united nation, not as against it, that he designed to strengthen. In the face of France, before the eyes of Christendom, for the prosecution of an occasional war with Philip, for the annexation of Wales and Scotland, or for the recovery of the Holy Sepulchre, a strong king must be the king of a united people. And a people, to be united, must possess a balanced constitution, in which no class possesses absolute and independent power, none is powerful enough to oppress without remedy. The necessary check on an aspiring priesthood and an aggressive baronage, the hope and support of a rising people, must be in a king too powerful to yield to any one class, not powerful enough to act in despite of all, and fully powerful only in the combined support of all. Up to the year 1295 Edward had these ends steadily in view; his laws were directed to the limitation of baronial pretensions, to the definition of ecclesiastical claims, to the remedy of popular wrongs and sufferings. The peculiar line of his reforms, the ever-perceptible intention of placing each member of the body politic in direct and immediate relation with the royal power, in justice, in war, and in taxation, seems to reach its fulfilment in the creation of the parliament of 1295, containing clergy and people by symmetrical representation, and a baronage limited and defined on a distinct system of summons.

But the design was not the ideal of a doctrinaire, or even of a philosopher. It was not imposed on an unwilling or unprepared people. It was the result of a growing policy exercised on a growing subjectmatter. There is no reason to suppose that at the beginning of his reign Edward had conceived the design which he completed in 1295, or that in 1295 he contemplated the results that arose in 1297 and 1301. There was a development co-operating with the unfolding design. The nation, on whom and by whom he was working, had now become a consolidated people, aroused by the lessons of his father's reign to the intelligent appreciation of their own condition, and attached to their own laws and customs with a steady though not unreasoning affection, jealous of their privileges, their charters, their local customs, unwilling that the laws of England should be changed. The reign of Henry III, and the first twenty years of Edward, prove the increasing capacity for self-government, as well as the increased desire and understanding of the idea of self-government. The writs, the laws, the councils, the negotiations, of these years have been discussed in this and the preceding chapter: they prove that the nation was becoming capable and desirous of constitutional action; the capacity being proved by the success of the king's design in using it, the conscious desire by the constant aspiration for rights new or old.

The adaptability of his people to the execution of his design may well have revealed to Edward the further steps towards the perfection of his ideal. The national strength was tried against Wales, before Scotland opened a scene of new triumphs, and the submission of Scotland encouraged the nation to resist Wales, Scotland, and France at once. In the same way the successful management of the councils of 1283 and 1294 led to the completion of the parliament in 1295. In each case the development of national action had led to the increase of the royal power. Edward could not but see that he had struck the very line that must henceforth guide the national life. The symmetrical constitution, and the authoritative promulgation of its principle, mark the point at which the national development and the fullest development of Edward's policy for his people met. He was successful because he built on the habits and wishes and strength of the nation, whose habits, wishes, and strength he had learned to interpret.

54 D. PASQUET

The phrase '*quod omnes tangit ab omnibus approbetur*' is, according to Stubbs, a summary of Edward's policy. The gathering of deputies from counties and towns to the parliament of 1295 was but an application of this principle. Deliberately for twenty years Edward prepared for this innovation. He perceived that the English people desired to take its place in the constitution of the country; and, when the appropriate moment seemed to him to have come, he called the whole nation to participate in the government of the realm. Two years later, it is true, he seems to have wished to retrace his steps. A violent conflict broke out between him and his subjects over his proposed expedition to Flanders. Edward confiscated the wool, seized ecclesiastical property and tried to levy aids to which parliament had not agreed. But that was because at the moment he was at war with Scotland and France and was also at odds with Boniface VIII. In these exceptional circumstances he tried to assume dictatorship and 'failing, he yielded gracefully'.

If Edward I really entertained the designs attributed to him, he should not be compared, as he is by Stubbs, to Alfonso the Wise, to Philippe le Bel, or to Saint Louis, but to one of those great men of rare political genius, who have at intervals appeared in human history, to Julius Caesar or to Augustus. But such designs are so utterly opposed to the conceptions of Edward's time and to his own authoritarian temperament as not even to have an air of probability. In 1305 Edward obtained the pope's cancellation of the Great Charter and his own release from all his promises to his people. How can we believe that, in calling the representatives of the counties and towns to his parliament, he desired of his own free will to share his power with the nation? We may further observe that the phrase, which is held to summarize Edward's whole policy, does not appear in the writ ordering the sheriffs to proceed to elections, but only in that addressed to the prelates. If, therefore, we wish to give it any precise significance, it can only be applied to the representatives of the inferior clergy. But in reality the phrase seems to have been a commonplace of thirteenth century political literature, borrowed, as Stubbs himself points out, from Justinian's Code. It is but a part of that store of philosophical maxims and flowers of rhetoric, on which English chancery clerks loved to draw, especially when addressing the clergy, who seemed to them more capable than the laity of appreciating elegance of style. Edward was so little disposed to see that what concerned all should be approved by all, that after 1295, as before that date, he often reserved the most important questions for the consideration of his barons or merely of his council, without calling representatives of the commons to a parliament.

It is clear that Edward's object, in assembling deputies of the counties and towns, was not to make them participate in his legislative activities. Legislation was a royal prerogative, in which subjects took no part, except to give counsel, when the king demanded it of them. . . . A considerable number of ordinances or statutes – there was then no precise distinction between these two terms – were promulgated by the king alone and as concessions to his subjects. Others were promulgated by the king, on the advice of his council. Others were promulgated by the king, on the advice of the prelates and barons. So little importance was attached to the presence and the opinion of the commons that in 1290 the statute *Quia emptores*, although it affected the knights, was promulgated a week before the delegates of the counties arrived at the parliament. Even when the knights and burgesses were present, it was not considered necessary to mention the fact. The statute of merchants of 1283, whose object was to facilitate the recovery of debts and which was drawn up at the parliament of Shrewsbury probably after consultation with the burgesses, contains no allusion to any such participation. The *Articuli super cartas* were promulgated in 1300, at the close of a parliament, at which representatives of the counties and the towns had been present, but probably after their departure. Only prelates, earls and barons are mentioned. The only laws of Edward I, in which the consent of the community or communities of the realm is mentioned, are the first and the last of his reign, the statute of Westminster of 1275 and the statute of Carlisle of 1307. As regards the latter statute, the king did not wish to have trouble with the Roman curia and therefore no doubt thought it best to shelter himself behind the united opinion of the whole nation. He accordingly decided to add 'the communities of the realm' to the list of those on whose counsel he had acted. It had been impossible to place the clergy on the list, but the mention of the communities gave increased authority to the decision taken. But too much importance should not be attached to this addition. In 1307, as in 1275, in the writs sent to officials for the execution of the law all mention of the communities of the realm has disappeared. The writs speak only of earls and barons.

Neither did Edward I summon the delegates of the commons in order to consult them on questions of general policy. This is so evident that it seems hardly necessary to waste time proving it. A few examples will suffice. In 1294 the decision to engage in war with France was taken in a parliament of barons in June; the knights of the shires were only summoned to the parliament of November. In 1301 the letter addressed to the pope, on the rival claims of the papacy and the English king on Scotland, bears only baronial names and seals and is dated the 12th February, thirteen days after the departure from parliament of the representatives of the counties and towns. . . .

Discussion of questions of general policy was long to remain reserved for the prelates and barons or even for the king's council alone.

The desire for financial support, on the contrary, has been considered by most historians to have been the principal cause for the convocation of deputies of the commons. Edward I, like his contemporary Philippe le Bel, was always short of money. The royal demesne was impoverished. The government of the kingdom was becoming more and more complex and more and more costly. The great undertakings of the reign, the conquest of Wales, the conquest of Scotland, the war with France, were very expensive. The king was thus forced by financial pressure to summon the representatives of his counties and good towns in order to obtain the necessary aids from them; and they used their financial power to diminish the royal prerogative by gaining ever-increasing concessions in matters of legislation and policy.

This theory is attractive. There is often a clear connection between the convocation of the knights and burgesses and the financial demands of the king. The concession made by them (or by the knights alone) is mentioned in the writs that order the collection of an aid in 1275, 1283, 1290, 1294, 1295, 1296, 1297 and 1301. A marginal note on the roll even tells us that the two assemblies of 1283, at Northampton and York, were expressly summoned *de subsidio petendo*. Unfortunately, we know that similar formulae are found in the writs of Henry III, although they were apparently not preceded by any convocation of representatives of the counties and towns. We are therefore forced to discount the value of the consent by the knights and burgesses. Further, Edward I, especially in the latter part of his reign, often assembled the delegates of the commons without apparently making any pecuniary demand from them. Such was the case in 1283 (at Shrewsbury), 1298, 1300, 1302, 1305, and 1307. The question is therefore not so simple as it might appear at first sight.

Although most of the views of Stubbs have been heavily attacked at one time or another, there are still a large number of historians who believe that political business was the prime function performed in early parliaments. In his study of parliaments under Henry III Professor Treharne has made one of the strongest modern assertions of this point of view. Professor Treharne has however avoided Stubbs's 'whig' preconceptions and attempted to relate the early growth of parliament to the political realities of the thirteenth century rather than the nineteenth. Only readers of another century will be able to judge how much he and other contemporary historians are influenced by twentieth-century prejudices and preconceptions.

55 R. F. TREHARNE

The men who framed the Provisions of Oxford [1258] were perfectly explicit upon the function and purpose of parliament as they understood the word and as they intended to operate the institution which it designated. For in their hands what had hitherto been merely an occasion was converted into a political institution, and a vague, un-

technical colloquialism became a clearly defined and precise constitutional term. They decreed that parliaments should meet three times a
year at specified dates almost mathematically equal intervals apart from
each other: they laid it down that to all of these parliaments the members of the council of fifteen and the twelve elected to represent the
communitas were to come without waiting for a summons, though they
might also be summoned specially for emergency meetings should need
arise. And the declared purpose of these parliaments is 'to review the
state of the realm and to deal with the common business of both the
kingdom and the king': the twelve are elected 'to treat at the three
parliaments each year with the king's council, on behalf of the *communitas*, upon the common business, the business of the king and of the
realm', and the *communitas* ratifies in advance whatever the fifteen and
the twelve shall do together. Parliament, in short, was to be the
systematized and organic form of the consultation between the king
and the *communitas* always implied in feudal custom, but now made
explicit. Its purpose was to ensure that this consultation should be
regular and frequent, that it should no longer be left to the king's whim
to decide when and whom he should consult, and that the consultation
should be completely effective in controlling royal policy in all matters
of the public interest. In particular, the aim of these consultations in
parliament was to reform the state of the realm by means of edicts and
ordinances discussed, adopted and promulgated in the parliaments
themselves, as was stated explicitly in the commissions issued for the
enquiry into individual grievances in August 1258, and in the proclamation of the Provisions and Establishments of Westminster in November
1259. The making of appointments and the control of foreign policy
through meetings of the parliament were further aspects of this insis-
tence upon consultation in parliament.

When, after their victory at Lewes on 14 May 1264, the reformers
once more controlled the government of England, the writs of summons to the two parliaments which they called, stated more explicitly
their conception of parliament as a forum for consultation, approval
and proclamation. The four knights summoned from each shire to the
June parliament of 1264 were to come 'to treat with us (and with our
prelates, magnates and other faithful men) concerning our business and
that of the realm'. The main purpose of that parliament was to adopt
the *Forma Pacis*, including the *Forma Regiminis*, which was to be the
provisional constitution of the government of England until a more
lasting constitution and settlement could be provided by means of

arbitration. The formal proclamation of this *Forma Pacis* describes it as 'an ordinance made in the parliament held at London about the feast of the Nativity of St John the Baptist last', and as having been 'enacted in parliament at London'; and again, as 'the ordinance made at London with the consent, approval and command of the lord king and of the prelates, barons and the *communitas* there present at that time'. The recalcitrant royalist Marchers, though they prudently disobeyed the summons, had, like the rest, been summoned 'to treat of the state of the king and of the realm'. The writs of summons issued for the famous parliament of January 1265 declared that 'the prelates, magnates and nobles of our realm have been summoned to our forthcoming parliament at London . . . for the matter of the release of Edward our eldest son and for other matters affecting the *communitas* of our realm'; that the barons and bailiffs of each of the Cinque Ports were to send four representatives to the parliament 'to treat with us and with the aforesaid magnates of our realm and to lend counsel on the aforesaid matters, since the king urgently needs their presence and that of our other faithful subjects'; other cities and boroughs were required, in similar terms, to send their representatives to the parliament, and from each county two knights were summoned 'to be present with us in our parliament at London . . . and to treat with us and with our counsel upon the release of Edward our dearest son, and to arrange security therefore, and also for other difficult business concerning our realm'. As the practice developed of widening the basis of parliament by extending its membership by means of representation, the writs of summons more than ever before emphasized its purpose as a consultative assembly for discussing, determining and proclaiming joint decisions upon the highest and the most general matters of public importance for the kingdom as a whole. Justice will still be done in parliament – witness the writs of summons to Peter of Savoy at Pevensey, John de Warenne at Lewes, Hugh Bigod at Bosham and William de Valence at Brehendon 'to come before us and our council in our next parliament at London on 1 June (1265) to do and receive justice'; or the implication in the grant to Isabella de Fors, 'until our next parliament at London on 1 June', of the custody of her late brother's lands; or the command to the overhasty bishop of Bangor to revoke the interdict which he has placed on the chapel of Llywelyn ap Gruffydd, 'or at least to respite it until our forthcoming parliament which we are to hold at Westminster, where you and the other prelates of our realm will be present at our command, so that then, having discussed these matters, we may do to both sides whatever in justice should be done'. But these judicial matters, however important or interesting in themselves, were merely items which it was convenient to settle at the forthcoming parliament: the purpose of the parliament itself remained essentially political.

The use of the word 'parliament' in this political sense grew up with the institution which it came to describe, though the germinating seeds of the institution may be discerned perhaps as much as thirty years before the term, in this special political sense, began to be applied to it. By 1240 the word, especially in its French form 'parlement', was in the air, in fairly common and unspecialized use among the men who together constituted political circles in England. Evidently these men were beginning to use the word to describe large and important political assemblies in which the king consulted with the great men of the land, both spiritual and secular, upon matters of state of all kinds. As yet this political usage was neither systematic nor exclusive, for some of the most important assemblies of the years between 1242 and 1258 were at no point in the chancery rolls described as 'parliaments'. But, though the term was at first slow to establish itself in the chancery records, it is highly significant that, while its first occurrence there, in 1242,[1] was casual, the second was portentous, for it shows that by 1244 the king's clerks had come to think of the famous meeting between King John and his barons in 1215 as 'the parliament of Runnymede'. Of the ten occurrences, on eight separate occasions, of the use of the word 'parliament' in the printed chancery rolls before 1258, only three were judicial in their context, the other seven being general or political and including such high matters as the refusal of the magnates to allow the papal grant to the archbishop of Canterbury of the first fruits of vacant benefices in lay gift, the consideration of the king's request for an aid from his magnates, and the withdrawal of the severe reassessment of the Crusading tenth made by the papal envoy Rostand. In face of this evidence, it is impossible to doubt the mainly political significance of the word 'parliament' used by the king's clerks in the chancery records before 1258: justice was indeed done at the parliaments, or at least during their time of session, but the parliament itself was essentially a political occasion for discussions between the king and his great men. So essential was the attendance of the magnates in great force when a 'parliament' was summoned that Henry thought it necessary to give formal written permission to a newly elected bishop who could not conveniently attend the parliament, and at the same time to

[1] See above no. 3 for an earlier occurrence in 1236.

insist that the bishop-elect should be represented by proctors with full powers.

We can only guess what brought the word 'parliament' into official use in the chancery records in this somewhat haphazard way in the years 1242–58. It is tempting, and not unreasonable, to link its appearance in the rolls with the recurrent political crises of 1242–44 over finance, military service, and the misconduct of the war in France, crises which led to repeated demands for political reforms foreshadowing so closely those which were eventually adopted at the Parliament of Oxford in 1258. Perhaps the word 'parliament' was used sufficiently often by those who urged reform for it to have become familiar and fairly common usage in political and governmental circles during these years, and so to have found its way without conscious premeditation into the official documents of the chancery. It is significant that in 1246, so soon after the ferment of the years 1242–44, Matthew Paris first used the word in his great chronicle, and that he should have felt it necessary to provide an explanation of the new word in high-sounding descriptive terms emphasizing the completeness of the assembly, the importance of the occasion, and the general character of the business to be treated, touching the whole state of the disordered realm.

This slow and haphazard beginning was suddenly and greatly accelerated, and was also given much sharper definition, by the revolutionary developments of the years 1258–65. Even if we omit the vitally important references in the texts of the Provisions and Establishments of Westminster, as well as those in the official records of Henry's complaints against Simon de Montfort, and of Simon's replies in 1260, we still find the word employed forty-three times in thirty-three different letters patent and letters close in the seven years between 1258 and 1265. Characteristically enough, after Evesham the word again became somewhat rare, occurring in the chancery rolls only five times in the remaining seven years of Henry's reign. While it would be absurd to attempt to draw precise statistical conclusions from evidence of this kind, we cannot escape the deductions which this overwhelming disproportion in frequency of usage forces upon us. Nor is it only a matter of frequency of usage: it is, even more, one of definition. The men of 1258 changed parliament from an occasion into an institution, an institution which they used as the fundamental source of authority for the government of England and for the adoption and execution of their plan of reform. To them parliament was no mere occasion for holding judicial pleas or settling fiscal transactions in the exchequer: it was the means whereby the king, in full consultation with the great men of the land and with such others as might be required, considered all the needs of himself and of his realm and people, and decided what action was required to satisfy those needs in every field – political, administrative, financial, military, diplomatic, or whatever else they might be, even were it ecclesiastical. Parliament was the seat of discussion and decision, and the source of all reform. It is not too much to say that they acted as if they saw in parliament the sovereign authority of the land, for the king was not to act without it, and he was bound to obey its advice. So frequently does the word appear in the chancery records during these seven years, and in so clearly-defined and fundamental a context, that it seems to have had for them something of the hypnotic appeal of a political slogan, the name of a magical panacea to cure all the ills of the age, like the 'constitution' of the continental liberals of the nineteenth century.

Because they could not trust Henry to decide the occasions and the frequency of the meetings of parliament, the magnates set themselves to regulate these matters by formal constitutional documents, written constitutions converting an irregular occasion into a formal institution with a defined and nominated membership meeting at exactly prescribed times and charged with highly important functions. We see in these selected texts how under the pressure of political exigency, they even extended the basis of the membership of parliament by calling in the representative element, speaking for the shires and the boroughs, to take part in the process of discussion and decision which was the essence of parliament. These same texts show us how these men sought to define the relations of parliament to the king, to the privy council, to the whole body of the *communitas*, and to the officials, clerks and servants who governed England in the king's name. In the record of the great debate between Henry and Simon de Montfort in the summer of 1260, as in Henry's insistent letters from France in January and February of that year, we can even see, sharply contrasted with each other, the royal and the Montfortian views of the essential nature of parliament. To the king it was a body existing only in virtue of his pleasure and his summons, having no authority save what it derived from him, so that it was indecorous and shameful to contemplate its meeting without him or against his orders, and treason to attempt to hold it in his absence or against his prohibition – a view which he still asserted in 1269, long after the troubles were over. To Simon, on the other hand, parliament was an institution created by the Provisions of

Oxford, which had given to it separate existence and independent authority, had prescribed the dates of its meetings and laid heavy responsibilities upon it.

This view of parliament could not prevail in the political climate of thirteenth-century England. Forced into premature development by Henry III's utter incompetence to cope with the problems of governing his kingdom, the reformers' conception of parliament was put to the test before the political education of the English baronage had advanced sufficiently to enable them to stand the strain imposed upon it. Kenilworth and Evesham were no more inevitable than Lewes had been: but it is hard to see how much longer Simon de Montfort could have kept England to his chosen path even had he escaped from the trap which the Lord Edward's military genius had so successfully improvised for him in the summer of 1265. In fact, Evesham put an end, for the time being, to the Montfortian view of parliament, and in the remaining seven years of Henry III's reign the Chancery records show the king's conception of parliament re-established. It is once more an occasion, rather than an institution; but, though it is now seldom mentioned, it is still an occasion of great moment, when the king will consult with his great men upon important matters of general public concern – the formal submission of rebels, the fate of the city of London after the rebellion, the projected crusade against the infidel, and the affairs of the realm at large. And the king's presence in person is essential to its meeting, for when illness prevents the enfeebled old king from attending parliament on the appointed day at Midsummer, 1269, he asks the magnates, 'out of reverence and honour for him', to await his coming to begin his colloquy with them. Parliament was, it seemed, back where it had been before 1258.

The appearance, however, was deceptive. After the tremendous events which had convulsed England so many times between 1258 and 1267, Henry's conception of kingship, already challenged as long ago as 1215, could not for long endure. The idea of parliament as the organized and regular means of consultation between the king and his magnates had in reality been impressed indelibly upon the political consciousness of all classes of Englishmen who played any part in public affairs, and the same Lord Edward who had done so much to bring to nought the parliaments of Simon de Montfort was, as king in his turn, to make parliament into one of the most important institutions in English political machinery. And despite the immensely important growth of the judicial and fiscal aspects of parliament in his reign, it remained what it had been from the first, an essentially political assembly. In France and in Scotland, as in most other medieval states, the corresponding national assembly became known as the Estates General or by some such term: in England the word 'parliament' prevailed. That the English parliament never dwindled to a mere court of law like the French 'parlements', and that our national assembly did not become known as another 'States General', was largely due, in the first place, to the fact which these instances from the chancery records of Henry's reign abundantly show, that, from the first uses of the word in matters of government, Englishmen thought of 'parliament' as a primarily political assembly; and in the second place, to the achievement of the reformers of 1258–65 in stamping that conception of parliament upon English political consciousness for ever.

Justice and Petitions in Early Parliaments

Scholars who see early parliaments primarily as political assemblies form, however, only one party among contemporary historians. Another group of writers has taken up Maitland's emphasis on the judicial aspect of early parliaments, almost to the exclusion of the many other categories of business transacted in parliament. Mr Richardson and Professor Sayles have been the strongest protagonists of this judicial point of view over the last forty years. Their many writings are represented here by extracts taken from the small book in which they recently not only restated their case, but set out to demolish the many criticisms levelled at it. Their critics are represented here by Professor Edwards who has been one of the most vigorous opponents of the idea that early parliaments were in essence only courts of law.

56 H. G. RICHARDSON and G. O. SAYLES

What was Parliament?

Now let us repeat what we said long ago, supported by a plenitude of evidence, 'that parliaments are of one kind only and that, when we have stripped every non-essential away, the essence of them is the dispensing of justice by the king or by someone who in a very special sense represents the king'. To these words and their implication, which have caused difficulty – unnecessary difficulty perhaps – we shall return. Let us say here that they are plainly contrary to all that Stubbs implied when, borrowing, as was his wont, an error of the Lords Committees, he spoke of a 'model parliament' in 1295; they are plainly contrary to what countless teachers, uncritically reproducing Stubbs, have proceeded to teach their pupils. The primary criterion by which an assembly is to be assessed is, we assert, that of function and not the presence or absence from the king's court of particular persons or some particular class of suitor. This criterion we believe to have been the contemporary criterion: function determined whether or not a particular session of the king's council was parliament and was so termed.

Like every judicial and administrative tribunal – and it is only gradually that the distinction between them becomes clear as the Middle

Ages advance – parliament evolves and changes. What may be said of it in the thirteenth century will not be true of it in the fifteenth: the parliament of *Fleta* is not the parliament of Fortescue. And since parliament was not the creation of a legislative act nor, so far as we can tell, a conscious creation at all, we cannot give a date to its inception. Bracton, conservative that he was, never uses the word parliament. He knows of an afforced court where the community of the realm and the baronage are present, but he gives that court no specific name. We can hardly be wrong, however, in equating Bracton's *universitas regni et baronagium* with the *commune* of the Provisions of Oxford [1258], who were to elect twelve representatives to meet the king and his council in parliament. But it is not every meeting between the council and the Twelve that constitutes a parliament. Since the position seems still to be misunderstood, let us explain what the arrangements were. It would have been clearly impracticable for the Fifteen, 'cunseilers le rei esluz', to be in constant attendance as a body upon the king, and in the Michaelmas parliament of 1259 the relation of the Fifteen to the small body of councillors attendant on the king was clarified. The Fifteen were to be represented by two or three of their number: these were to be '*mesne gent*', that is of middling status, words which exclude bishops and earls. Their invidious task was to decide whether any weighty affair (*grant bossoine*) that might arise could be decided by their advice or could be deferred until the next terminal parliament or, if it could not be delayed, justified summoning by writ the whole of the Fifteen. Now it seems clear from the terms of the chancellor's oath that a weighty affair meant, at least normally, the grant by the king of wardships, money or escheats of any considerable amount, for such grants could not be made without the assent of the 'great council' or the majority of them. It seems also clear that these afforced meetings would not be specially summoned parliaments but afforced councils, for which provision had been made at Oxford, to which both the Fifteen and also the Twelve might be summoned. Here, then, we have assemblies of the same composition, some of which, those meeting at fixed terms, are parliaments, while others, meeting occasionally and not periodically, are not parliaments. We see that the insurgent barons have seized upon the word 'parliament', a popular word and hardly yet a word of court, and have applied it to one kind of afforced council. In doing so they have given 'parliament' a technical meaning, for periodicity implies definition: there cannot be a periodical occurrence of something that is not defined. What the technical meaning of parliament was we shall examine in the light of such evidence as is available; but we may say, in advance, that there seems no reason to suppose that Henry III's parliaments differed in character from those of Edward I nor that their distinguishing characteristic was not the dispensing of justice.

These two points we must emphasise. First, parliament is an afforced meeting of the council: it is an occurrence, an occasion, not yet a separate court with a continuous existence like the courts of common law. This is made clear by Henry III when he speaks of the parliament 'quod habuimus cum magnatis nostris apud Oxoniam' in the summer of 1258. And secondly, there are other afforced meetings of the council, not distinguishable in their constitution, which are not parliaments. We must not imagine that these two kinds of council meetings were altogether novel in 1258 and that in the Provisions of Oxford we have an act of creation. Parliaments *eo nomine*, as well as afforced councils or sessions of an afforced 'great court', were already well known. The barons did not invent the distinction: they adopted it. Doubtless, without their intervention, parliaments would have become distinguished from other meetings of similar constitution and would have been held at regular terms, for such a development took place at much the same time in France. The barons did no more than precipitate the event.

Yet the advantage of regular parliaments was obvious. As the fountain of justice, the king was under a duty to afford relief to his subjects, relief which, it was admitted, was not always available to them in the ordinary course. When Henry had forbidden the barons to hold a parliament in his absence, he had nevertheless expressed his wish that the justiciar, Hugh Bigod, should, with the aid of the council, administer justice to all and sundry. This alternative was possible because the justiciar was in a very special position: the office had been revived in 1258 by men who had a notion of its glorious past when the justiciar had been the king's *alter ego*. To Hugh Bigod Henry had himself committed the custody of the kingdom, though he did not intend to delegate the power to hold parliaments. Outside parliament Hugh Bigod and other specially appointed justices had, it is true, been diligent in itinerating the country for the purpose of hearing plaints, but evidently this was no adequate substitute for the higher justice men might expect from the king's council in parliament. With the royalist victory at Evesham, the office of justiciar had been swept away, and there was no conceivable alternative to parliament if there were to be righted wrongs that the ordinary course of the law would not touch. It is not surprising therefore that, after Henry III had been gathered to his fathers and old quarrels had been largely forgotten, the new king should have reinstituted regular terminal parliaments, though now they were to be held twice a year only, in the Easter and Michaelmas terms. The need for them, or at least their popularity, is evident, for the plaints which reached the king's council at these sessions soon became an almost unmanageable flood.

Justice in Parliament

If there was an undeniable likeness between parliaments and great councils, why then do we lay stress upon the difference between them? It is because, as we have said, the difference is fundamental. We believe, let us repeat, 'that parliaments are of one kind only and that . . . the essence of them is the dispensing of justice'. If this were not so, it would be difficult to understand why the author of *Fleta* should have described parliament as he did or how the Ordainers [1311] could have obtained the conception of parliament that patently informed their decisions on the functions to be discharged in future parliaments. It would be equally difficult to understand why the surviving records of the parliaments of the first two Edwards (the period with which we were primarily concerned when we first used the words we cite) are so overwhelmingly the result of the dispensation of justice. If we were writing of a later period, we would not employ quite the same words, though they apply with equal force to the early years of Edward III. Parliament, said Adam of Orleton, was convened 'pro justicia omnibus exhibenda'; and Adam, as a minister and spiritual peer of long experience under Edward II and Edward III, can hardly be accused of error. But at no period, so it seems to us, can the essential purpose of great councils be so described. We know of no contemporary text that would lend colour to such a thesis nor, numerous as great councils were, have they left behind them any record suggesting that men commonly resorted to them to sue for justice.

Now, despite the wealth of contemporary authority, our conclusions on the nature and function of parliament have been challenged. To disarm criticism we might perhaps have claimed, in the ironical phrase of Maitland's, that we were 'not departing very far from the path marked out by books that are already classical'. Did not the Lords Committees declare, in the light of the evidence known to them, that in the reigns of Henry III and Edward I parliament was the name given to 'an assembly . . . acting generally as the king's ordinary council or as a court of justice'? Did not Stubbs take the same view when he stated the obvious truth that 'most of the early documents preserved under that name [*sc.* the Rolls of Parliament] belong to the sessions of the council for judicial business'? We do no more than assert that there were not several kinds of parliament, as classical teaching held, but one kind only and that if some parliaments were 'general' – the contemporary adjective for those more numerously attended – they were nevertheless 'ordinary' parliaments. Why then should the difference between the classical position and our own appear so wide? Is it not because we reject in its totality Stubbs's conception of a 'parliamentary constitution' as 'the English system' of government in the Middle Ages, even though the qualification be added that this 'was by no means the whole of the system'.

In the dust of controversy there seems to be some likelihood that Stubbs's own teaching may be obscured. Let us then recall his words. 'We must be content', he said, 'to understand by the name of parliament all meetings of the national council called together in the form that was usual at that particular time.' By implication he plainly excluded 'the sessions of the council for judicial business' which were nevertheless called by contemporaries parliaments and which were 'held, as the Provisions of Oxford had ordered, at fixed times of the year'. Under 'the parliamentary constitution . . . the clergy, the barons and the communities' were 'associated for financial, legislative and political action', and, whatever had been the shortcomings in the past, the parliament of 1295 'was to be a model assembly . . . serving as a pattern for all future assemblies of the nation' or, as Stubbs said elsewhere, was 'a perfect representation of the three estates . . . and a parliament constituted on the model of which every succeeding assembly bearing that name was formed'. The diffuseness of Stubbs's exposition and his neglect to resolve apparent inconsistencies between statements made in different contexts render it far from easy to form a coherent picture of the parliament of his imagination. We have done our best, by piecing together passages sometimes wide apart, to present a true and intelligible account, without, we trust, distortion or misrepresentation. This, at least, can be said: not the most ingenious of interpretations can reconcile Stubbs's conception of parliament with *Fleta*'s – the conception of parliament where 'the king in council holds his court in the presence of prelates, earls, barons, nobles and others learned in the law'. Stubbs's parliament is not conciliar in this sense: his parliament is a national council, 'the concentration of the three estates'. Nor, in Stubbs's view, were the representatives of the commons on an inferior footing to the other 'estates': 'under Edward II, Edward III and Richard II', he asserted, 'the third estate claimed and won its place as the foremost of the three'. The picture thus presented is not one of the English parliament of contemporary documents, not the parliament of history, but something imaginary masquerading as history. It is, if you will, anachronistic, a projecting into the past of a 'parliamentary constitution' which Stubbs believed, without justification, to have existed in the later Middle Ages.

One of the curiosities of historiography is that, just as French scholars have been inclined to minimize the part played by the thirteenth-century parliament of Paris in administrative and political matters, so English scholars have tried to wish away the judicial functions of the early English parliament. Stubbs was nearer to the truth than he imagined when he said that 'the parliament of Paris [under Philippe le Bel] may be generally compared with the special judicial session or parliament of the council' or, again, 'the point at which the two constitutions approximated more nearly than at any other in the middle ages' was the end of Edward I's reign in England and the reign of Philippe le Bel in France. It may seem astonishing that Stubbs could approach so near to the realities of history and yet persist in his dogma of an English 'parliamentary constitution', which falsifies his teaching throughout. He could, indeed, keep himself in countenance only by asserting that parliaments were of three kinds and then, because the records did not bear him out, abusing the Rolls of Parliament for their confusion.

57 SIR GORONWY EDWARDS

1258

The earliest extant description of periodically frequent parliaments in England is implicit in two familiar clauses of 'the provisions of Oxford': their substance is summarized in the contemporary memorandum thus:

> Il fet a remembrer ke les XXIV unt ordene ke treis parlemenz seient par an: le premerein as utaves de Sein Michel, le secund le demein de la Chandelur, le terz le premer jor de June ceo est a saver treis semeines devant le Seint John. A ces treis parlemenz vendrunt les cunseillers le rei esluz [i.e. the council of 15] tut ne seient il pas mandez pur ver le estat del reaume et pur treter les cummuns bosoingnes del reaume et

del rei ensement; e autre fez ensement quant mester serra per le mandement le rei.

Si fet a remembre ke le commun eslise xii prodes homes ke vendrunt as parlemenz et autre fez quant mester serra quant le rei u sun cunseil les mandera pur treter de bosoingnes le rei et del reaume, e ke le commun tendra pur estable ceo ke ces xii frunt: e ceo serra fet pur esparnier le cust del commun.

[It ought to be recorded that the twenty-four have ordained that there shall be three parliaments each year: the first (shall begin) a week after Michaelmas, the second on the day after Candlemas, and the third on the first of June, that is to say three weeks before St John's day. The elected councillors of the king (i.e. the council of fifteen) shall come to these three parliaments whether they are summoned or not, to review the state of the kingdom and to discuss the common needs of the kingdom and of the king; and similarly at other times when it is necessary by the summons of the king.

It is to be recorded that the community shall choose twelve wise men who shall come to the parliaments, and at other times when it is necessary, when the king and his council shall summon them, to discuss the needs of the king and the kingdom, and that the community shall consider whatever the twelve shall do as established: and this shall be done to spare the cost to the community.]

It is of course agreed that in this specific form – the fifteen counsellors afforced by twelve 'prodes homes' on behalf of 'le commun', meeting periodically on three particular dates – the parliaments envisaged by the Provisions of Oxford did not survive the short period during which the Provisions were effectively current. But it is also agreed that the idea of holding parliaments consisting of the king's counsellors afforced by 'prodes homes' of various kinds and meeting periodically several times a year, continued to flourish long after 1258, and was acted upon pretty consistently. Moreover, just as it is quite clear that these periodical parliaments continued to meet long after 1258, so also there are indications suggesting that the same idea had been current and had been acted upon before that date. Mr Richardson has noted two early references to parliaments in the Close Rolls respectively of 1242 and 1248. Now the former entry speaks of a 'parliamentum regis quod erit Londinii a die Sancte Johannis Baptiste in unum mensem', and the latter mentions a parliament 'quod erit in octabis Purificacionis'. It is a noteworthy coincidence that the two feasts to which the meeting-dates of these very early parliaments in 1242 and 1248 are thus keyed – St John Baptist and the Purification – appear also as two of the three feasts to which the meeting-dates of the periodical parliaments in the Provisions of Oxford are keyed. These periodical parliaments prescribed in 1258 were therefore no transient phantoms conjured out of the void by the authors of the Provisions of Oxford. So what the Provisions say about the function of those parliaments becomes significant. Their function is described twice, in two distinct sentences of identical import: 'pur ver le estat del reaume et pur treter les cummuns bosoingnes del reaume et del rei ensement', and 'pur treter de bosoingnes le rei et del reaume'. Pollard's suggestion that the barons of 1258 demanded frequent parliaments 'for the justice therein dispensed' is thus shown by the barons' own statements to be quite unconvincing: they describe the function of parliaments in the widest of terms – terms which doubtless include, but which also certainly transcend, the dispensing of 'justice'.

1280

During the half-century between the first and the second of our recorded demands for frequent parliaments there comes a familiar document which is very relevant to the present discussion. Everyone agrees that the petitions brought into these early parliaments were sometimes (and perhaps usually) very numerous, and that it was mainly through these petitions that parliaments became involved in 'judicial' activities. In the Close Roll of 8 Edward I (1279–80) there is enrolled an important chancery memorandum of the procedure that was followed in dealing with these petitions:

> Because the people who came to the king's parliament are often delayed and disturbed, to the great inconvenience of them and of the court, by the multitude of petitions which are offered before the king, of which petitions the greater part could be disposed of by the chancellor and by the justices, it is decreed that all the petitions which pertain to the great seal should come first to the chancellor, and those which pertain to the exchequer shall come to the exchequer, and those which pertain to the justices or law of the land shall come to the justices, and those which pertain to the Jewry shall come to the justices of the Jewry. And if the matter is so important or involves the king's grace to such an extent that the chancellor or the others cannot deal with it without the king, then they shall bring it with their own hands before the king, to learn his will in the matter; so that no

petition shall come before the king and his council except by the hands of the aforesaid chancellor and the other chief ministers; and thus the king and his council can, without the burden of other business, attend to the weighty business of his realm and of his foreign lands.

It will be seen that the *modus operandi* is to reduce to a minimum the number of petitions that have to be considered in parliament by the king and his council. The memorandum states that the greater part of the petitions presented could be disposed of by the chancellor and by the judges, in consultation with the appropriate ministers, and then lays down that no petition shall be brought before the king and his council unless it involves business that is 'so great or so much of grace' that 'the chancellor and the others' cannot handle it without the king. Then comes the final sentence, which is the important passage in the present connection: only the selected petitions are to be brought before the king and his council,

> ensi ke le rey e sun consail pussent sanz charge de autre busoignes entendre a grosses busoignes de sun reaume et de ses foreines terres.

The memorandum thus assumes that the king and his council will, during the time of parliament, have 'grosses busoignes de sun reaume et de ses foreines terres', to which they must be able to attend without the distraction of 'autres busoignes'. Now some of these 'grosses busoignes' may well arise out of some of the select petitions that will have been reserved for consideration by the king and his council. But we can hardly suppose that all the 'grosses busoignes' will arise in that way. Quite irrespective of petitions, if the king desires to have any matters whatsoever considered in parliament – not only taxation or legislation or France or Scotland or the papacy, but also any other subject such as we find included in those written 'arrays' of agenda that were commonly drawn up before parliaments met – we may reasonably suppose that the king and his ministers will ensure that such matters shall rank among the 'grosses busoignes'. Naturally such business is bound to be very varied, and no one can expect that taxation, or legislation, or what not, will turn up in every parliament. Nevertheless, the authors of the memorandum of 1280 proceed on the assumption that in every parliament there will always be 'grosses busoignes' of one sort or another over and above the multitude of petitions, and that most of those petitions must therefore be sloughed off and left to 'le chanceler et ces autres'. In other words, the king's officers in 1280 expect as a matter of course to encounter in every parliament two things – petitions (i.e. 'justice') and 'grosses busoignes'. Mr Richardson and Dr Sayles, on the contrary, maintain that we must not necessarily expect more than one – 'justice'. 'Justice' was doubtless the one thing that interested 'the people', 'the litigants and suitors and clerks', the generality of the 'Englishmen living between 1272 and 1327'. But at least some few Englishmen of that period had an equally deep interest in the 'grosses busoignes'. Admittedly those few Englishmen were very few. Yet they were the makers and builders of parliament. They were the king and his officers. These in 1280, like the barons previously in 1258, evidently thought that the function of parliaments always transcended the mere dispensing of 'justice'.

If we are to reach an adequate view of the ideas underlying the English parliament, the dispensing of 'justice' must be given its due place among the functions performed in the early parliaments. Formerly, historians accorded to 'justice' less than its due place. Latterly, they have given to it more than its due place. The functions performed in these early parliaments cannot be satisfactorily appraised from a single point of view. *Fleta*'s classical description, for instance, forms part of a chapter in which he is giving a list of the various royal tribunals that exercise judicial functions: in such a context, it is very proper that he should mention only the judicial functions that are performed in parliament – the functions other than judicial are irrelevant to his purpose. We shall get equally one-sided views of parliamentary functions if we regard them from the standpoint only of the generality of Englishmen, or from the standpoint only of the king and his counsellors: both parties were concerned in parliament, and the functions performed in it need to be appraised from both points of view. Of the business done in parliament, what specially interested the generality of Englishmen was the dispensing of 'justice'; but what specially interested the king and his counsellors were the 'grosses busoignes'. We must set beside *Fleta* the two other early accounts of parliamentary business contained in the less specialized contexts of the Provisions of Oxford of 1258 and of the chancery memorandum of 1280: both these documents describe parliamentary functions in the widest and most comprehensive terms. Evidently the competence of king in council in parliament was not a 'judicial' competence. It was a general competence. It was an omnicompetence. Parliament was a 'high' court not merely because it was judicially above other courts, but also because it was in itself more than a judicial court: it was an omnicompetent organ of government at the summit of lay affairs in England. Nor can we justly conceive its omnicompetence as something consisting of a basic nucleus of 'judicial' competence, to which king or barons might on occasion 'add' various 'other things' – but only as detachable 'non-essentials' which historians must now 'strip away'. Parliament's robe of omnicompetence was not a thing of shreds and patches: it was a seamless whole.

The essential ambiguity of much of the source material over which historians are arguing is illustrated here by two documents relating to the trial of David of Wales in parliament in 1283. This case could be used as an example of the judicial function of parliament, but it could be equally used to support a view that parliament was essentially concerned with politics, which were on this occasion masquerading under the guise of justice.

58 WELSH ROLL 1283

The king to the mayor, citizens and sheriffs of London. With how many kinds of fraud and deceit the men of the Welsh language, like foxes, have attacked our ancestors, ourselves and our kingdom for as long as the memory of man can recall! How many massacres they have made of the magnates, the nobility and others, whether English or foreign, whether young or old, women or children! How many castles and manors of ours and of other inhabitants of this kingdom they have set on fire! The tongue of man can scarcely recount how many times they have disturbed and troubled our kingdom, without fear of God or man. But let us say no more of the past, for every ear in our kingdom has now heard how in these days, Llewelyn the son of Griffith, formerly Prince of Wales, and David his brother, spurning the fealty which they had duly made to us, and unable to relinquish their former habits, suddenly burnt our towns, with even more treachery than usual, and, alas, killed certain of our faithful subjects, and burnt others, and committed yet others to horrible dungeons, and how with rash boldness they presumed to attack our castles, and cruelly shed the blood of the innocent. After the conversion of the sinner, God waits for a longer time, but if he becomes hardened, he permits him to fall. Since it appears that He wished to put an end to these frauds and deceits, to these burnings and inhuman slaughterings, God first killed the prince

[Llewelyn] and, after capture by men of his own tongue, at length consigned to our prison David, who was almost the last survivor of this family of traitors. Thanks be to God for this, for we believe it to be his doing. We wish to discuss with our faithful people what ought to be done to David, who we rescued when he had been banished, who we nourished when an orphan, who we endowed from our own lands, and to whom we gave a place among the magnates in our palace. We therefore command you that you cause to be chosen two of the wiser and more suitable citizens of the city and send them to us, that they may be with us at Shrewsbury on the day after Michaelmas (30 September) to speak with us and others about these things. And do not fail in this in any way.

Witnessed by the king at Rhuddlan, 28 June.

Similar writs were sent to twenty other cities and towns, to all the counties, to ten earls, a hundred barons and nineteen other named individuals.

59 ANNALS OF OSNEY

About Michaelmas the king held his parliament at Shrewsbury having summoned thither the magnates of his kingdom and the mayors of the cities of England. By his orders David, who had been captured at Rhuddlan, was brought there and judicially condemned, by the consideration of the gathered magnates, who thought that his treachery deserved it, to a death unheard of in earlier times. First he was pulled asunder by horses, secondly he was hanged, thirdly he was beheaded, fourthly his heart and entrails were drawn out for burning, and fifthly his body was divided in four parts to be hung up separately in the four quarters of England, whilst his head was carried away to London by the citizens who were present, to be placed, as a notable spectacle, on the Tower of London next to the head of his brother Llewelyn.

Taxation in Early Parliaments

When historians have looked at early parliaments as a whole, they have considered the political, or judicial, functions of paramount importance. When, on the other hand, they have concentrated on the representative elements in these parliaments, that is to say the knights, burgesses and lower clergy, they have found that consent to taxation occupies a much more prominent place. Professor Stephenson approached this on a comparative basis, examining parallel developments in England, France and Germany to demonstrate the importance of taxation in the evolution of political representation in each of these countries. Professor Mitchell approached the question of consent to taxation as an aspect of a fuller examination of taxation in medieval England, and followed Dr Pasquet in seeing consent as related to ease and speed of collection rather than as a constitutional necessity. In his general survey of the thirteenth century Professor Powicke has very lucidly summed up the effects of consenting to taxation in parliament.

60 CARL STEPHENSON

Familiar as is the subject of urban liberties, one of its fundamentals still needs emphasis – the public basis of the town's establishment. Mere ownership of the soil did not suffice for creating a privileged municipality: that necessitated the tenure of immunities which could be shared with a group of subjects. The lord of a town was the person who chartered it. As he chartered it, so it was said to stand on his domain; for that expression, in the political sense, meant the territory under his immediate jurisdiction. And if under feudal custom the ordinary baron possessed the legal faculty of conferring bourgeois status, that is only added testimony to prove the public nature of his authority. Thus the typical emancipation charter to a community was not the act of a master freeing his bondmen; it was a grant of territorial franchise. It customarily restricted the exercise of the political rights – judicial, military, and fiscal – which the grantor held within the locality, and also guaranteed to all settlers freedom from the exactions of their previous lords. Moreover, this liberty, except for specified reservations, applied even to immigrant serfs. Everywhere the precedence of territorial over personal rights was advertised by the famous law of a year and a day.

In this way, and only in this way, can the taxation of the medieval town be satisfactorily explained. The urban settlement, because it was located within a lord's territorial immunity, was subject, unless he chose to relax it, to his exclusive and unrestrained power of tallage. But as a matter of fact, the exaction, like arbitrary *corvées* and unlimited military service, was found incompatible with the interests both of the bourgeois and of their patron. So it tended to disappear. The most highly privileged towns gained complete exemption, often with the guarantee that they should be liable only for freely granted subsidies. . .

[In France] Within each great fief custom normally permitted the lord, lay or ecclesiastic, to levy a subsidy when confronted by some special need. The aids thus taken were seignorial, rather than feudal, for they were commonly paid by both noble and non-noble tenants. Except on definitely recognized occasions, the former could be expected to pay only voluntary contributions, and the effect of municipal charters was to place many towns in somewhat the same advantageous position. But in any case the outcome was not so much a matter of law as of political strength. A weak lord was hardly able to collect even the more regular aids, while the mere request of a powerful prince, no matter what he asked for, could be ill refused. An autonomous city state might dispense with all chartered privilege, but no amount of written guarantees prevented extortion from an actually dependent community. To interpret medieval taxation as following a set of rigid legal principles is to miss the point completely.

In order to get what money he required from an ordinary town the lord had only to negotiate for a grant, enlarging upon the urgency of his need, emphasizing the benefits secured from him in the past, and hinting the misfortune that his displeasure might occasion in the future. And if necessary, he was always willing to issue the letter of no prejudice for which his chancery kept a stock of forms on hand. It is true that auxiliary troops or money compositions were occasionally levied from towns, but such a practice could introduce no new principle, for municipal charters commonly restricted military service as well as tallage. If most taxes were levied because of wars, they were none the less taxes. The only way in which the French king, or one of his great vassals, could secure a general subsidy from all his dependents was by negotiating with each important individual or group. From that system to the calling of estates was but a step. How Philip IV [1285–1314] and his successors used such meetings for fiscal purposes is quite familiar. And throughout the provinces from Flanders to Béarn, whether held by king or count, the same phenomenon recurred. In proportion to its wealth and political solidarity, the bourgeoisie secured power in the central councils.

In Germany the situation was the same. The towns, either free of the old *Bede* or obliged to pay only fixed sums, were still solicited for extraordinary aids. And again the custom of dickering with each community was in time succeeded by the calling of representative assemblies. Even under Rudolf of Habsburg [1273–91] the *Reichsstädte* came to send deputies for making a grant to the king, and within another century many territorial diets had appeared in connection with similar practices on the part of the *Landesherren*.

If now we turn back to England, in spite of all insular peculiarities, we find a familiar situation. The royal boroughs, it is true, had with slight exception never been exempted from tallage; but in the king's hands that exaction had corresponded rather with the extraordinary aids than with the *taille* of the Continent. That the boroughs were as legally liable for the imposition as lawyers could make them is beyond doubt. However, this did not prevent their objecting to the tax. The action of London, to my mind, should be interpreted, not as an appeal to, but as a protest against the law. When, during the crisis under John, the city asked that it be exempted from tallage and recognized as having the right to grant its aids, it was merely echoing a demand raised by the bourgeoisie in all quarters. Nor, in an age when mere villages were securing such guarantees in France, could one repulse be expected to end the Londoners' agitation. Indeed, there is plenty of evidence to show that the tallage continued to cause bitter opposition until it was dropped in favor of the new parliamentary grants.

To explain the origin of the House of Commons as a purely insular phenomenon is surely mistaken. Any one who studies the mass of relevant material on the Continent can hardly escape the conclusion that the representation of the towns there was the logical outcome of a new system of taxation – one forced upon princes whose necessary expenditures were far exceeding their ancient sources of income, and one which had grown up with the towns themselves. To say this is not to imply that all representative assemblies were called to grant taxes: the system was obviously useful in many ways. But in proportion as fiscal necessity controlled the later fortunes of the estates so it must have dominated their creation.

Knowing how both the earlier and later evolution of parliament turned upon matters of taxation, I find it hard to discount that factor as determining Edward I's policy. Even in connection with the counties, the representation of which was the most peculiar feature of the English system, fiscal considerations can by no means be ignored. Many writers on the subject have pointed out that, thanks to the Norman perpetuation and improvement of the ancient shire court, the lesser barons and other freeholders of the kingdom had come to be grouped in legally organized communities, or communes. How useful they had been to the king in police, justice, and other local affairs is a commonplace. But was that usefulness in itself enough to account for the knights of the shire as an estate in parliament? I do not think so. By associating them with the other sections of the council, Edward was able to assure the financial support of a very important element in his state, and one which strict feudal law would have prevented his taxing. But in this respect, as in all, his policy was distinctly anti-feudal, and in following it he was not without precedent.

So, too, while making allowance for the importance of judicial and administrative work, I still feel that the incorporation of the burgesses as a permanent element in the great council was due primarily to the cash which the king was thereby enabled to get. For though he was not legally forced to tax the towns with their consent through deputies, he undoubtedly found it easier to do so. It was a political necessity that faced Edward, as it faced the other princes of the age. Indeed, if any of them had been strong enough, would he not have levied his imposts despotically? . . .

On ultimate analysis, it seems to me that in the organization of representative institutions in Western Europe we encounter the necessary result of a social revolution. This revolution, the product of a commercial revival, had created a new moneyed class, the support of which proved a decisive factor in the rebuilding of the European monarchies. For intelligent princes were quick to see that they stood to gain infinitely more from the good will of the rising burghers than from an outworn system of hated exactions. Accordingly, the tallage, together with other obsolete manorial arrangements, was generally abandoned in the towns, and less obnoxious payments were substituted. Especially by means of subsidies called voluntary, seignorial taxation was not only continued but enormously enhanced. Bourgeoisie and monarchy formed a famous alliance, which, breaking the political dominance of feudalism, eventually produced the modern state. That the men whose wealth had long been the chief reliance of indigent but ambitious princes should be given a voice in the reorganized central councils was quite inevitable.

Thus the same statesmanship that in the twelfth century had led to the granting of liberal municipal charters gave the towns representation in the fourteenth. Though the parliamentary system was ordained by the sovereign for his own convenience, that convenience was largely dictated by his need of taxes.

61 S. K. MITCHELL

Let us review the changes in the notion of consent to taxation that reflect the modification in the social structure of England. We begin with the feudal Anglo-Norman customary organization using an income derived entirely from dues and one special extra source of supply, the feudal gracious aid, an occasional resource. The latter was founded on the principle that in time of great need the vassals ought to come to their lord's assistance, first in services and payments in kind and, by a later interpretation, with money. It was only an occasional levy, taken under extraordinary circumstances. Very soon the council began to base it upon a unit of land or other property, as a result of which the tax was automatically exacted for the king from property holders who were not tenants of the king and hence owed him nothing; such was the use of the danegeld, which was abandoned and then revived as the carucage, of the aid on knights' fees, and the tax on movables and revenues. The authorizing body was the great curia regis. Thus unintentionally and without deliberation the king began to authorize an occasional levy of a general tax on the property belonging to nearly all property holders in the realm regardless of their status in society. The consent of the curia regis to such a levy bound people who were not summoned or consulted. It facilitated later the substitution of corporate for individual consent. As has been said, although the aid was of grace, an obligation seems to have bound the tenant to grant the aid. The reigns of Richard I and John resulted in a crisis in the relations between king and barons, one subject in dispute being the levy of both aid and scutage. The exciting cause was the increased frequency with which both were taken, particularly scutage. The regulation as given in Articles XII and XIV of Magna Carta declared that neither could be taken as a custom – only by the consent of the great curia regis could they be levied. Thus two facts are to be noted in 1215 in this connection: first, that the barons had the feeling that aids should be regulated, and second, the emphasis on the part to be played in the regulation by the great curia regis, that is, by the barons themselves. The reign of Henry III established the custom that the great council could refuse as well as grant the aid; the notion was established that taxes on movables were essential from time to time, the form that the aid was to take. Though not formally declared, in fact, consent became corporate. Under Edward I we see the truth of these generalizations made for Henry III. In addition, on the initiative of the king, the custom was established that had already been used occasionally in the later years of Henry III, though not in connection with taxation, viz., summoning representatives of the shires to associate themselves with the great council in granting an aid on the property on all the holdings of tenants in chief. Thus the authority of the great council to consent or refuse established under Henry III continued, but for some reason not clearly understood the king decided to associate elected knights of the shire with the great council in the grant. Perhaps they thought to secure better cooperation in the assessment and collection. Perhaps the growing money economy suggested a doubt of the capacity of the council to grant taxes on property not their own. Anyhow the two bodies cooperated in granting taxes on the same property. The demesne continued to negotiate with royal justices who went on iter as in the past (except in 1283) till 1295, when towns and boroughs were summoned by representatives to meet with the council and vote aids. Notice that the reasons for the use of representatives suggested above did not apply to the demesne. The only reason in their case was ease and speed, for at the date they began to use representatives the aid on movables was a convention both in frequency and in amount. Hence its grant could be satisfactorily and easily made by deputies.

62 SIR MAURICE POWICKE

Taxation, indeed, was the crucial problem. We have already seen how, by way of understandings between pope and king, the clergy were brought into the fold to be shorn. The lay subsidies became a normal source of revenue in a more domestic way. They were an expression of a social unity which they did much to create. They were taxes, not on land, but on the goods or movables of all members of the community except the king at one end and those whose goods were valued at less than a certain minimum at the other end of the social scale. Other exemptions were due to particular reasons or special favour; thus the men of the Cinque Ports and other ports would be exempted because they contributed to the building of the king's ships; and active service in the army was a natural ground of exemption. The tax levied on the value of the goods assessed varied in Edward's reign from a ninth in 1297 to a thirtieth in 1283 and 1306–7. There were nine such taxes in the thirty-five years of the reign, two before 1290, seven between 1290 and 1307. In 1290 a most important change, suggesting, though not due to, an intention that this extraordinary levy had come to stay, was made in the process of collection. Hitherto a tax of this kind had come only casually within the purview of the exchequer. Its proceeds had generally been set aside for a special purpose. It had been collected in various places, and paid out, as required, to those concerned or into the king's wardrobe or to his foreign bankers, only occasionally into the treasury. In 1290, after Kirkby's successor, William March (*de Marchia*), had become treasurer, the tax granted in this year was placed under the direct control of the exchequer. This was part of a larger plan. While he was in Aquitaine the king had realized the need for a financial organization of the duchy independent of the seneschal, centralized at Bordeaux; and his decision, after his return to England, to make the exchequer in Westminster responsible for all the income of the Crown was doubtless influenced by his experience in the south. The new policy was not always effective but its results in the case of taxation were both immediate and lasting. Henceforth the proceeds of the lay subsidies were paid into the treasury either in cash or receipts for cash which had been paid elsewhere in accordance with writs of assignment or other writs; records of receipts and expenditure were kept by the officers of the lower exchequer on their receipt and issue rolls; the final audit was made in the upper exchequer. The subsidies became the most important of the 'foreign' accounts administered by the exchequer.

The most striking fact revealed by a general survey is the absence of local opposition to the assessment and collection of these subsidies. Here and there a steward tried to prevent the intrusion of the taxers into the lands of his lord; now and then minor disturbances are recorded; but there would seem to have been no serious resistance. On the other hand, as the subsidies became more frequent, the proceeds decreased.

While the fifteenth of 1290 brought in nearly £117,000, the ninth of 1297, a much heavier tax, brought in only £34,419. Of course, there was a great difference between the grateful mood in which the fifteenth of 1290 was granted and the war-weariness and impatience with which the ninth – the heaviest and last of four annual taxes – was received. Moreover, in 1297 the method of assessment was changed. The valuation was made by sworn men of each vill, not, as had previously been the practice, by twelve men of the hundred who valued the goods of every tenant in every vill with the assistance of the reeve and four men of the vill. With one exception, in 1306, this easier method continued until the process of assessment ceased in 1334, to be replaced by a fixed payment, and, as time passed, multiples of payment, from each unit of assessment, that is, each vill and borough. The change made in 1334 was a temporary expedient to avoid corrupt practices; but the careful allocation made by collective agreement in this year between officials of the exchequer and the localities endured for nearly three hundred years. It is easy to imagine the state of things which made the adoption of a fixed and unchangeable sum such a relief to the central authority. Between 1275 and 1332 the country had been subjected eighteen times to a searching visitation. Chief taxers in each shire had had to arrange for the assessment of the goods of every householder, in every grade of society. They had been provided with detailed but variable and perplexing instructions about taxable goods and the goods exempt from taxation, instructions which they must interpret as best they could in the light of customary regard for the maintenance of life and for standards of living. Most of the local assessments, made by neighbours, were beyond the cognizance of the chief taxers. Their writs and returns, priceless to the social historian, are also so full of anomalies that only rough-and-ready principles can be deduced from their precise details. Behind the scenes, where peasants and burgesses wrangled about what should or should not be taxed of their stores and clothes and household utensils, peace can only have been preserved by timely concessions and convenient oversights. Yet, in the course of Edward's reign, over £400,000 were raised from lay subsidies. How was it done?

There can be no doubt that, beneath all their grumbling and evasions, these lords, knights, burgesses, and peasants had become aware of a common obligation. Their acquiescence was certainly not a form of inertia; its roots lay deeper than any respect for the constitutional niceties which may perplex the historian, for very few of them could have had even the vaguest ideas about such matters. They inherited the silent garnered experience of centuries in the common life of home, village, parish church, market, hundred, and shire; they had learned that the natural and ordered activities in which they shared, in the fields, in the courts, on juries and commissions, in watch and ward, on hue and cry, were but parts of a greater whole and subject to a wider loyalty, to whose calls they must respond, as they responded when their landmarks were removed or a felon was at large. They were susceptible to propaganda as they were to the influence of local loyalties, feuds, and passions. And when, through sheriffs and tax collectors, the king took them into his confidence, he had this in mind. Neither he nor those whom he addressed had any precise conceptions of representation or consent, in the sense . . . emphasized by later historians. That the talk in and after the meetings of the courts in which the representatives of shires and boroughs were selected was important in the history of political education nobody should deny; but the primary intention of the royal writs was to state how and why something was to be done, to associate the future taxpayers with the government and, as far as possible, to enlist loyal support in the interests of the common good. The widespread application throughout western Europe of the legal principle that those concerned in a matter should concur in what was done had meant this, though, especially in ecclesiastical quarters, it might mean a good deal more. The representatives who came to parliament with full powers came to 'hear and do what was necessary for the common convenience of the realm' (1300) or, in more generous terms, 'to treat, ordain and do' what was required to avoid the dangers which threatened the realm (1295). We do not know exactly how they did this, or to what extent they were given or took the opportunity to make themselves better informed and to express their opinions, short of formal sessions and votes. They did enough to justify the statement that they had granted an aid. Then in the writs appointing tax collectors and writs ordering the sheriffs to help the collectors, the consent of the various classes of the community to a 'gracious' or 'courteous' subsidy was described, 'as if to remind a reluctant population that they are committed by their representatives to the payment of the tax'.

It was not only in parliament, however, that consent to taxation was given. In 1294 Edward I obtained the grant of a tax on wool exports from an assembly of wool merchants, and intermittently over the next sixty years similar

*assemblies were summoned, to which historians have given the high-sounding
title of 'The Estate of Merchants'. In her masterly survey of the medieval
English wool trade Professor Power summarized much of what is known of this
nebulous body and described the stages by which control of taxation on wool
passed from their hands into those of parliament.*

63 EILEEN POWER

If the development of parliament was thus bound up with royal finance,
it immediately becomes clear why the early stages of its history ran in
double harness with the history of another body to which historians
have given the name (the somewhat misleading name) of the Estate of
Merchants, and why it was only with the dissolution of that other body
that parliament emerged as a single body in control of taxation. The
appearance of a separate body of merchants – or rather of wool merchants – was due to the character of the particular tax that evoked
it: a tax on the export of wool. It is important to remember that the
wool merchants were only a section of the merchants engaged in
foreign trade, and a still smaller section of the general merchants of the
country. The burgess members of any Edwardian parliament comprised, in addition to the handful of big traders usually concerned in
foreign trade, a great mass of respectable middling members of town
gilds. Some of the big capitalists were wool exporters, some members
of merchant gilds were up-country wool middlemen. But the bulk
were concerned not merely in wool but in all sorts of miscellaneous
commodities, the groceries, merceries, haberdasheries, foodstuffs and
what not, of everyday trade in innumerable boroughs and market
towns. It is this great miscellaneous interest which was represented by
the burgesses in parliament, and among these burgesses the wool interest
had only a modest proportional representation. But economically the
wool merchants were an over-powerful group, because it was they who
handled the staple commodity of England, the one which could be
taxed, and when taxed provide an important proportion of the revenue.
It was almost inevitable in these circumstances that side by side with a
parliament which was only just finding its feet there should stand this
other body with its special interest and its special powers – the body of
wool merchants.

Indeed, for forty years after the *Confirmatio Cartarum* [1297, *see below* no. 65] the king went on negotiating with the merchants. From time to time he put on an extra tax on wool, yet never got into trouble unless it looked as though the tax would be heavy and more than temporary. Then the country began to get restive at once. On one occasion only, in 1333, did parliament raise any objection, and then it objected that the people were damaged and not that it had not consented.

The second phase in our story begins with the Hundred Years War. In 1336 the king was in urgent need of money for war. He had got from parliament a tenth and fifteenth on movables, but that was not enough. So in September there were issued summons simultaneously for a great council and an assembly of merchants at Nottingham. The great council granted another tenth and fifteenth and the assembly of merchants granted a 40*s* 'maltote' on export of wool. But it was now clearly realized that the 'maltote' would hit the growers, and be opposed by them, and that their objections had to be forestalled. So with the imposition of the 'maltote' an attempt was also made to fix a scale of minimum prices payable to growers.

With this attempt at a compromise a new era opens. In spite of the fixed price schedule, the merchants are agreeable because they have obtained, as their *quid pro quo*, a monopoly in the export of wool, and a consequent prospect of passing the tax to the foreign consumers. In the next year, to mark the compromise, there begins a great series of loans and taxes *in* wool, which are raised from growers and handled by merchants. And throughout the period the three forces, the king, parliament and merchants, are involved in a major constitutional readjustment, and the issue slowly and finally shifts from abolition to control. The parliament continues its traditional opposition to 'maltote'. It demands its abolition in 1339, and several times prefers large grants in wool to the tax. But it is gradually and grudgingly converted to the view that the king must have it, and then it begins to demand to control it. Parliament gets to this point in 1340 and grants the tax for one year only. But when the year is up the king keeps it on as a 'maltote'. Parliament requests its abolition in 1343 but agrees to a compromise, and grants it for three years with revised minimum prices. At the end of the period, the king keeps it on as a 'maltote'. The parliament demands abolition again in 1346 and 1348, and it is not until 1350 that it at last reconciles itself to the tax, grants it, and henceforth converts it into a permanent parliamentary subsidy, though it is still talking about the possibility of superseding it as late as 1362. But during this period the issue has definitely shifted, though with the utmost reluctance on the part of parliament, from abolition to control. Rather than have an extraordinary 'maltote' granted by merchants, parliament has agreed to a regular subsidy granted by itself.

In 1254 Henry III was in Gascony in urgent need of money for the war there. In this letter the regents, Henry III's Queen, Eleanor, and his brother, Richard, earl of Cornwall, report to him on their attempts to obtain a subsidy. It is apparent that already by 1254 the prelates cannot grant a subsidy, without the assent of the lower clergy, and the magnates do not do so without the assent of the lower laity. Representative knights of the shire were summoned to an assembly later in the year, perhaps in consequence of this refusal of the magnates to commit anyone to taxation apart from themselves. The text does not permit us to postulate that as early as 1254 the magnates felt themselves unable to bind their social inferiors. All previous lay subsidies had been granted by assemblies which, as far as the evidence goes, probably consisted solely of magnates. Nevertheless the vertical bonds of society were so much weakened by 1254, and the political and economic power of the gentry had grown so much that it was possible for the magnates, when faced with a demand for a subsidy for a purpose of which they disapproved, to side-step the issue plausibly and leave the regents with the problem of obtaining consent to taxation on a broader basis.

64 QUEEN ELEANOR AND RICHARD OF CORNWALL 1254

. . . May your reverend lordship know that the lords the Earl Marshal and John Baliol were delayed on the sea by contrary winds for twelve days. They reached us in England on 4 February. We held 'treaty' with the prelates and magnates of your realm of England, on the matter of your subsidy, both on 27 January before the arrival of the Earl and John and after their arrival. . . . And the archbishops and bishops told us that if the king of Castile attacks you in Gascony each of them will aid you from his own goods, in such a way that you should be eternally grateful. But they have been able to do nothing about making an aid to you from their clergy without the assent of those clergy; nor do they believe that their clergy can be induced to offer you any aid, unless the tenth . . . [already granted and now due] . . . is withdrawn. . . .

And they will apply themselves diligently to persuading the clergy subject to them to come to your assistance . . . and they will have *tractatus* with them; but at the date when the bearer of these letters leaves, no subsidy has as yet been granted by the said clergy.

Furthermore, as we have notified you elsewhere, if the king of Castile attacks you in Gascony, all the earls and barons of your kingdom who are able to make the crossing will come to you in Gascony with all their force. But we do not believe that we shall be able to get any aid to meet your need from the other laity who will not cross to join you, unless you write to your vicegerents in England, that they will cause the great charters of liberty to be firmly held, and that this will be firmly commanded by your letters sent to every sheriff of your realm, and publicly proclaimed throughout every shire of the realm. In this way, they will be greatly inspired freely to offer you an aid, for many complain that the said charters are not held by the sheriffs and other bailiffs of yours as they ought to be held.

It is to be noted by your lordship that since we shall hold *tractatus* with the clergy and laity at Westminster about the said aid, a fortnight after next Easter, we beg your lordship to write back with as much speed as you can to inform us of your pleasure in the above matters. . . .

Given at Windsor, 14 February, in the 38th year of your reign [1254].

In 1297 Edward I, hard pressed by political circumstances, faced with war in both Flanders and Scotland at the same time, was compelled to yield to the claims of the more vocal part of his baronage. Under pressure he confirmed both Magna Carta and the Forest Charter and added the following clauses, promising not to levy any future taxes, whether direct or indirect, without the common assent of the whole kingdom. The magnates' intention in extorting this promise was to ensure that the king was in future obliged to obtain some sort of consent from them, but they did not yet specify that such consent must be obtained·in parliament. The objectionable wool tax had been negotiated with the wool exporters, and not with the wool producers upon whom it fell in reality. The most important wool producers, however, apart from ecclesiastical corporations, were the great magnates who ran sheep ranches in the Welsh Marches, in the Peak District or on the Yorkshire Wolds. No taxation without common consent in 1297 meant at least 'no taxation without magnate consent', if not something rather broader. Like King John, Edward I sought and obtained papal absolution from his promises. Confirmatio Cartarum, *like the original*

Magna Carta, soon ceased to be binding, and it was not until 1362 that it was finally and definitively established that consent to any taxation, whether direct or indirect, must be obtained in parliament, and that the commons must participate in granting it.

65 STATUTE ROLL 1297

And whereas some people of our kingdom are fearful that the aids and taxes (mises), which by their liberality and good will they have heretofore paid [*fait*] to us for the sake of our wars and other needs, shall despite the nature of the grants, be turned into a servile obligation for them and their heirs because these [payments] may at a future time be found in the rolls, and likewise the prises that in our name have been taken throughout the kingdom by our ministers; therefore we have granted, for us and our heirs, that, on account of anything that has been done or that can be found from a roll or in some other way, we will not make into a precedent for the future any such aids, mises, or prises.

And for us and our heirs we have also granted to the archbishops, bishops, abbots, priors, and other folk of Holy Church, and to the earls and barons and the whole community of the land, that on no account will we henceforth take from our kingdom such aids, mises, and prises, except by the common assent of the whole kingdom and for the common benefit of the same kingdom, saving the ancient aids and prises due and accustomed.

And whereas the greater part of the community all feel themselves gravely oppressed by the *maltolt* on wool – that is to say, 40s from each sack of wool – and have besought us to relieve them [of the charge], at their prayer we have fully relieved them, granting that henceforth we will take neither this nor any other [custom] without their common assent and good will, saving to us and our heirs the custom on wool, wool-fells, and hides previously granted by the community of the kingdom aforesaid.

In testimony whereof we have caused to be written these our letters patent. Given at Ghent, November 5, in the twenty-fifth year of our reign.

Legislation in Early Parliaments

66 HELEN CAM

There has been so much discussion, and that so learned, of the nature of law in the Middle Ages, that it will be well for me to begin with a disclaimer. What I am concerned with is not so much law as laws, not so much theory as practice, not so much forms as forces. The great American school of legal historians may be right in saying that none save God could *make* law in the Middle Ages, but the student of medieval English government is confronted with assizes, establishments, provisions, ordinances, proclamations, and statutes that men observed or infringed and that judges enforced. They existed, and they mattered; they are both a monument to human activity and an indication of human intentions and opinions. In asking how and why they came to be there I am seeking the originating impulse for legislation rather than investigating its technical validity or the authority and status of the legislator. . . .

Who made the laws in medieval England? That is the question that I want to put, limiting myself to the last three centuries of the Middle Ages, to which the bulk of the enacted laws belong. . . .

There are three main sources of legislative activity in medieval England: the directive or planning urge in the ruler, the need for clarifying and defining experienced by the judicature, and the demand from the ruled for redress of grievances.

To the first source, the desire of the executive for order, we can attribute a large part of the legislation of the thirteenth century – such measures, e.g., as the police code built up by Henry III and Edward I from the Assize of Arms to the Statute of Winchester, the order for the holding of hundred courts in 1234, the succession of decrees on the coinage, the series of Exchequer ordinances down to Stapleton's of 1323, and Edward I's great Statute of Wales, the first colonial constitution. We have a glimpse of one of the departmental discussions, which produced such regulations in the preamble to the *Provisio super vicecomites et clericos suos* of 1298, which shows how three bishops, the king's treasurer, the barons of the exchequer, the justices of the bench, and others of the king's council, being assembled in the Exchequer on the feast of St Valentine, had before them the problem of the literate but dishonest clerk who made out writs for levying excessive dues, and thus involved his illiterate but innocent chief, the sheriff, in penalties for extortion. They took counsel for a remedy and provided that henceforth the clerk should share his master's responsibility to the Exchequer. Official decrees of this sort might or might not need wide publicity, and a large proportion of them were not promulgated in parliaments. I do not propose to discuss them at length; administrative legislation is with us today and we know all about it and its sources. But the directive impulse of the administration, and above all of the council, is a continuing influence throughout the Middle Ages, originating, selecting, and amending the measures that become laws, not least in the period when the forms of legislation would seem to suggest a receptive rather than constructive attitude on the part of the government.

The second source, the judicature, is most important in the first of our three centuries. The judgment in a particular case, formally recorded as a precedent for the direction of future judges and litigants, belongs to the period when parliaments are still pre-eminently judicial occasions, and there are several instances of such *ad hoc* legislation on the rolls of Edward I's parliaments. The Statute of Waste of 1292, as is well known, is the judgement in the case of *Butler* v. *Hopton* after long discussion among the king's justices in full parliament. The two 'explanations' attached to the Statute of Gloucester, in effect revisions of a clumsily drafted enactment, have been traced by Mr Sayles to two lawsuits, of 1278 and 1281, in which Eleanor Percy and the mayor and bailiffs of London, respectively, were involved. The Ordinance *de Proteccionibus* in 1305 arose out of the particular grievance of the prior of St Oswald's, who could not get redress from a defendant who was wrongfully pleading the king's protection. In 1315 the *specialis petitio* of Katharine Jordan as to some sharp practice in a plea of Novel Disseisin produced a *generalis responsio* imposing penalties to be enforced by the justices in all such cases. The transition from judicial to legislative remedy is perhaps indicated in a petition of 1318, when, in response to Robert of Mouhaut's complaint as to the penalizing of an attainted jury, the council reply that to change the laws of the realm requires the greatest deliberation, and that in full parliament. Aside from judgments, it was, of course, in the great statutes of Edward I from 1275 onwards, modifying and defining the operation of the Common Law, that the judges made their greatest contribution to the statute book.

But the most abundant source of law-making is the third: public demand, direct or indirect, implicit or explicit; and parliaments were at once the field in which such impulses could work and, as time went on, the institution by means of which men could assert and enlarge their claims to law and justice. It is mainly, though not solely, with legislation in parliaments that we shall be concerned.

Eileen Power has depicted the interplay of motives among the different parties concerned in the establishment of parliamentary control of the wool taxes. I should like to glance at another example of economic legislative experiment involving various interests, and consider the Statute of the Staple of 1354.

The staple for English merchants set up by Edward I had been at Bruges, Antwerp, and St Omer by turns when, in the Parliament of York in 1318, the question of the establishment of home staples was mooted, and a conference was arranged in the following year between the merchants and the Exchequer officials with others of the council, which reported in favour of the establishment of home staples. Political factions in the council, it seems, held up action till 1326 when, under the influence of the younger Dispenser, ordinances made 'by us and our council for the common profit and relief of the people of all our realm and power' set up the fourteen home staples and laid down regulations for native and alien merchants, purchasers, and manufacturers. In 1328, however, the matter was reopened and the different towns were asked to send delegates to an assembly of merchants at York. The London delegates, writing back to the city for further instructions, indicate the difficulties of the assembly; the towns cannot agree, the merchants of the staple want a foreign staple, and they are all afraid of incurring the enmity of the king and council if they fail to make a recommendation. The compromise suggested by the city fathers in their reply was in fact accepted, the ordinances of 1326 were repealed in the Parliament of Northampton, and free trade 'after the tenor of the Great Charter' was established for the time being. A petition from the good folk of the community in the Parliament of York of 1334 for the restoration of the home staples was rejected and in 1340, the war with France having begun, Edward III established an overseas staple at Bruges in the lands of his continental ally. In the April parliament of 1343, in response to an inquiry from the council, the merchants put forward a long and reasoned statement in favour of home staples, but foreign policy still outweighed their arguments and it was not till 1353 that they had their way. In September of that year a Great Council was held, expressly to deal with the maintenance and good government of the staple. A set of carefully drafted ordinances, drawn up by the king's council at least three months earlier, according to Mr Richardson, was read aloud to the prelates, magnates and commons assembled in the White Chamber of Westminster Palace; any amendments proposed to be given in writing. The commons demanded a copy of the ordinances; one was given to the knights and another to the burgesses, and after great deliberation had amongst themselves they gave their opinion in writing. The magnates having read and discussed this written statement, the ordinances were issued in their final form. Only one amendment of the commons is recorded; they proposed to add eight more towns to the list of staples, bringing the number up to seventeen. The king accepted the suggestion only as far as regarded Canterbury 'in honour of St Thomas'. The commons further petitioned that the articles of the ordinances should be recited at the next parliament, and entered on the roll of parliament, so that ordinances and agreements made in council should not be on record as if they had been made in common parliament, and to this the king assented. Thus in the following April the chief justice expounded to the lords and commons in parliament how the king had established the staple in England, and how no staple could be maintained without fixed laws and customs, and therefore he had deputed the wise men of his council and the prelates, dukes, earls, barons, justices, serjeants, and others of the commonalty to ordain and make such laws and ordinances; and because he wished them to endure for ever he now caused them to be recited in parliament to endure for ever as a statute. Once again the knights of the shire were invited to get written copies and study them and, if they wished, propose amendments in writing. And after good deliberation the commons found the ordinances good and profitable for king and people and prayed that they might be confirmed, putting forward a number of supplementary proposals, most of which were accepted, and the ordinances, being confirmed, with these additions, by the king and the magnates, were finally placed on the statute roll.

So much for the genesis of the Statute of the Staple of 1354, the fruit of thirty-five years of bargaining, diplomacy, and compromise between king, merchants, burgesses, magnates, and council. . . .

As regards the medieval statute there is a good deal to be said for Dyer's description of the preamble to a statute as 'a key to open the minds of the makers of the act and of the mischiefs they intend to remedy'. I will quote some of Edward I's alleged reasons for legislation in chronological order. 'Because our lord the King greatly desires to redress the state of the realm where it needs amendment, and that for the common profit of Holy Church and of the realm' (1275); 'the king providing for the fuller administration of right as the royal office demands' (1278); 'because merchants have fallen into poverty through failure to recover their debts' (1283); 'to make good the oppressions and defects of former statutes' (1285); 'of his special grace, and for the affection that he bears towards prelates, earls, barons and others of his kingdom' (1290); 'since the Abbots of Fécamp and St Edmunds and divers others supplicated in parliament' (1290); 'at the instance of the magnates of his realm' (1290); 'on the grievous complaint both of religious and of others of the kingdom' (1292); 'understanding by the public and frequent complaint of the middling folk . . . we have decreed in parliament for the common welfare' (1293); 'having diligently meditated on the defects in the law and the many grievances and oppressions inflicted on the people in time past we wish to provide a remedy and establish the certainty of the law' (1299); 'in favour of the poor workmen of this city who live by the work of their hands, lest they should lack meat and be impoverished' (1302); 'since those who have been put out of the forest by the perambulation have made request at this parliament' – that is, the parliament of 1305, on whose rolls four such petitions are recorded.

If these preambles give the key to Edward's mind, we seem to see a benevolent and order-loving legislator, passing from concern for a complete and coherent system of law to a growing consciousness of personal and class grievances calling for redress. Without any intention of calling the nation into partnership with him, it is clear that Edward was to some extent permitting his subjects to suggest, if not dictate, matter for legislation.

The Omnicompetence of Parliament

This section on the functions of early parliaments has been divided into sub-sections dealing with politics, justice, petitions, taxation and legislation. This division and categorization goes back to Maitland (see above no. 52), but it is well to end the section with Professor Powicke's warning against 'too eager definition' and Professor Edward's salutary reminder of the lack of differentiation in function in early parliaments, and of their omnicompetence even in the period before these assemblies came to include representative elements.

67 SIR MAURICE POWICKE

The mystery which attends on the beginnings of parliament is not peculiar to these particular happenings. It is the mystery which attends on all beginnings, when men are doing things because they are convenient and do not attach conscious significance to them, still less consider what the distant outcome of their acts may be. The word was in the air, the materials were to hand. To track down every nerve in the body politic and locate each impulse, as though they carried some secret message, is as futile as to read into the rivulets which compose the upmost waters of the Thames a foresight of the wharves and shipping in its spacious estuary. Nor should we injure the fragile uncertainties of these beginnings by too eager definition. Some would deny any relevance to the great dispute about parliament in the tendencies at work in the court of King Henry. Others would press too hard the coincidence of interest between the meetings of the great council and the arrangement of judicial business in the law terms. It is safer to state the facts. 'Parliament' was not what lawyers call a term of art. It might merely mean a colloquy or it might describe a meeting of magnates summoned to a stated place at a stated time for a particular purpose. In neither case did it suggest specialized functions. A baron in the Welsh marches whose bailiff gathered the vassals together for business had his parliament; and when Marchers and Welshmen met in conference they had a parliament. Similarly, the tradition of great annual feasts attended by the king's vassals had never been lost, but their regularity had been broken, whereas the great councils summoned to treat with the king on the affairs of the realm had too often assumed the character of parleys between divided interests. In Henry's reign under new conditions the Norman tradition tended to revive, yet at the same time the great councils tended to express an independence of their own. This does not mean that there were two kinds of parliament, but that there was a distinction between the conditions which made the king and his servants on the one hand and the magnates on the other aware of the value of parliament. In Edward I's time the coincidence in time and place between parliaments regarded from these two points of view is complete. Parliaments, except possibly, though not certainly, during Edward's absence in Gascony (1286–9), were held nearly every year, once, twice, or thrice, generally in Westminster and notably at Michaelmas and Easter. The presence of knights and burgesses was not yet a criterion of parliament; it became a general rule only during the first quarter of the fourteenth century. A parliament, we are told, implied the judicial activity which arose, as we have seen, from the co-operation of king and administration in the affairs of state. If this activity were not exercised in an assembly, even though knights and burgesses were present, the assembly was not, we are told, described in official documents as a parliament. Yet developments in England were due to the appreciation of the twofold nature of parliament, whereas in France, where the stress lay on its judicial nature, the history of parliament took a different course.

King and magnates were more closely allied than they knew. Their quarrels were domestic, inside the great house of the king. Their relations had been defined in the great councils of 1234, and when the charters were confirmed in 1237. Their troubles were largely due to bad temper. On both sides, nay, on all sides intelligence and good sense were marred by lack of restraint. In 1255 the marshal, Roger Bigod, earl of Norfolk, whose wife was a daughter of William the Lion, interceded with Henry for Robert de Ros, the lord of Wark in Northumberland. Robert had incurred Henry's displeasure by his tactless tutorship of the young king of Scotland and the young queen, Henry's daughter. Henry, as usual, flew into a rage and called the earl a traitor. 'You lie,' said the earl, 'I have never been a traitor nor shall I ever be. If you are just, how can you harm me?' The King retorted: 'I can seize your corn and thrash it and sell it.' 'Do so,' said the earl, 'and I will send back your threshers without their heads.' Friends interposed to separate the pair; but, adds Matthew Paris, the windy words bred anger and hatred.

History, even constitutional history, is the history of persons. We are dealing with men who lived well, loved tournaments, and liked romances better than law books. And Henry had the tongue of an asp.

68 SIR GORONWY EDWARDS

If then we reject the latter-day doctrine that the dispensing of 'justice' was the 'essence' of parliament, and that the other functions – summarized in 1280 as 'attending to the great business of the realm' – were merely something 'added', and were therefore something 'non-essential' which may and should be 'stripped away'; must we therefore proceed now to reverse the doctrine, and say that 'attending to the great business of the realm' was the 'essence' of parliament, and that the dispensing of 'justice' was the 'non-essential' function which was 'added' and which may therefore be 'stripped away'? The answer is that neither function may rightly be 'stripped away' – that is, if we wish to see the pre-representative parliament as it really was. The evidence as a whole indicates that the functional 'essence' of the pre-representative parliaments, so far from being 'judicial', consisted rather in *not being* 'judicial'. Important 'judicial' functions could be, and often were, performed in parliament, but the essence of its functions was not specifically judicial, any more than it was specifically legislative, or specifically taxative, or specifically anything. The essence of its function consisted in being *unspecific*, in being *omni*competent, in ranging over the whole field of lay government, in exercising (always, of course, in association with the king, who was 'its head, its beginning and its end') those functions of government which, in the earliest extant description of English parliaments, are summarised as 'viewing the state of the realm and treating the common business of the kingdom and of the king'.

It seems, then, that if we are to understand the medieval English parliament as it really was, we must regard it as having been in origin not 'a high court of justice', not a high court *of* anything, but simply a high court. The medieval king, in England as in some places elsewhere, was deemed to act always (as the phrase went) 'with counsel'. Sometimes, indeed, that counsel might be regarded as 'evil counsel', but good or evil it was 'with counsel' that the king was deemed to act. In England it was in parliament that the king found counsel at its amplest, so it was in parliament that his power was legally at its highest. That was why parliament was a 'high court' and why king in parliament was omnicompetent. Such was the essence of the pre-representative parliament in England. To it the king and his ministers added the representatives of shires and boroughs. These representatives enlarged the existing amplitude of parliament with a new amplitude because, humble vessels though they were, yet legally they were vessels of power: the king commanded them to bring – and they duly brought – to parliament from the local communities of shire and borough a *potestas* that was called *plena*. This 'full power' was, as the solitary chronicler who mentions the summoning of representatives duly points out, a 'potestas obligandi comitatum, et faciendi quod per consilium regis ordinaretur'. This fusion of the omnicompetence of the pre-representative parliament with the full power of the representatives to 'obligate' the local communities persisted beneath 'the drums and tramplings' of five centuries, and thereby provided the groundwork of ideas for that doctrine of parliamentary sovereignty which became, from a legal point of view, 'the dominant characteristic of English political institutions'.

The Great Variety of Business in a Single Parliament

The narrative of the Hilary parliament at Lincoln in 1316, which was one of the focal points of the reign of Edward II, is taken from the memoranda kept at the time by the king's express order by William de Ayremynne, who was one of the inner group of civil servants and is thought by some historians to have been the author of the Modus (see above no. 25). Apart from the very short narrative passage in the memoranda of the Lenten parliament of 1305, it is the first 'parliament roll' which is not exclusively a record of cases and petitions dealt with in time of parliament, and as such it anticipates the type of narrative record kept by the clerks of parliament after 1330. It reveals a mixed pattern of politics, taxation, legislation, justice and administration, with politics in the foreground. It is not however the only record of this parliament. Sewn up together with this parchment sheet or membrane are seven other sheets which include a variety of matter. The second membrane, also written by Ayremynne, describes the argeement between the earl of Lancaster and the king in parliament, and the third contains a statute made then, together with the settlement of a brawl in parliament between two magnates, and a case in parliament involving the abduction of an heiress by a magnate. The other membranes each cover a single subject. One deals with diplomatic negotiations between the king and the count of Flanders over a number of years, but without any apparent relationship to this parliament, whilst the others concern lawsuits. Two of the cases were certainly opened by petitions to the king in this parliament, but were carried on and brought to a conclusion later. Although the other three suits may equally have started in the same way, only the narrative of their later development is recorded. The whole 'roll' was printed in Rotuli Parliamentorum, I, 350–64. In addition to these eight membranes sewn together, another totally separate 'parliament roll' also survives from the same meeting which contains forty petitions to the king in parliament. These were printed in Rotuli Parliamentorum, I, 334–49, with the exception of one entry which was omitted and only appeared in the Rotuli Parliamentorum Hactenus Inediti, p. 63. Over and above these two 'parliament rolls' there are numerous entries in the close and patent rolls relating to this parliament. These record the letters sent out by the chancery. Many of them, such as the writs of summons, or the writs de expensis, add nothing to our knowledge of what was done in parliament. Others add only a little to our knowledge, such as the writs concerning the application of the forest laws or those about raising the army which was to go to Scotland. A third group refers in passing to events which we would not otherwise have known to have taken place in parliament, the discussion of a clerical subsidy, and of loans by various prelates, the decision that all holding lands worth above £50 a year should take up knighthood, or the setting up of a committee to deal with Scottish affairs. Of this information from 'official' sources, only Ayremynne's memoranda and the following membrane are here translated, although a considerable amount of extra information has been added from other sources. All such inserted matter has been placed in square brackets to distinguish it from Ayremynne's narrative.

69 PARLIAMENT ROLL 1316

Memoranda of the Parliament of Edward, King of England, son of Edward, formerly King of England, summoned and held at Lincoln on the quindene of St Hilary in the ninth year of the said king [27 January 1316], drawn up by William de Ayremynne, clerk in the royal chancery, nominated and specially deputed for that purpose by the king.

On Wednesday, the day after the quindene [28 January], the King who was staying in the residence of the Dean of Lincoln, made his entry into a chamber there in which the prelates, earls and others were assembled, and caused his wishes to be expounded in public by William Inge, one of the royal justices of the Common Bench:

The King much desired that the Parliament, which he had called for various and difficult business concerning himself and the condition of his kingdom, and in particular his land of Scotland, as set out in the summons to it, should be held with the utmost speed that should conveniently be possible. The King (wished) that this and other business to be dealt with in this parliament should similarly be speeded up, since he had great concern for the prelates, earls and others who had come from distant parts, for if his stay there should be long, it would prove tedious and burdensome for them, because of the high cost of provisions, which was then much greater than usual. [*Two successive harvest failures throughout western Europe brought about exceedingly high prices and a famine from which perhaps as many as a tenth of the population died.*]

Since Thomas, earl of Lancaster, and certain other magnates of the kingdom had not yet arrived, on whose advice the king wished to proceed in these difficult matters, the king wished to postpone the completion of this business until the arrival of these magnates. Nevertheless he enjoined the assembled prelates, earls and others to meet daily and continue the parliament, dealing with other business until the arrival of the absent magnates.

John de Sandale, the Chancellor, was ordered to receive the proxies and excuses of those prelates and others summoned to Parliament who were not coming. He and others, whom the king would associate with him, were ordered to examine them, and to file away the acceptable reasons for absence, if those excused had sent adequate proxies, but to bring to the king the names of those who were not coming, and who had either not excused themselves or not sent proxies, so he could then order what should be done.

And the king associated Walter of Norwich, Treasurer of England, and William Inge with the Chancellor.

The same day it was agreed that petitions should be received and dealt with as was formerly customary in other parliaments, and that they should be received until the day after the Purification and the day after that [3 and 4 February]. Robert de Askeby, a clerk of the chancery and Adam de Lymbergh, one of the remembrancers of the exchequer were nominated to receive the petitions which concerned England, and Master Edward de London, also a clerk of the chancery, and Master William de Maldon, one of the chamberlains of the exchequer, to receive the petitions of Gascony, Wales, Ireland and Scotland. Proclamation was made accordingly. After this the Chancellor and the Treasurer, and the Justices of both Benches were ordered to have a written abstract made of any business pending before them in their courts which could not be concluded out of parliament, and to refer it to parliament so that due action could be taken there.

On the following Thursday it was agreed to proceed with petitions until the arrival of the earl of Lancaster and the other absent magnates. Bishops John of Norwich, John of Chichester and Roger of Salisbury, with Edward Deyncourt, Philip de Kyme, John de Lisle, a baron of the exchequer, Henry Scrope, a justice of the Bench, and Robert de Bardelby, a clerk of the chancery were nominated to hear and deal with the petitions which concerned England. Bishops Henry of Winchester, Walter of Exeter, and John of Bath and Wells, with William

Inge and Masters Roger de Rothwell, Richard de Plumpstok, Thomas de Cherleton and Henry de Canterbury, clerks, were nominated for petitions about Gascony and the [Channel] Islands. Ralf Fitzwilliam, Master William de Birston, archdeacon of Gloucester, Master William Walewayn, escheator south of the Trent, with John Bush, Philip de Turville and John de Lisle, clerks, and John de Mutford, a Justice of assize, were nominated for petitions about Wales, Ireland and Scotland.

On the following Saturday, in the presence of the king, Humphrey de Bohun, earl of Hereford, addressed the prelates then present, on behalf of the king, about the petitions which the prelates had presented to the king on a previous occasion about the state of the church. He said that those petitions to which sufficient answers had been given, would be duly observed, and that replies which were less than satisfactory would be amended, and that reply would be made to those petitions to which no reply had yet been made, as should seem most advisable for the welfare of king, kingdom and church, [after discussion] between the king's council and the prelates and magnates.

[*Discussion of the so-called* Articuli Cleri *was brought to an end later in the year at the Michaelmas Parliament in York, when the conclusions were entered on the Statute Roll. They are printed, with translation, in* Statutes of the Realm, *I,* 171–4, *and it is apparent from the opening paragraph that the real work on this 'statute' was done in this Hilary parliament at Lincoln.*]

On the following Sunday, in the chamber of the king, the bishops of Norwich, Chichester, Exeter and Salisbury were sworn into the king's council. On the same day the king appointed the bishops of Norwich and Exeter, with John of Britanny, earl of Richmond, and the earl of Pembroke, to act during his absence on his behalf in parliament, until the arrival of the earl of Lancaster and the other magnates.

Afterwards on February 12th, a Thursday, in the hall of the dean of Lincoln, in full parliament, in the presence of the earl of Lancaster and the other magnates who had earlier been absent, but had now arrived, the king caused the reason for summoning parliament to be declared. He asserted that he had caused parliament to be specially summoned for the affairs of his land of Scotland, which was partly occupied by his enemies. He asked and enjoined the prelates, magnates and others of his faithful servants and subjects assembled there to advise him in this business and give him suitable assistance. After this it was agreed that the prelates and magnates should meet on the next day, Friday, in the chapter-house of the cathedral, to discuss this business.

On Friday [13 February] they met in the chapter house and discussed various matters among themselves, and in the end it was agreed, at the bidding of the king, to meet again on Saturday, at the house of the Carmelites in the city, to deal with the same business.

On Saturday [14 February] it was agreed to repeal a proclamation fixing maximum prices for oxen, cows, sheep, ducks, chickens and other provisions, and to let them be sold instead for 'reasonable' prices, as had previously been customary. Writs, under the great seal of the king, were prepared accordingly.

The same day agreement was reached on a Statute of Sheriffs and Hundreds, which is contained in another roll. [*It in fact appears on the third membrane sewn up with this roll, as well as in the Statute Roll. Printed, with translation, in* Statutes of the Realm, I, *174–5.*]

On the following Tuesday [17 February] in the presence of the king, and of the prelates and magnates, the bishop of Norwich, by command of the king, read out the foregoing conclusions, and added that the king wished the Ordinances, formerly made by the prelates and magnates and accepted by him [in 1311], to be observed in all points, and also the Perambulations of the Forest made in the time of Edward his father, reserving to the king the points in which he disputed those Perambulations. Letters and writs were made out accordingly, as are contained in another roll.

The copies of letters and writs enrolled in the patent and close rolls give rather more information, and reveal that there must have been considerable discussion of forests in parliament. They explain that the question had been raised in the form of a petition to the king in parliament on behalf of the prelates, earls, barons and community of the realm complaining against infringements of the perambulations, by which the bounds of the forests were fixed. They explain also that the king's dispute with the perambulations consisted of his wishing to reafforest any lands omitted from them which had been forest in the time of Henry II. And they reveal the means of settling this dispute. An inquest was to be held on 25 April before the royal council at Westminster, at which two knights from each shire were to be present as well as all the forest officials, who were to come with their records. Records in the possession of former forest officials or their descendants were to be sent, and the Exchequer was to produce any relevant documents, including Domesday

Book, so that the king should have the best possible opportunity of proving his case.]

The Bishop (of Norwich) also said certain things on behalf of the king addressed to the earl of Lancaster, which are contained in another roll [*in fact they are contained in the second membrane, translated below pp. 209–10*].

On the following Friday [20 February] the magnates and the community of the realm granted the king one able-bodied foot-soldier from every township in England, except from the cities, boroughs and royal demesne, for his Scottish war. Such foot-soldiers were to be provided with 'aketons' and bascinets [helmets] and armed with swords, bows, arrows, slings, pikes or other arms suitable for foot-soldiers. And the men [of the township] shall provide the arms of the foot-soldiers at their own expense, and the expenses of the soldiers on the way to the place to which the king shall summon his army for his war, and their wages after their arrival, for sixty days at most, while waiting there or proceeding on the King's service, at the rate of fourpence a day for each infantryman. If a town has a market and is able to bear the cost of more than one infantryman, it shall bear a greater expense. And the king agreed to grant letters patent on behalf of himself and his heirs to the magnates and community of the realm, guaranteeing that this grant of foot-soldiers should not be used as a precedent in future to the prejudice of them or their heirs. On the same day, by the advice of the magnates, the king ordered that all his 'servitium debitum' [the feudal army] should be called out for this campaign, and should be at Newcastle-on-Tyne on the quindene of the Nativity of St John the Baptist [6 July]. [*Although there is no mention of it in Ayremynne's Memoranda the close rolls provide evidence that all those with a landed income of £50 a year or more were to be compelled to take up knighthood, by a regulation made in this parliament, presumably to augment the feudal army in the Scottish campaign.*]

[*On the back of the membrane there is a note to the effect that:*]

The citizens, burgesses and knights of the shires who came to parliament, granted the king, as an aid for his Scottish campaign, a fifteenth part of such movable goods as the citizens, burgesses and other inhabitants of the cities, boroughs and royal demesne had at the previous Michaelmas. For this purpose any cities, boroughs or royal demesne which are in other hands for a term of life count as being in royal hands.

[*There is no note, however, to the effect that the clergy present in parliament met and discussed a grant, but failed to make one through a misunderstanding. They were later convened again in convocation to make a grant, according to the close rolls.*]

[*On the second membrane is a fuller account of the events of 17 February*:]

On the Tuesday before Lent, in the parliament of King Edward at Lincoln, in the presence of the king, and of the prelates, magnates and others who were assembled for parliament, the Bishop of Norwich, by the king's command, explained the reasons why the king had summoned the parliament and other business concerning the king as contained in another roll [*in fact in the first membrane of Ayremynne's memoranda, see above pp. 207–8*]. He further went on to address certain words to Thomas earl of Lancaster, on behalf of the king, in order to remove certain doubts which the earl was said to entertain concerning the king. He assured him that the king had acted sincerely and honestly towards him and the other magnates of his realm, and held them, as his faithful liege men in his special royal good will as was fitting. And he said that the king wished the earl to become head of his council, and asked him, on behalf of the king, and of the prelates and magnates present, to agree to assume that post effectively, and to give appropriate aid and counsel in the affairs of the king and the kingdom as he was bound to do. And the earl, thanking the king, humbly asked to be given an opportunity to consider the matter before replying.

And afterwards the earl was sworn of the king's council in the following words:

Our lord King Edward, by the grace of God king of England, with the prelates, earls and barons of his land in full parliament has requested his dear cousin Thomas earl of Lancaster to become his principal counsellor in all great and weighty matters concerning himself and his kingdom, to seek out with other prelates, earls and barons what should be most profitable for himself and the kingdom. Thomas earl of Lancaster has therefore agreed to be of the council of the king, with the other prelates, earls and barons, for the great love that he has towards his lord the king, and for the common welfare of the kingdom, and because the king has covenanted to keep to the ordinances and uphold the rightful laws in all respects, and also in the hope of being able to amend many things which are amiss in his household and kingdom. However if the king does not follow the advice given by him and the others of his council in matters concerning his household and his realm, then the earl of Lancaster, after he has pointed this out to the king, and if the latter still does not redress matters according to the counsel given by the earl and others, can then discharge himself from the royal council without evil intention, reproach or ill will. No business concerning the king and his kingdom shall be undertaken without the assent of the earl and of the other prelates, earls and barons who have been ordained to counsel the king. And if any of those prelates, earls or barons in advising the king, or otherwise, shall do anything prejudicial to him or his kingdom, he shall be removed [from the council] at the next parliament on the advice of the king himself. And so on from parliament to parliament with regard to each of them [i.e. the councillors] according to the faults found in them. In witness whereof this statement of the conditions made by the earl of Lancaster shall be entered in the roll of parliament.

A statement in these terms was handed to William de Ayremynne, clerk, by the treasurer, Walter, bishop of Norwich, and Bartholomew de Badlesmere with the instruction from the king that William should have this statement enrolled word for word in the parliament roll. Nevertheless that statement is sewn to this roll [*and it still is. Comparison of the entry in the roll with the attached piece of parchment, from which the earl perhaps read out his conditions in parliament, shows with what exactitude the latter was copied. The earl's statement of conditions is in French, the remainder of the roll is in Latin.*]

In Perspective

To put the origins of parliament in perspective we must turn away from the thirteenth and fourteenth centuries and must look at the successive metamorphoses of the institution over the succeeding six centuries, and its transplantation and adaptation to the needs of new countries in the Americas, Africa and Asia.

Although the outward forms of parliament, as they were formalized in the fourteenth and fifteenth centuries, remained much the same until the nineteenth century, the spirit of parliament completely changed. Medieval conceptions of sovereignty were displaced in England in the seventeenth century. The political balance between crown and community irrevocably altered at the same time, and so did the relative importance of the two houses. The seventeenth-century revolution in constitutional realities, although not in constitutional forms, has of course since been overshadowed by the nineteenth and twentieth-century revolution in both form and reality.

It is not the parliament of medieval Europe which was the archetype on which the institution has been modelled in ex-colonies, but that transformed modern English parliament, with its emphases on the primacy of the lower house, the party system, the responsibility of ministers, universal suffrage, the secret ballot, and constituencies rather than communities, which are all so totally dissimilar to the medieval original.

Further Reading

Until now there has, surprisingly, never been a complete book devoted to the origins of the English parliament, although Edward Miller, *The Origins of Parliament* (Historical Association, 1960) is a valuable introductory pamphlet.

For any particular topic in the early history of parliament it is best to refer to the list of sources and to read in full the relevant books and articles from which excerpts have been included in this volume. As will be seen, most of these sources are articles and many of these may therefore not be readily accessible. It is to be hoped that one of the principal values of the present volume will be that it brings together in one place adequate extracts from a wide range of publications which are no longer generally obtainable. Readers may, however, be alarmed that so many, so contradictory, assertions appear here unsupported by footnotes to indicate the evidence for them. Those who care to pursue the full version of the books and articles cited here will usually find that the authors have provided ample evidence for their arguments. Such readers may, however, be astonished to discover that different authors cite the same evidence to support opposite conclusions.

Three general articles on the English parliament which have not been quoted in this volume are T. F. T. Plucknett, 'Parliament', *The English Government at Work, 1327–1336*, ed. J. F. Willard and W. A. Morris, I (Medieval Academy of America, 1940), pp. 82–128, Geoffrey Templeman, 'The History of Parliament to 1400', *Birmingham Historical Journal*, I (1948), pp. 202–32, reprinted in *The Making of English History*, ed. R. L. Schuyler and A. Ausubel (1952), pp. 109–27, and J. S. Roskell, 'Perspectives in English Parliamentary History', *Bulletin of the John Rylands Library*, XLVI (1964), pp. 448–75.

The most useful work on Europe in general is Antonio Marongiu, *Il Parlamento in Italia* (Milan, 1962). Although ostensibly devoted to Italy, over 300 pages of Professor Marongiu's work are devoted to a comparative study of parliaments elsewhere in western Europe. This is at present by far the most up to date and comprehensive study of medieval parliamentary institutions in any language, and it is also very useful as a bibliographical guide. An English translation is now being prepared by Dr Stuart Woolf for Eyre and Spottiswoode. A great many important contributions, on various parts of Europe, have appeared in the twenty-eight volumes of *Studies presented to the International Commission for the History of Representative and Parliamentary Institutions* (1937–65). Of these one could single out for particular mention E. Lousse, *La Société d'Ancien Régime* (1943) and the two volumes of the *Album Helen Maud Cam* (1960 and 1961).

The original source material for early parliaments in England has mostly been in print for a very long time. Most of the rolls of parliament were published in the eighteenth century as *Rotuli Parliamentorum* in six volumes (1783), but a few more have been published since. H. Cole printed some in *Documents Illustrative of English History* (Record Commission, 1844), F. W. Maitland printed the roll for 1305 as *Memoranda de Parliamento* (Rolls Series, 1893), and H. G. Richardson and G. O. Sayles some further fragments in *Rotuli Parliamentorum Hactenus Inediti* (Camden Society, 1935). Most of the surviving writs of summons to parliament and a great deal of other relevant material was published by Sir Francis Palgrave as *Parliamentary Writs* (Record Commission, 1827–34). Much of the legislation in parliament can be found in *Statutes of the Realm* (Record Commission, 11 vols., 1810–28). The chronicle narrative sources for the period largely appeared in the Rolls Series (1858–97).

List of Sources

The letter 'T' indicates that the passage has been translated for this publication.

PART ONE

1. R. H. LORD, 'The Parliaments of the Middle Ages and the Early Modern Period', *Catholic Historical Review*, XVI, 1930, pp. 125–8, 140–3.
2. R. F. TREHARNE, 'The Nature of Parliament in the reign of Henry III', *English Historical Review*, LXXIV, 1959, pp. 590–2.
3. Unpublished Coram Rege Roll in the Public Record Office, London, KB. 26/116C, m. 2d. T. I am much indebted to the discoverer of this entry, Mr. C. A. F. Meekings of the Public Record Office, for providing me with a transcript. It will appear in the printed *Curia Regis Rolls*, vol. XV as no. 2047.
4. HUMBERT DE ROMANS, *De Eruditione Praedicatorum*, Book II, part 2, chapter 86, ed. Margarino de la Bigne, *Maxima Bibliotheca Veterum Patrum*, XXV, Lyons, 1677, pp. 559–60. T, using the Rheims–Douay Bible for quotations from the Vulgate.
5. *Cortes de los antiguos reinos de Leon y de Castilla publicadas por la Real Academia de la Historia*, I, Madrid, 1861, pp. 39–40. T.
6. 'Sententia de iure statuum terrae', *Monumenta Germaniae Historica*, Legum, IV Constitutiones, II, Hanover, 1896, no. 305, p. 420. T.
7. W. STUBBS, *Select Charters*, 9th edn, Clarendon Press, Oxford, 1913, p. 354. T.
8. E. BARKER, *The Dominican Order and Convocation*, Clarendon Press, Oxford, 1913, pp. 73–6.
9. A. MARONGIU, *Il Parlamento in Italia*, Giuffre, Milan, 1962, pp. 52 and 56. T. I am grateful to Dr Stuart Woolf, who is producing an English edition of this book, for checking my translation.

PART TWO

10. E. LOUSSE, *La Société d'Ancien Régime*, 2nd edn, I, Editions Universitas, Louvain, 1952, pp. 41–4.
11. J. DHONDT, '"Ordres" ou "Puissances" l'example des États de Flandre', *Annales: Économies, Sociétés, Civilisations*, V, 1950, pp. 290–1.

12. F. L. GANSHOF, *Feudalism*, 3rd English edn, Longmans, 1964, pp. xv–xvi.

13. M. BLOCH, *Feudal Society*, English edn, Routledge and Kegan Paul, 1961, pp. 442–4.

14. *Ibid.*, pp. 69–71.

15. S. PAINTER, *Studies in the History of the English Feudal Barony*, Johns Hopkins Press, Baltimore, 1943, pp. 193–7 and 44–5.

16. HENRY DE BRACTON, *de Legibus et Consuetudinibus Angliae*, translated by Sir Travers Twiss, II, Rolls Series, 1879, p. 237.

17. G. T. LAPSLEY, 'Buzones', *English Historical Review*, XLVII, 1932, pp. 565–6.

18. R. F. TREHARNE, 'The Knights in the period of Reform and Rebellion 1258–67: A Critical Phase in the Rise of a New Class', *Bulletin of the Institute of Historical Research*, XXI, 1946, pp. 2–4.

19. R. F. HUNNISETT, *The Medieval Coroner*, Cambridge University Press, 1961, pp. 170–1 and 173.

20. J. C. HOLT, *The Northerners*, Clarendon Press, Oxford, 1961, pp. 59–60.

21. K. B. MCFARLANE, 'Bastard Feudalism', *Bulletin of the Institute of Historical Research*, XX, 1945, pp. 162–3.

22. Translated by B. Wilkinson, *Constitutional History of Medieval England 1216–1377*, III, Longmans, 1958, p. 224.

23. E. MILLER, 'The English Economy in the Thirteenth Century: Implications of Recent Research', *Past and Present*, XXVIII, July 1964, pp. 26–9.

24. MATTHEW PARIS, *Chronica Majora*, V, Rolls Series, 1880, p. 22. T.

PART THREE

25. MODUS TENENDI PARLIAMENTUM, ed. M. V. Clarke in *Medieval Representation and Consent*, Longmans, 1936, pp. 374–84, T, but using parts of the translation by B. Wilkinson in *Constitutional History of Medieval England 1216–1377*, III, Longmans, 1958, pp. 351–8. While this book has been in the press the first complete translation of the *Modus* has appeared in J. J. Bagley and P. B. Rowley, *A Documentary History of England*, I, Penguin, 1966, pp. 171–87.

26. M. V. CLARKE, *Medieval Representation and Consent*, Longmans, 1936, pp. 196–201, 203–7.

27. F. W. MAITLAND, *Memoranda de Parliamento 1305*, Rolls Series, 1893, pp. xxxv–xxxviii, xlvii.

28. As no. 22, vol. III, pp. 305–6.

29. *Rotuli Parliamentorum*, II, 1783, p. 65. T.

30. T. F. TOUT, *Chapters in the Administrative History of Medieval England*, ii, Manchester University Press and Longmans, 1920, pp. 146–9.

31. J. S. ROSKELL, 'The problem of the attendance of the Lords in Medieval Parliaments', *Bulletin of the Institute of Historical Research*, XXIX, 1956, pp. 198–9.

32. D. PASQUET, *An Essay on the Origins of the House of Commons*, English edn, Cambridge University Press, 1925, pp. 234–5. T.

33. *Parliamentary Writs*, ed. F. Palgrave, I, 1827, p. 165. T.

34. As no. 32, pp. 223–8.

35. As no. 33, vol. I, pp. 150 and 156. T.

36. *Ibid.*, p. 49. T.

37. J. L. STRAYER, *Studies in Early French Taxation*, Harvard University Press, 1939, p. 113. T.

38. *English Historical Review*, XL, 1925, p. 585. T.

39. M. MCKISACK, *The Parliamentary Representation of the English Boroughs during the Middle Ages*, Oxford University Press, 1932, pp. 119–20, 125–8, 133–4.

PART FOUR

40. R. W. and A. J. CARLYLE, *A History of Medieval Political Theory in the West*, v, Blackwood, Edinburgh, 1928, pp. 471–4.

41. W. ULLMANN, *Principles of Government and Politics in the Middle Ages*, Methuen, 1961, pp. 20–1, 150–1, 232–4, 254–5, 190–1.

42. AQUINAS, *Selected Political Writings*, ed. A. P. d'Entreves, translated by J. G. Dawson, Basil Blackwell, Oxford, 1948, pp. 145, 149, 151.

43. MARSILIUS OF PADUA, *The Defender of the Peace*, translated by A. Gewirth, Columbia University Press, 1956, pp. 45–6.

44. G. POST, 'A Roman legal theory of consent, *quod omnes tangit*, in medieval representation', *Wisconsin Law Review*, 1950, pp. 66, 76–8.

45. As no. 22, vol. III, p. 311.

46. Translated by Ewart Lewis, *Medieval Political Ideas*, I, Routledge and Kegan Paul, 1954, pp. 279–80.

47. *The Digest of Justinian*, translated by C. H. Monro, I, 1904, pp. 23–4.

48. As no. 22, vol. I, pp. 175–7.

49. *The Song of Lewes*, edited and translated by C. L. Kingsford, Clarendon Press, Oxford, 1890, pp. 43–54.

50. As no. 46, p. 280.
51. *The Mirror of Justices*, edited and translated by W. J. Whittaker, Selden Society, 1895, pp. 7, 8, 155–6.

PART FIVE

52. As no. 27, pp. xlviii–lvii, lxxvi–lxxxii.
53. W. STUBBS, *The Constitutional History of England*, 3rd edn, II, Clarendon Press, Oxford, 1883, pp. 301–4.
54. As no. 32, pp. 172–8.
55. R. F. TREHARNE, 'The nature of Parliament in the reign of Henry III', *English Historical Review*, LXXIV, 1959, pp. 604–10.
56. H. G. RICHARDSON and G. O. SAYLES, *Parliaments and Great Councils in Medieval England*, Stevens, 1961, pp. 6–11, 30–3.
57. J. G. EDWARDS, '"Justice" in Early English Parliaments', *Bulletin of the Institute of Historical Research*, xxvii, 1954, pp. 38–41, 53. Translation of the memorandum from the 1279–80 Close Roll inserted from no. 22, vol. III, p. 144.
58. As no. 33, vol. I, p. 16. T.
59. *Annales Monastici*, ed. H. R. Luard, IV, Rolls Series, 1869, pp. 294–5. T.
60. C. STEPHENSON, 'Taxation and Representation in the Middle Ages', *Anniversary Essays in Medieval History by students of Charles Homer Haskins*, Houghton Mifflin, Boston and New York, 1929, pp. 304–5, 307–12.
61. S. K. MITCHELL, *Taxation in Medieval England*, Yale University Press, New Haven, 1951, pp. 234–5.
62. F. M. POWICKE, *The Thirteenth Century*, 1st edn, Clarendon Press, Oxford, 1953, pp. 523–7.
63. E. POWER, *The Wool Trade in English Medieval History*, Oxford University Press, 1941, pp. 65–7, 80–2.
64. As no. 22, vol. III, pp. 260–1. (Much abbreviated translation.)
65. As no. 22, vol. I, p. 228.
66. H. M. CAM, 'The Legislators of Medieval England', *Proceedings of the British Academy*, XXXI, 1945, pp. 127–30, 132–4, 136–7.
67. F. M. POWICKE. *King Henry III and the Lord Edward*, I, Clarendon Press, Oxford, 1947, pp. 340–2.
68. J. G. EDWARDS, *Historians and the Medieval English Parliament*, Jackson for Glasgow University, 1960, pp. 23–4, 41–2.
69. As no. 29, vol. I, pp. 350–3. T.

INDEX

Abbots, *see* Prelates

Amiens, award or mise of (1264), 132–3

Aquinas, St. Thomas, 16, 116, 118, 122–6

Aristotle, 16, 118, 120–2, 124–7

Ayremynne, William de, 203–4, 208–10

Barker, Sir Ernest, 35–7

Barons, *see* Magnates

Bench, justices of the, 81, 89, 149, 151–2, 194, 205; Common Bench, 90, 204; King's Bench, 90, 152

Bishops, *see* Prelates

Bloch, Marc, 47–54

Borough representatives, *see* Burgesses

Bracton, Henry de, on *buzones*, 59–60; on the community of the realm, 169; on the courts, 152; on the king, 124, 131–2, 139

Burgesses in parliament, 5–6, 11–15, 35, 79–81, 88, 98, 100–3, 108–11, 189, 208; election of burgesses to parliament, 103–7; coroners as burgesses, 63

Buzones, 7–8, 59–60, 63

Cam, Helen, 194–8, 213

Carlyle, R. W. and A. J., 115–17

Chamberlain, King's, 85; *see also* Exchequer

Chancellor, 80–2, 84–5, 89–90, 149, 175–6, 205

Chancery, 89–90, 93, 149; clerks of, 205; masters of, 89; officers of, 4

Cinque Ports, 78–9

Citizens, *see* Burgesses

Clarke, Maude, 77, 82–8, 91

Clergy, 146–7; lower clergy, 192; representatives of lower clergy in parliament, 5–6, 12–14, 78, 81, 84, 88

Cole, H., 213

Common Pleas, court of, *see* Bench

Commons in Parliament, 100–11, 146, 156–60, 182, 188; *see also* Knights of the shire *and* Burgesses

Community, 115–18, 120–1, 124–6, 138; of the realm, 5, 16, 80, 95, 123–4, 141, 169, 208

Confirmatio Cartarum (1297), 110, 190, 194–5

Convocation, 13, 36–8

Coram Rege, court, 151–2; rolls, 28, 151–2; *see also* Bench

Cornwall, Richard earl of, 191–2

Coroner, 6–7, 59, 63–4

'Corporatist' theory, 43–6

Cortes, 2, 21–5, 32–3

Council, king's, 4, 87, 89–90, 92–3, 150, 206, 209–10; in parliament, 80, 84, 86–94, 145–53, 176–7

Council, Great, 92–3, 184–5

County court, *see* Shire court

David of Wales, 178–9

Dhondt, J., 43, 45–6

Diets in Germany, 2, 21–5, 32–3, 182

Dominicans, 29, 35–8

Earls, *see* Magnates

Edward I in 1305 parliament, 145–6; his grand design for parliament, 154–7

Edward II in 1316 parliament, 204–10, absent from parliament, 206

Edwards, Sir Goronwy, 168, 173–8, 199, 201–2

Eleanor of Provence, queen of Henry III, 191–2

Elections to parliament, 103–7

Escheators, 62–4, 206

Estates, assemblies of, in France, 2, 21–5, 106, 128, 167, 181–2

Estate of merchants, 13, 189–91

Exchequer, 89–90, 93, 186; barons and

219